THE NATURE OF HOME

Lisa Knopp

The *Nature* of *Home*

A Lexicon and Essays

University of Nebraska Press
Lincoln and London

Publication of this volume was assisted by The
Virginia Faulkner Fund, established in memory
of Virginia Faulkner, editor-in-chief of the
University of Nebraska Press.

Library of Congress Cataloging-in-Publication Data
Knopp, Lisa, 1956–
The nature of home / Lisa Knopp.
p.   cm.
Includes bibliographical references.
ISBN 0-8032-2754-X (cloth: alk. paper)
1. Knopp, Lisa, 1956–   2. Lincoln
Region (Neb.)—Biography.   3. Lincoln Region
(Neb.)—Description and travel.   4. Lincoln
Region (Neb.)—Social life and customs.
5. Natural history—Nebraska.   6. Knopp, Lisa,
1956—Philosophy.   7. Women authors,
American—Biography.   8. Home—Psychological aspects.
9. Nebraska—History—Miscellanea.   10. Nebraska—
Biography—Miscellanea.   I. Title.
F674.L7 K58   2002
978.2'293—dc21
2002017972

"N,,

This book is dedicated to my elders,
Mae and Arthur Parris,
Pertsie Parker, Ruth Knopp

Contents

Preface

This is a book about home—what home is, how one might find it, what it means to be at home or away from home or homeless, what might change one's idea of home, how the presence or absence of home affects the way that one feels, thinks, and acts, both as an individual and as a member of a community, society, or nation. This book is called *The Nature of Home* in part because when I hear the word *nature*, two meanings immediately come to mind: the essential character of a thing or being; and the nonhuman, nonhuman-made part of our world that includes the flora, fauna, geography, and weather patterns. Both definitions apply.

These essays were written over a two-and-one-half-year period, a period that began with my return home to Lincoln, Nebraska. When I embarked on this project, I had a title for my book, but no plan other than to write about whatever struck my fancy. Yet the collected essays seem to reveal a scheme, design, method, plan. The essays move from an exploration of an awareness of home that is geographical and bodily to one that is more culturally, even politically, based and finally to one that is more abstract and portable. The individual essays, all written as "stand-alone" pieces, radiate more significance, impart more meaning, bear more weight when seen as parts of a whole. I could not have planned any of this.

Between each of the twenty-two longer essays is a brief, transitional interlude that I call a "lexicon entry." A lexicon is a word-book or dictionary as well as the vocabulary of a compartment of knowledge, sphere of activity, region, or person. Each of the twenty-two lexicon entries combines the definition provided by that greatest dictionary of all, *The Oxford English Dictionary*—whose twenty half-volumes I visit frequently at Lincoln's Bennett Martin Public Library—along with my private or idiosyncratic definition. Hence, these lexicon entries present a vocabulary of home that is both widely held and singular.

Each entry for the six hundred thousand word forms included in *The Oxford English Dictionary* contains the variant spellings, pronunciations, definitions, the earliest recorded use of a word, and, in the case of an obsolete word, its last recorded use. When one imagines how people delineated and named objects, experiences, and ideas, when one considers how words encode the values and preoccupations of a culture, when one knows where a word has been, how it has changed, and analyzes the implications of those changes of meaning, words become far more than mere labels, the medium through which messages about immediate concerns are sent and received. Indeed, words can take us home; words can keep us from home; words and combinations of words can be a home.

If I had written this book when I was younger, I would not have felt the structural or philosophical need for the lexicon entries. But then again, at twenty, thirty, and even forty, I would not have written a book about such a familiar, common, everyday topic as home. Then, I had other fish to fry. But in my early forties, finding my belonging-place and positioning myself there became my grand necessity. In part, this book is the account of that journey. Equally influential is that at age forty-four I am less inclined than ever to believe that anything—historical events, millennia, essays, moments of extraordinary awareness, the connections between organisms—ever completely ends. Anything charged with significance persists in the individual or the collective memory and determines how we approach the next event, millennium, essay, luminous moment, or relationship. The lexicon entries permitted me to be more didactic or suggestive, more tightly or widely focused than I had felt appropriate in one or more of the longer essays, to contradict a position that I had just set forth, to strengthen connections or set up reverberations between the essays on either side of the entry or in other parts of the book, to continue an essay even after I had seemingly ended it. The lexicon entries were liberating since they permitted me to cross self-imposed boundaries. My sincere hope is that these definitions and essays will encourage, even guide, the reader in her or his own border crossings.

Given the breadth of my subject matter, it is fitting that the essays in this collection are of various forms and styles. Some essays are au-tobiographical, while others are more outwardly directed. Some essays are narrative, some are lyrical meditations, and yet others are rather scholarly excursions into the past. In most essays, I have simply cited the authors and titles of my information sources and provided more complete citations in the references section at the back of the book. Two biographical essays ("Affinity," about Frank Zybach, inventor of the center-pivot irrigator, and "Backdrop," about Elizabeth Dolan, whose murals grace the walls of the University of Nebraska State Museum) have no previous literary treatment, and so I have used more formal documentation within the essays to indicate the sources of information used. Two other essays ("Far Brought," about J. Sterling Morton's efforts to remake the grasslands as eastern woodlands, and "Homestead National Monument Album," about the myths, realities, and legacies of the Homestead Act) also include more formal documentation since both offer reinterpretations of subjects in Nebraska history about which a great deal has already been written. Finally, in some essays, I have changed the names and identifying details of some of the people men-tioned in order to protect their privacy.

Because an exploration of the meanings of home must begin with an exploration of a physical place, a particular spot on the earth, *The Nature of Home* is also a book about Nebraska, especially southeastern Nebraska. But the specific place that I have chosen is of less importance than the fact that I have chosen a place and entered into a committed, faithful relationship with it. Sometimes I wish that I had more lifetimes, so that I could know what it is like to be at one with a damp, beech-and-hickory forest, a dry, piñon-pine-covered mountain, a great northern lake, a city of many millions of people, cars, and starlings. But a deep and full exploration of one's geographical home and how the nature of that place influences the nature of the home that she carries within her requires an abiding devotion to one place, the place that belongs to her and she to it. At this point in my journey, I can say that the rewards of such a commitment are generous and constant.

Acknowledgments

I gratefully acknowledge the editors of the following publications in which portions of this book first appeared: *Organization and Environment* (12 [September 1999]: 325–31) for "The Memory of Trees"; *Southern Indiana Review* (8, no. 1 [2001]: 55–67) for "A Salt Marsh Reclamation"; *Shenandoah: The Washington and Lee University Review* (49 [fall 1999]: 5–13) for "In the Air"; NEBRASKA*land* (77 [October 1999]: 24–25 and 77 [June 1999]: 28–29) for "Necessary, Honorable Work" and "Common Miracles", respectively; *Heritage of the Great Plains* (30 [fall/winter 1997]: 27–41) for "Homestead National Monument: An Album"; *Connecticut Review* (22 [fall 2001]: 189–95) for "My Place of Many Times"; *Seeding the Snow* (5, no. 1 [spring/summer 2001]: 13–16) for "Inherent Value"; *Michigan Quarterly Review* (40, no. 4 [fall 2001]: 713–25) for the following lexicon entries—"Home," "Hearth," "Body," "Sojourner," "Nostalgia," "Relic," "Niche," "Settle," "Citizen," "Neighbor," "Heaven," and "Homewell"—which appear as an essay entitled "Household Words"; and ISLE (*Interdisciplinary Studies in Literature and the Environment*, 9, no. 1 [winter 2002]: 189–202) for "Mammoth Bones." In addition, "My Place of Many Times" was listed as one of the notable essays of 2000 in *Best American Essays, 2001*, edited by Kathleen Norris and Robert Atwan.

I also gratefully acknowledge the insights of Robert Root Jr. and Kent Ryden whose comments on this manuscript showed me what this book is about and George Corner, Collection Manager, Department of Vertebrate Paleontology, University of Nebraska State Museum in Lincoln, for his contributions to "Backdrop" and "Mammoth Bones."

A fellowship from the Nebraska Arts Council helped make this book possible. Warmest thanks!

THE NATURE OF HOME

Nostalgia

European medical men first diagnosed homesickness in the seventeenth century among Swiss peasants who hired out as soldiers in foreign countries. For some of these mercenaries, homesickness was a fatal condition. In his 1688 medical treatise, *Dissertatio de Nostalgia oder Heimweh*, the Swiss physician Johannes Hofer called this body- and soul-sickening longing for home *nostalgia* (*nostos* meaning "homeward journey"; *algos* meaning "pain" or "sorrow" in Greek). Nostalgia is a longing to go back—to homeland, hometown, house, hearth, family. In short, to wax nostalgic is to yearn to return to that faraway, long-ago placetime that is home. For me the curiosity is not that some soldiers, immigrants, refugees, nursing-home residents and first-year college students suffer from the insomnia, absent-mindedness, loss of appetite, melancholy, and general wasting away associated with extreme homesickness or home-withdrawal, but that some do not.

1. Homecoming

"Home," says Louise Erdrich, "is the place we head for in our sleep." For a long time, that place for me was Burlington, Iowa, my birthplace and the setting for most of my childhood. But in my early thirties, I transferred my allegiances about 350 miles west to southeastern Nebraska. I can list the conscious reasons why southeastern Iowa could no longer be home. First one of my brothers was offered a job near Cleveland, Ohio; then another brother and his family located there; then my parents moved southwest of Cleveland following their early retirement; and in 1997 my grandmother moved from an Iowa to an Ohio nursing home, where she remained until her death three years later. In my parents' Ohio house are the furniture, wall hangings, bric-a-brac, foods, and aromas that I associate with home; yet the flora, fauna, weather, building, and land-use patterns in which this house is set are too unfamiliar, too eastern. Nor is this place steeped in memories and stories. North-central Ohio is not, nor will it ever be, my home.

But memories and stories are not enough for southeastern Iowa to continue to be home. Now, the only family members I have in my Mississippi River hometown are in Aspen Grove Cemetery. When I return to Burlington, I am a visitor, staying in the Ramada Inn, eating at Abe's Family Restaurant and Steak House, visiting my native haunts without a local guide or companion. While I need to return to southeast Iowa periodically so that I can see the sites, or what remains of the sites, of many of my most pungent childhood memories (the old public library where four generations of my family borrowed books, the cobblestone alley where I dug crinoids from the crumbling alley walls, the ghost-infested house where I spent my teen years, the bends and islands in the river, the hospital where so many of my kin were born or died), I have no present life there to hold me in place.

In *Earth Muse: Feminism, Nature, and Art*, Carol Bigwood defines home as "a nomadic place, an unfinished place of variable historical and geographical boundaries, but a belonging-place nonetheless." I can list the conscious reasons why Nebraska is now my belonging-place. When I was four and five, my father worked at the CB&Q railroad shops in Havelock, Nebraska. Consequently, I began the first of twenty-some years of schooling at Hartley Elementary in Lincoln, Nebraska. Fresh out of college I was hired to teach English at Westside High School in Omaha. After three years of teaching, I returned to southeastern Iowa, where my son, Ian, was born (though he was conceived in Nebraska) and I attended graduate school in western Illinois. Four years later, Ian and I moved to Lincoln. During the seven-year period that followed, I published my writing, married, bore a daughter, Meredith, earned a Ph.D., and divorced. And during that time, I became aware of the natural world in a way that I had not been before. Thus, the first and only landscape I've known both objectively and intimately is Nebraska's grasslands.

Perhaps like monarch butterflies who migrate north from Mexican forests in relays each spring and summer, the females laying their eggs along the way, new generations replacing the old, I too was driven to this place by a memory older than me. When I returned to Lincoln for graduate school, I rented an apartment and later a house in the Russian Bottoms north of the train yards, a neighborhood settled by Germans from Russia in the latter years of the nineteenth century. Each evening I walked this neighborhood, learning its history from the buildings, the residents, and later, from books. Upon hearing my last name, some of the elderly residents asked if they could heft my long, hay-colored braid to see if it was as heavy as a mother's, grandmother's, sister's, wife's. An old man who lived across the alley often tried to converse with me in a language that resembled German. Several years later my brother showed me what he had collected about Knopp family history. He discovered that our paternal great-grandparents' first attempt at homemaking following their arrival in America in the 1890s was not in Burlington, Iowa, but in Hastings, Nebraska.

These Knopps (pronounced Kuh-nop') already knew something of exile. When the German government demanded military service of their men in the eighteenth century, they moved to Russia at the invitation of Catherine the Great, a German. For over a century, my father's father's people lived in insular German communities and farmed the Ukrainian steppes during their sojourn until again military service was demanded of them, this time by the czar. My father's family did not leave soon enough: Knopp males were conscripted into the Russian army or the Russian navy. In Nebraska, my grandfather's people were neither Germans nor Russians, but Germans from Russia or "Roosians." A few years after their arrival in Hastings, Nebraska, years made difficult by a long, severe drought, my Knopp ancestors settled in Iowa, where rain was more plentiful and the Mississippi ran its banks most springs. There they were simply Germans.

Perhaps other reasons that I neither know nor can name bind me to this place, not a place in which I sojourn, but a place to which I belong and that belongs to me.

What caused my flight from my belonging-place was an ended marriage. At the time, I supposed that a greater physical distance between my ex-husband and me would cure me of the love I still felt for him, and after years of part-time teaching at the University of Nebraska, I suddenly needed a full-time income and my own health insurance. The job I found—a tenure-track position as a professor in a university where I designed and taught courses that mattered to me (American Autobiography, Literary Journalism, American Travel Literature, Early American Literature)—bought physical security for me and my children. Yet this job was in a place so unprairielike that I found it uninhabitable and too far from my young daughter, who spent more time with her father in Nebraska than with me. Every day that she and I were apart broke my heart.

I began taking my daily five-mile walks after dark so that I would not have to see the place in which I lived. But the darkness couldn't hide enough. When I glimpsed the shelves arranged with art or bric-a-brac in a living room of one brightly lit house, my stomach churned. How could anyone like this place enough to go to the trouble of arranging her living room in a homey manner? I wondered. Once Meredith and I hiked with friends at a regional state park with a one-hundred-foot-tall intermittent waterfall, lush ferns, wild geraniums, blooming pawpaws, and other damp, southern species. Beech, tulip poplars, and sugar maples formed the dense closed canopy of what ecologist E. Lucy Braun calls the "western mesophytic" or medium-moist forest that stretches from southwest Ohio to northern Mississippi. It is the type of landscape most people imagine when they hear the terms *nature* or *wilderness*. It is the type of landscape that most people consider beautiful. But the dense forests and rugged hills blocked out so much sky and light that I felt oxygen-deprived and disoriented. Everything—soil types, landforms, flora, fauna, aromas, lack of sky, the depth and length of the seasons—was wrong because it was different from home, the template against which I compare all other landscapes. The overwhelming presence of this unprairielike landscape so exhausted me that I could barely complete the one-mile loop through the nature preserve. When I reached the top of the hill and found myself in a sumac grove with fewer tall trees and more sky, my weakness, breathlessness, and nausea abated.

My dislike of this southeastern landscape affected my view of the people, too. Once, I went to a lovely arts festival in a clearing in the forest. Artists and craftspeople demonstrated how they tanned leather, threw pots, carved ornate walking canes, wove baskets, hooked hemp rugs, and blew glass. A drama troop gathered our children, dressed them in filmy scarves and glitter, and helped them stage a play about kind wood nymphs and an evil lumberjack. The local natural foods cooperative sold rich, fruit-filled pastries. But I was too sick to eat or to enjoy the play. Many of the people attending the festival were so deeply drawn to this landscape—tupelo swamps, bald cypress, holly and magnolia trees, bright songbirds, orchards, vineyards, exhausted coal mines, little towns where the Great Depression had not yet ended—that they made their homes on the edge or between fragments of the national forest. These people, many of whom I knew, possessed qualities that I admired: intelligence, resourcefulness, respect for the land, uninstitutionalized spirituality, a brushy unkemptness. But they were such a distillation of the place that I could not stand to be with so many of them at once. I wanted to be with people who were at home with bigger skies, clearer light, fewer trees, rolling fields of corn, beans, wheat, alfalfa, and cattle, longer winters, drier summers, wilder springs (sultry one day, blizzardy the next), golden autumns, an American Indian presence, the near presence of a "pioneer" past. I wanted to be with other people who shared my sense of Nebraska as a belonging-place. I wanted to live on that electric edge where the Midwest ends and the West begins.

During my three-year exile in the "estranging-place," the asthma that sometimes kept me sedentary during my childhood and early twenties returned. I required more and more medication to be able to breathe freely. At times I was overcome with painful waves of colitis that left me exhausted. Now I know that the latter is an allergic reaction to wheat, which appeared, curiously, while I was living in a region where the soil is too poor and wet to support wheat fields. All I knew at the time was that I was suffocating, turned inside out, sleepless with grief and estrangement.

The only times I felt deeply happy during my three-year stay in the estranging-place were when I went to Nebraska to visit people and places. Just north of St. Joseph, Missouri, I knew that I was on the outskirts of home because there I saw more cottonwoods in one glance than I had seen in a dozen Sunday rambles in the estranging-place. When I saw the razorback loess hills on the east side of the Missouri River and the gently rolling hills on the west side, I breathed deeply, finally filling each alveolus. By the time I crossed the wide and sandy Platte, I was humming with energy. But it was a tainted happiness, since I knew that I had to return to the estranging-place.

During my first year in exile, I tried hard to create the connections that might transform the new place into home—or to at least make it homier. I joined a church and was elected to the pastoral relations committee and the church board. I, who so love prairies that I saw trees as intrusions, marched in a logging protest and wrote numerous letters to save the forest. I kept company with one man and then another, believing that by binding myself to a person who was rooted in the place that I could bind myself to the place. But in both cases our togetherness lacked luster and momentum. I spent my weekends exploring the small towns and natural areas in the region so that I could carry a map of its terrain and its natural and human-made landmarks in my head. I began writing a book about this biological crossroads where organisms associated with the Ozarks, the Smoky Mountains, the coastal plain, and the southeastern edge of tallgrass prairie reach the limit of their respective ranges. And too, I explored the human history of this place, a cultural crossroads where the South and the Midwest met. But instead of profiting from that blend, I found this place so liminal that it lacked the charm of either region.

I waited, but connectedness did not come. Perhaps the obstacle was my unwillingness to be made over in the image of a new land. Perhaps the obstacle was my belief that I could not with integrity commit myself to a new land, since I already had a belonging-place. When I found that none of my efforts at connecting were catching and holding, I strengthened my lifelines to home. I maintained better contact with some of my Nebraska friends than I had when they and I lived in the same city. I maintained my membership in the church in which I had married, in which both of my children had spent significant parts of their childhood, a church that fed my spirit. I maintained my friendship with a man on Nebraska's death row, a man who insisted that God had sent me to the estranging-place for a reason, to which I should submit. I continued sessions with my Jungian dream analyst in Nebraska by telephone, since I did not trust anyone to plumb my depths who lived in a place where my bodymind felt so sick. I filled the reading lists in the courses I taught with a disproportionate percentage of Nebraska authors—Loren Eiseley, Tillie Olsen, Mari Sandoz, Willa Cather, John Neihardt. When clothes, gadgets, or appliances that I brought from home wore out or broke, I simply stored them, as if they possessed an energy that I might need someday. And I surrounded myself with tangible reminders of home: dried stalks of big and little bluestem, clusters of cottonwood leaves, ceiling-high paper birch boughs, the brown-and-black-striped tail feather of a meadowlark, the segmented abdomen of a fossilized trilobite that once drifted in the Paleozoic sea that covered what is now Nebraska. In the office in my house I hung a large road map of Nebraska and a photograph of the *Sower*, Lee Lawrie's twenty-seven-foot bronze statue that tops the four-hundred-foot central tower of the Nebraska capitol. This slim, muscular man carries his seed bag slung over his right hip; his left hand is cupped, ready to sow. He stands on a gold-glazed tiled dome: ripe wheat fields or the grasslands in autumn. Over my desk in my university office I hung photographs of a sod house that once stood in Custer County, Nebraska; of Omaha dancers at the Pine Ridge agency in South Dakota in 1891; of the Ponca chief, Standing Bear. He stands before a fake rock covered with fake foliage and a backdrop painted with what looks to be a rugged seacoast: not Nebraska. His hair is long and adorned with a large white feather, a bear-claw necklace hangs from his neck, his left hand grips a tomahawk, his shining eyes look faraway.

I was in the estranging-place, but I was not of it. I was of my belonging-place, but I was not in it. I was a soul separated from its source. I was homeless.

Even though the Poncas had never fought U.S. soldiers, Congress decided to include them in the list of northern tribes to be exiled to Indian Territory following the Battle of the Little Bighorn. In 1877 soldiers drove the Poncas out of their ancestral home in northeast Nebraska to Indian Territory in what the Poncas called the Warm Land, a place now widely known as Oklahoma. The Ponca historian Peter Le Claire observed that "the warm moist climate" in the Warm Land "so differed from the dry bracing air of their Nebraska home" that it made his people sick. "Homesickness," wrote Le Claire, "worst of all diseases in the misery that it carries, was in every lodge." During their first year in exile, 158 of the 700 Poncas died. During the winter of 1878–79 the eldest son of Chief Standing Bear grew very ill. Before he died, the boy made his father promise to carry his body the five hundred and some miles to Má-azì, the Ponca burying ground on the bluffs above the Missouri River. When the boy died, Standing Bear placed his body in a wagon, which he hitched to two skinny horses. The grieving father and some sixty other Poncas set out for home. Along the way they rested among their friends and allies, the Omaha, on their reservation in northeast Nebraska.

Because the Poncas had traveled without the U.S. government's permission, that old Indian fighter, General George Crook, commander of the Department of the Platte, sent a guard to arrest them and imprison them at Fort Omaha. But Crook was so moved by the plight and courage of Standing Bear and his followers that he refused to transfer them to Indian Territory as ordered. Federal Judge Elmer S. Dundy suggested that Standing Bear issue a writ of habeas corpus upon General Crook so that the Ponca chief could have his day in court. The general agreed to this plan.

On April 18, 1879, in *Standing Bear v Crook*, Standing Bear's attorneys argued that he "and any other Indian had the right to separate themselves from their tribes and live under protection of United States laws like any other citizen." Judge Dundy ruled that an Indian is a person within the meaning of the law and that, in the words of historian Dee Brown, "the right of expatriation was a natural, inherent, and inalienable right of the Indian as well as the white race."

The choice of the word "expatriation" suggests that home is with one's people and that Standing Bear's decision to leave Indian Territory was a decision to exile himself. Apparently Judge Dundy did not understand that for some, home is geographically bound. Apparently he did not understand that for some the land is a living entity with whom they are covenanted. So Dundy's ruling that Standing Bear was being held illegally and was free to come and go as he pleased meant that Standing Bear had to chose between home with his beloved people and home in his beloved land. Fortunately, a commission appointed by President Hayes in 1880 worked out an arrangement whereby all Poncas who wanted to return to their ancestral home could do so. Unfortunately, corrupt officials forbade many Poncas from leaving the Warm Land. One-fourth of the nation's 833 members were allotted lands along the Niobrara River to be held in severalty—by individual ownership. Following his release from jail, Standing Bear and his followers completed their journey to the burial grounds, where they buried the chief's son among his ancestors. Standing Bear spent the rest of his earthly life at home near the Swift Running Water, the Niobrara.

I knew that I would only get sicker, perhaps even die of the misery that is homesickness if I remained in the estranging-place. I knew that I needed a radical ritual to move me from a place of lack and loss to a place of wholeness. I needed a ceremony to take me home. Yet no ceremony I knew of seemed fitting. And, too, I doubted that in my sick and weakened condition that I alone had the physical and psychic energy to create and sustain a ceremony. Nonetheless, I would try.

I brought my tangible lifelines to the middle of my living room floor. I spread out deer antlers, hawk and meadowlark feathers, stalks of prairie grasses, a cluster of dried cottonwood leaves, my pictures of Standing Bear and the *Sower*, the ceiling-high paper birch boughs like those that grew near the Niobrara, and all the broken and worn-out things I had brought from Nebraska: a jammed electric pencil sharpener, an air purifier that shot sparks, a now worn-out, deodorant-stained, machine-embroidered, white cotton dress that I had bought at the Latvian Lutheran Church rummage sale in the Russian Bottoms, and the shards of a hand-painted glass egg given to me by a Chinese student at the University of Nebraska. I thanked the objects for helping to keep me alive and beseeched them to pull me home. These relics of home, charged as they were with the energy of home, would stir the ether, move the Spirit to compassionate action, and kindle my faith in my own power to move hills and forests: to return myself to my belonging-place.

Next I spread out acorns, a raccoon skull and ribs, songbird feathers, a turtle carapace, a few knobby feet of bald cypress root, the beaked, woody, grenadelike fruits of the sweet gum, and the orange, yellow, and gray body and wings of a royal walnut moth, all gathered in the dark, damp forest. I told these forest mementos that I did not blame them or their belonging-place for my condition and appealed to them to push me home. These foreign objects, charged as they were with the energy of someone else's home, would also stir the ether, move the Spirit to compassionate action, and kindle my faith in my own power. In the powerful presence of these objects and energies, I prayed until my skull tingled.

In the dream that followed the ceremony I was seeking to buy a house in a Lincoln neighborhood, the Highlands, a metaphorical misnaming since the actual neighborhood called the Highlands is farther west than the one I was dreaming about. In my dream I wondered if it was foolish for me to be buying a house in a place where I had no means of earning money. I decided that it was not.

At an earlier point in my life I had often parked my car at my son's preschool at the top of the hill about which I was dreaming and walked the two miles to the university in the morning and back again in the afternoon, usually stopping on the bridge over Oak Creek to observe muskrats building dens, Canada geese preening, a fox slipping through the brush, a great blue heron stalking. Sometimes I saw a person—though never the same one—sleeping beneath the bridge.

In my dream I crested a rocky bluff, whose incongruous presence surprised me. I followed a winding, descending path around the bluff to a cave in the rock, a small rocky beach, and smooth water. As I approached the shoreline, one bristled black nose after another broke the water surface. With astonishing speed a herd of seals emerged from the water and slapped their flippers and torsos across the narrow beach toward me. I was afraid that in their pleasure at my presence they would knock me down; so I ran toward the ascending path. Out of the corner of my eye I saw behind me a tall, slim woman of about fifty, walk from the area of the cave toward me. I knew that she was courageous, serene, and wise. Though the two of us may have been the only ones who knew of this unexpected and magical place, we said nothing to each other. When I awakened, I was at peace. Without a doubt, I was going home. And soon.

"Seals live in two realms," my dream analyst explained. "They can live on dry land or they can stay submerged for long periods of time while they explore the bottom of the sea. You ran away from the seals because you are not yet ready to explore the depths with them—depths which the woman, your guide, has already experienced. More immediately the dream is telling you that if you want to come home, you have to take a risk. If you take this risk, you will receive guidance."

A few months after my ceremony and dream, I was offered, quite unexpectedly, a very good part-time position mentoring graduate students in a creative writing program in Baltimore, Maryland. I only had to be on campus for two weeks in August. The rest of the time I would work at home, reading the manuscripts and book reviews that my students sent me, responding to them by telephone and electronic mail. While the job offered no security, no benefits, and less than half my present salary, it offered enough that I could live where I belonged if I lived frugally.

Yet when I was first invited to apply for the job in Baltimore, I declined. I was still hoping to be offered one of the teaching positions that I had applied for within or near southeastern Nebraska. And, too, I reasoned that I needed the summer to rest, write, and be with my children before I began a new job in the fall. I simply didn't have time to prepare to teach a workshop that would take me away for half the month of August. But then I remembered that in the past my prayers had never been answered in quite the manner I expected. Usually, what I needed was just around the corner, the next-of-kin, glimpsed in the periphery, caught by the hem, still part of the background. Sometimes, it approached from behind. Once I loosened the hold that my expectations had on me, I realized that my ceremony and prayers had evoked this job offer. Once I resigned from my job as a professor and returned home, a series of part-time jobs appeared: secretary at my church, private writing teacher, book reviewer for a major newspaper, substitute teacher in the public schools, interim administrator at the college where I teach. Such support came because I had made a leap of faith and had acted upon that faith.

Though my choice was irresistible, it was not without problems. Many nights when I should have been sleeping, I stared into the darkness and made lists of what my children and I could do without (garbage service, first-run movies, air conditioning, newspaper subscriptions, long-distance telephone calls, organic foods, machine-dried clothes, anything bought firsthand). Again and again, I mentally budgeted my small future income. I wondered how I would support the three of us if one of us became very ill or if I had to replace my car. Faith, I told myself. Faith will make this work. I thought often about Jesus' disciple, Peter. The moment Peter thought about the impossibility of walking on water, he began to sink. I could sustain myself in my belonging-place as long as my faith exceeded my doubts.

I gave my ceiling-high paper birch boughs to my neighbor, a displaced Texan, set some of my broken and worn-out possessions by the curb in front of my house, where they quickly disappeared, and began packing.

The geographer Yi-Fu Tuan writes that "an environmental value requires its antithesis for definition. . . .'Home' is a meaningless word apart from 'journey' and 'foreign country'; claustrophobia implies agoraphilia; the virtues of the countryside require their anti-image, the city, for the sharpening of focus, and vice versa." Without my journey into exile in a foreign place, I would not know with such deep certainty where my home is and why I must live there.

Though my monthly income is wildly unpredictable, ranging from far less to just a little more than my family needs, I have bought a house and sleep well. Most weekends I explore near and far places that I have added to my map of home: tallgrass prairie remnants in eastern Nebraska and northeastern Kansas; the salt marshes of Lancaster and Saunders Counties; the Loess Hills of western Iowa; the braided Platte; little towns in the Sandhills; the rugged, ponderosa pine-covered cliffs, canyons, and buttes of the Panhandle; the rolling, sand-sage prairie or the sharp ridges and ravines of the dissected plain of southwestern Nebraska; the history of the land and people of the city in which I dwell; the sites of old or vanished settlements, of battles, of sacred encounters. Each day I become more inhabitory. Each day the distinction between where I live and who I am becomes more blurred.

On an overcast afternoon in mid-September, Meredith and I are hiking the golden prairie at Crane Meadows Nature Center, nestled between two channels of the Platte between Alda and Wood River, Nebraska. The little bluestem seed heads are ripe and hairy, the stems purple. We drop to our knees to inhale the vanilla scent of the lady's tresses orchids, which grow in the damper spots on the prairie. We peer into a badger den, only a few days old yet already abandoned for another home. We marvel at the hard bulb within the goldenrod stem where the female goldenrod gallfly has laid her eggs and exited through a neat hole. We imagine the one-half-million sandhill cranes that will feed and dance here on the Platte River sandbars next spring.

We enter a small grove. Perhaps as many as two hundred monarch butterflies drift and flutter and light in the trees, studding the branches with orange. They are working their way south to their winter home in Mexico, a home they have never seen. Next spring, their descendants will return to drink milkweed juices, to rest in the trees, to fill the air with orange shimmers in a place they've never seen but will recognize at once as home.

I wish them well on their journey.

Home

The Germanic words for home may have been derived from two Indo-European words: *kei*, which means "lying" or "settling down," "a bed or couch," as well as "something beloved"; and *ksêmas*, which means "safe dwelling." These linguistic ancestors also yield the Greek *koiman*, "to put to sleep," which is the root of *koimeterion*, a "sleeping place" or "cemetery." In time, the word for "home" in several European languages (*ham* in Anglo-Saxon; *heimr* in Old Norse; *háims* in Gothic; *kemas* or *kaímas* in Lithuanian; *caymis* in Old Prussian, and so on) also came to mean a "village, town or collection of dwellings." Home is both a community and a safe beloved place to lay down your living or dead body for the night or for eternity.

Now, we use the word *home* to refer to one's fixed residence, the center of domestic life and interests as well as the center of the neighborhood, city or town, state and region to which one properly belongs, in which one's affections center, in which one finds refuge or rest. But in the past several decades in the United States, Australia, and increasingly elsewhere, home also has come to designate a building that is a place of private residence. According to the real estate industry's limited and desacralized definition of the word, home is just a physical structure, one's mailing address, for the time being. This makes light of the fact that some of the despair felt by people living in refugee camps or "homeless" shelters is that they are not homeless. They know where home is or was or should be. They know it as the place where they would most prefer to lay their bodies down, the place they dream of when they sleep, a place and circumstance that can't be bought or sold, that persists even when taken from them by bombs, tanks, tornadoes, wrecking balls, or eviction notices.

2. Far Brought

On May 14, 2000, Ian and I strolled through the arboretum near Arbor Lodge, the Nebraska City mansion where Carrie and J. Sterling Morton and their four sons once lived. When I had visited this state historical park over a decade earlier, I had sought nineteenth-century Nebraska history. But this time I sought natural history: the lay of the land, evidence of what the land, flora, and fauna had been, what it is now.

On this May morning, the hilltop arboretum was cool, damp, dark, and rather foreign-looking. And for good reason. Some of the more than 260 species of trees and shrubs included in the arboretum are native to Nebraska. But most species are not. *Ginkgo biloba*, Yulan magnolia, Norway spruce, sassafras, Chinese chestnut, Scotch pine, swamp white oak, golden rain tree, Japanese pagoda, tulip poplar, London plane, white pine and bald cypress are native to other parts of the continent or world and thus are exotics or aliens.

My son and I paused before a grove of American chestnuts. In 1904, imported Asian chestnuts hosted a fungus to which they were immune but the native chestnuts were not. Within forty years of its introduction, the blight had completely eradicated American chestnuts, once the dominant tree in northeastern deciduous forests. The Mortons' grove escaped the blight because of its location in a part of the continent where American chestnuts don't naturally grow and where people had not yet begun planting the blight-bearing imported chestnuts. But the Mortons' grove of white pines did not fare as well. Sterling had planted them in 1891 to prove that the eastern white pine, native to parts of eastern Canada, the northeastern United States, the Appalachian Mountains, and the Great Lakes region, could grow in Nebraska. This pine, accustomed to more moisture and less extreme temperatures, perished in the drought of 1937. Shortly thereafter, the grove was replanted. The stories of the groves of these two imported species contrasts with that of the native Osage orange hedgerow that the Mortons planted almost a century and a half ago. Four of these spiny trees persist to this day.

Ian and I completed our stroll at the Prairie Plants Garden, which was added to the arboretum in 1979 by the Nebraska Game and Parks Commission. I suspect that Sterling, who preferred what he called "far brought"–over native species, would have approved such an inclusion in his arboretum since it reminded visitors what the land was like before he had improved it.

From the moment they arrived in Nebraska Territory, the Mortons had designs upon the land. In 1854 Carrie and Sterling claimed and purchased a quarter section of land just west of Nebraska City, on the highest ground in the area, now the site of Arbor Lodge. When facing the Missouri River just a few miles east of their claim, they saw bluffs covered with the western edge of the oak-hickory forest and flood plains wooded with native ashes, willows, box elders, and cottonwoods. Because the then untamed Missouri flooded frequently and fiercely, scouring the lowlands of saplings and drowning older trees, the Mortons saw a riparian forest that was forever young. When they turned their backs on the river, they saw grassland, broken by woodlands clumped near rivers and streams and in the lowlands. Once this grassland extended, more or less, from the Rockies into central Illinois, from southern Saskatchewan into north-central Texas. Once prairie was our continent's largest and most characteristic biome. When the Mortons settled in Nebraska, they saw prairie that was relatively healthy and intact. Periodic wildfires, droughts, the integrity of plant communities, and grazing by bison, pronghorns, mule deer, and elk kept the prairie safe from the encroachment of trees and other woody plants.

Apparently the Mortons did not consider the grasslands comforting or homelike. Sterling and Carrie spent their childhood and early adulthood in and around Detroit, Michigan, an area forested with aspens, beeches, birches, elms, maples, oaks, cedars, firs, hemlocks, white pines, and spruces. But their earliest memories were set in even more eastern forests: Sterling was born in Adams, New York, on April 22, 1832;

Carolyn Joy French was born in Hallowell, Maine, on August 9, 1833. The bluffy, timbered Missouri River, that easternmost edge of Nebraska Territory, might have resembled the Mortons' geography of home. But the landscape that the Mortons saw when they faced west was entirely Other.

Because they broke the prairie on their claim in 1855, the Mortons knew something about prairie plants. In his 1871 address at the opening of the University of Nebraska, Sterling said, "One of the grandest of material labors is the reduction of untried lands to tillage" (Olson 157). By "grand," I do not know if he was referring to what he perceived to be the lofty task of converting any landscape to productive cropland or orchard or if he meant that the job was "grandly" arduous. Certainly, the latter was true. Those who used wooden or iron plows had to stop frequently to clean the sticky prairie soil off the moldboard. In *Where the Sky Began: Land of the Tallgrass Prairie*, John Madson writes that the roots of the bluestems and prairie clovers were so tough and wiry that sometimes they damaged plows and injured draft animals. And breaking the tallgrass prairie was noisy work. The sodbusters called the leadplant "prairie shoestring" because when its strong roots were cut by a plow, they popped like breaking shoestrings. Nor was one plowing enough to subdue the prairie. The aerial and subterranean parts of the dominant tall grasses—Indian grass, big bluestem, and switchgrass—are roughly equal, with the seed heads waving six to ten feet above the ground and roots burrowing as far into the earth. While the aerial parts of little bluestem rise only a couple feet, the roots plunge twice that far. The roots of prairie forbs are even more remarkable. The roots of members of the sunflower-aster family can extend eight to twelve feet. The fleshy taproot of the purple coneflower extends ten or more feet. Roots of the leadplant extend sixteen or more feet. In healthy, undisturbed prairie, the sod is so crowded with roots, that alien species—blue grass, leafy spurge, maple trees—can't gain a toehold. Because most of the prairie's biomass is beneath the earth's surface, the plants are safe from droughts, fires, harsh winters, hordes of insects, and big native grazers. Thus the Mortons and other sodbusters found that the tough, deep roots of prairie plants had to be broken again and again before the land was safe for corn and wheat, planted fence row to fence row.

Because the Mortons farmed and kept orchards, they knew something about the extraordinary fertility of prairie soil. But they probably didn't know what accounted for it. When the last ice sheets of the

Pleistocene melted about twenty-five thousand years ago, vast stretches of dried mud remained. High winds carried the fine dust particles (*loess*, an Old German word meaning "light" or "loose") south into what is now Nebraska, Iowa, and western Missouri. Because glacial drift contains a larger variety and greater quantity of the soluble minerals that plants use for food, the soil formed from loess is superior to soil formed from native bedrock.

The fertility of "prairyerth" is also due, in part, to an abundance of humus, the dark, organic residues formed when bacteria and fungi break down dead plants, animals, and insects: plant food. Madson says that in forest soils, the twenty to fifty tons of humus per acre are concentrated on or near the earth's surface. In unbroken prairie soils as much as 250 tons of humus per acre is distributed from the surface to the subsoil. Prairie plants are well nourished from seed head to root tip.

Yet no matter how much the rich, fertile soil yielded, Morton failed to see that treelessness and barrenness are not equivalent states. No matter how much money Morton made from the hogs, corn, and fruits he raised on prairie soil, he spoke of and acted with hostility toward the native landscape. In the March 12, 1870, issue of the *Nebraska City News*, of which he was the editor, he wrote of the need to "battle against the timberless prairies." In his 1872 "Fruit Address" to the Nebraska State Horticultural Society, Morton proclaimed that his goal was to make Nebraska our nation's "best timbered state." Sterling's biographer, James C. Olson, writes that on Christmas 1876, Paul Morton gave his parents letterhead stationary that bore an engraving of their house, Arbor Lodge, in the upper left-hand corner. Stuck in Sterling's farm journal is a sheet of this stationery on which he had scribbled: "From a photograph of house taken by Dr. Smith of Nebraska City in summer of 1876. Had the Dr. set his camera in the same place twenty-two years before it would have been a picture of barren prairie so far as the eye could see without a tree in sight" (245).

Of course Morton wasn't the first to be distressed by the "timberlessness" of the plains. When the first white immigrants arrived in what is now Nebraska, 3 percent of the state was forested, or rather, 97 percent of the area was grassland—tallgrass prairie in the eastern third of the state; mixed grass in the Sandhills and south-central part of the state; short and mixed grasses in the Panhandle. This landscape didn't satisfy the overwhelming majority of the immigrants who were what Kansas historian James C. Malin called "Anglo-American forest men." Part of the baggage these newcomers brought with them from Europe or the eastern United States was, in Malin's words, the belief that "the presence of forests was natural and the absence of trees was an unmistakable sign of deficiency or abnormality of nature" (2). So, when immigrants, who rarely if ever had seen the sun rise or set on an unobstructed horizon, arrived on the Great Plains, they felt overwhelmed, frightened, or diminished by the open land and sky. Many of them were so fixated on the lack of trees that they could not see the grasses, the rich soil, the integrity of the prairie communities. Shortly after his arrival in Nebraska, Judge Edward R. Harden of the territorial supreme court wrote to his wife in Georgia that he was catching the first boat home and would never return to Nebraska Territory: "It is poor country no Timber, sickly, and out of the world and settled up with Savages" (27). One of those savages, Omaha chief Big Elk, told members of Major Stephen H. Long's 1819 expedition, "If I even thought your hearts bad enough to take this land, I would not fear it, as I know there is not wood enough on it for the use of the whites" (Rice B2).

Nor was Morton the first immigrant to dream of remaking the prairie. In "Women and the 'Mental Geography' of the Plains," Sandra L. Myres writes that many newcomers to the plains "believed that the real physical world which they saw about them could be transformed by an increased population and the application of modern science and technology" (42). The science and technology offered by Samuel Aughey, a land speculator, chairman of the Natural Sciences department at the University of Nebraska and first director of the University of Nebraska State Museum, was simple though arduous. Aughey believed that one had only to plow the grasslands to produce a more agreeable, more eastern landscape. In his 1880 *Sketches of the Physical Geography and Geology of Nebraska* Aughey asserted that by breaking "primitive" prairie soil, one could increase absorption of rainfall, which in turn increased evaporation, which in turn increased rainfall. Aughey's views, popularized by Charles D. Wilbur, were repeated in the diaries and journals of diverse grassland settlers. For instance Elizabeth (Mrs. George) Custer wrote, "The cultivation of the ground, the planting of trees, and such causes, have materially modified some of the extraordinary exhibitions that we witnessed when Kansas was supposed to be the great American desert" (Myres 42).

Morton did not come to Nebraska Territory because he loved the land; rather, he came, according to his biographer, "for the express purpose of achieving fame or wealth, preferably both." Immediately upon his arrival Morton went to work on his dual goals of becoming rich and famous and of creating a home place that resembled the home he had left. He succeeded on both counts. Among Morton's worldly accomplishments were: the founding of Nebraska's first newspaper; election to the territorial legislature within a year of his arrival and several times thereafter; appointment as secretary of the territory by President Buchanan in 1858; appointment as secretary and acting governor of the territory for a term running from 1858 to 1861; selection as the Democratic nominee for governor in 1866, 1882, 1884 and 1892, as well as to the U.S. Senate and House of Representatives (he lost each race); an attorney for several Chicago corporations; coauthor with Albert Watkins of the three-volume, posthumously published *Illustrated History of Nebraska*; and appointment to the cabinet as U.S. secretary of agriculture during President Cleveland's second administration (1893–97). According to his biographer, Morton was "a conservative from a section of the country that seemed for a time to produce only radicals; a man, who, though virtually always in the minority, was ever a force to be considered." Morton supported free traders, the gold standard, the rights of labor, and the Confederacy. As a well-paid lobbyist-publicist for the Burlington and Missouri River Railroad, Morton opposed the Granger Movement, the farm organization that secured the passage of laws limiting railroad rates.

As Sterling's wealth and fame grew, so did Arbor Lodge, from a four-room cabin in 1855, to a thirty-room, neocolonial mansion at the time of his death on April 27, 1902. Sterling and Carrie's son, Joy, the founder of the Morton Salt Company, continued his parents' expansions and renovations. When Joy and his family donated the property, which had served as their summer get-away, to the state of Nebraska in 1923, Arbor Lodge included fifty-two rooms.

Sterling was also successful in his goal of re-creating his estate in the image of his old home in the East. Immediately upon arriving on his quarter section, he began planting trees. Dr. George L. Miller, founder and editor of the Omaha *Herald* (now, the *Omaha-World Herald*), wrote in the May 13, 1868, issue of that paper of his friend's landscaping activities: "The farm itself bears the most gratifying evidence of Mr. Morton's early appreciation of what was needed to make it yield the solid as well as the luxurious comforts of Home. His orchards, numbering hundreds of apple trees, remind one of those a century old in the East. . . . All around that splendid farm may be seen proof of the constancy with which Mr. Morton has given direction to fruit and tree culture. He is constantly sticking the 'cuttings' or roots or fruit of forest trees into the ground" (Olson 156).

Morton was not content to transplant native cottonwoods from the riverbanks and bottoms. When County Commissioner Oliver Stevenson brought seed potatoes back from a trip to Pennsylvania, Morton wrote in the February 2, 1867, issue of the *Nebraska City News*: "If every Nebraskan who visits the East would look after matters of this kind, and emulate Mr. Stevenson by introducing new and improved kinds of grains, vegetables, and fruits the whole State would be much benefited" (Olson 158). Morton hoped that tobacco and hemp would become "staple products of Nebraska." Likewise he introduced Suffolk pigs into Otoe County, adding imported fauna to the imported flora. When Carrie returned from a trip to Pike's Peak, she brought an Engelmann spruce seedling in a tomato can to add to the arbor. Sterling's only opposition to alien species was that "far brought" trees didn't grow as easily as native trees, which added ammunition to the arguments of those who believed that apples and pears could not be grown on Nebraska soil.

Nor was Morton content to forest just his own property. On January 4, 1872, he offered a resolution to the State Board of Agriculture, of which he was a member, to establish a tree-planting holiday. The board accepted the proposal and offered one hundred dollars to the Nebraska county agricultural society and twenty-five dollars' worth of books on farming to the individual Nebraskan who properly planted the largest number of trees on the holiday. Two board members wanted to call the holiday Sylvan Day, which Morton rejected since it only referred to forest trees. Arbor, on the other hand, referred to all trees. The name Arbor Day was unanimously accepted.

The next step for Morton in reconstituting the landscape was to compel individual Nebraskans to plant trees. In his famous "Fruit Address" before the State Horticultural Society, also on January 4, 1872, he linked the planting of trees with home, culture, and morality:

> There is comfort in a good orchard, in that it makes the new home more like the "old home in the East," and with its thrifty growth and large luscious fruits, sows contentment in the mind of a family as the clouds scatter the rain. Orchards are missionaries

of culture and refinement. They make the people among whom they grow a better and more thoughtful people. If every farmer in Nebraska will plant out and cultivate an orchard and a flower garden, together with a few forest trees, this will become mentally and morally the best agricultural State, the grandest community of producers in the American Union. . . . If I had the power I would compel every man in the State who had a home of his own, to plant out and cultivate fruit trees. (Olson 163)

Such sentimentality and boosterism were readily accepted and re- peated. On Nebraska's first Arbor Day, Lincoln's *Daily State Journal* charged every property-owning Lincolnite to "put out a tree or two, if not more, with his own hands, if necessary." Moreover, the editor wished that "business of all kinds could be suspended" so that every person "capable of making a hole in the ground" could plant something— tree, shrub, or even a rose bush—in recognition "that this is a treeless country, and that what nature has left unfinished, the enterprise of Nebraskans will complete. Nebraska only lacks trees to be the Elysium of the continent" (Rice B2).

On April 10, 1872, the first Arbor Day was celebrated. Much to Morton's disappointment, the eight hundred trees that he planned to plant on his farm didn't arrive in time. James S. Bishop, a farmer who lived four miles southwest of Lincoln, planted ten thousand trees— cottonwoods, soft maples, Lombardy poplars, box elders, and yellow willows. He won the state fair premium for the finest grove of cultivated timber in the state. On the first Arbor Day, Nebraskans planted more than one million trees, though the editor of the *Nebraska Farmer* claimed that twelve million was a more accurate count. On that first Arbor Day, Morton was positively effusive. In a letter to the *Omaha Daily Herald*, he wrote: "Then what infinite beauty and loveliness we can add to the pleasant plains of Nebraska by planting forest and fruit trees upon every swell of their voluptuous undulations and, in another short decade, make her the Orchard of the Union, the Sylvan queen of the Republic" (Olson 165).

Arbor Day sponsors wanted a celebration every year and a forest for every farm. In 1874, the legislature set aside the second Wednesday of every April as Arbor Day, a legal holiday. In 1874, Morton's sometimes friend, sometimes foe, and fellow orchardist, Governor Robert W. Furnas, issued a proclamation encouraging Nebraskans to celebrate the new holiday. That Arbor Day, Morton noted in his diary that he set out two hundred elms, ashes, and lindens on his farm.

In 1885, the Nebraska State Legislature moved the date of Arbor Day to April 22, Morton's birthday. (Ironically, Earth Day, first celebrated in 1970 coincided with the celebration of Arbor Day.) By 1892, forty-one of the forty-two United States (Delaware being the one exception) as well as several other countries celebrated the tree-planting holiday. In 1895 the state legislature passed a resolution that Nebraska be known as "the Tree Planter's State," a nickname that persisted until 1945 when Nebraska was redubbed "the Cornhusker State." By 1900, seven hundred million trees had been planted in the Midwest alone. In 1972, the centennial of the first Arbor Day, Nebraskans planted seven million trees. Now the holiday is celebrated in every state on a date or dates established by each state's legislature. Now the green road signs welcoming travelers to Nebraska identify our state as the "Home of Arbor Day," asking us to identify ourselves by a movement that sought to make Nebraska look like something other than Nebraska.

The movement to forest the grasslands has had almost a century and a half of political backing in the form of cash incentives from both the state and federal governments. In 1869 the state legislature exempted one hundred dollars' worth of property for every acre of trees planted and maintained. Since most farmers paid their entire tax bill by planting trees, the incentive became too costly for the government and the law was repealed in 1877. Under the federal Timber Culture Act of 1873, anyone who qualified for a homestead could acquire an additional quarter section by planting forty acres "of the same trees" and tending them for ten years. Later the law was revised so that one had only to maintain ten acres' worth of trees for eight years.

The Kinkaid Homestead Act of 1904, sponsored by Congressman Moses P. Kincaid of O'Neill, Nebraska, provided 640 acres for homesteaders in northwestern Nebraska and free tree seedlings to any homesteaders or farmers living west of the hundredth meridian. In 1924 this legislation was replaced by the federal Clarke-McNary Act, by which two million trees per year were sold to Nebraskans at cost for farmstead and feedlot windbreaks. Through this program more than sixty million trees were planted in Nebraska. New Deal projects planted many thousands of miles of shelterbelts in the Midwest and the Great Plains to reduce erosion. In 1902, University of Nebraska botanist Charles Edwin Bessey persuaded President Theodore Roosevelt to provide

206,028 acres of land in the Sandhills, an area dominated by mixed-grass prairie, for what would become the largest, human-made forest in the United States: the Nebraska National Forest.

Planting the prairie with pine forests, orchards, windbreaks, and arbors may seem benign compared to turning it under and either asphalting it or replanting it with nonnative grasses and crops. Yet each of these activities were and are inspired by the same mind set: seeing the land and those who dwell upon it as a commodity or resource. According to this philosophy, land that lacks immediate and practical use is without value and can be remade according to the owner's desires—desires that are usually inspired by economic self-interest, such as Morton's. And so forests continue to be leveled, wetlands drained and filled, deserts forced to bloom like a rose, and the grasslands broken.

To the Anglo-American forest people, the planting of almost any tree was and is desirable, since it converts the ugly and barren into the beautiful and productive. Yet tree planting can have disastrous consequences when the species planted is inappropriate for a place. Alien plant species steal moisture, nutrients, and sunlight from native species. In the absence of natural predators, "far brought" species have no checks on their ability to reproduce and can quickly overtake a habitat. Since ecosystems are comprised of complex, intricate interdependencies, the insertion of an alien species into an exquisitely balanced ecosystem or the displacement of a native species from its exquisitely balanced belonging-place affects countless other organisms, in great or small ways.

The Russian olive, a native of southeastern Europe and western Asia, was introduced in the United States in the late 1800s and widely planted as a windbreak. Since then, this aggressive species has invaded riparian areas that were historically open and has lowered the water table. Those riparian areas dominated by dense stands of Russian olives do not host the same rich diversity of bird species (piping plovers, least terns, and sandhill and whooping cranes, to name but a few) found on open sandbars, fields, and prairies dominated by native plant species. Likewise, the Siberian elm, native to northern China, eastern Siberia, Manchuria, and Korea, was introduced in the United States because of its fast growth and ability to withstand summer droughts and cold winters. Consequently, this species was the most widely planted shelterbelt tree in the 1930s and the dominant species in Nebraska's urban forests. This elm produces many hundreds of samara (one-seeded, winged fruit) per tree. The wind-disseminated seeds sprout quickly and easily, forming dense thickets of seedlings on disturbed prairie, making it even more unlikely that the land will return to a vigorous, healthy state. In short, tree planting is desirable only if one selects species that preserve the integrity and stability of the native ecosystem. In some cases, the best way to contribute to the well-being of an ecosystem is not by planting trees but by removing "weed" trees.

I do not hold Morton, Furnas, Kinkaid, Bessey, and the other forest people accountable for what they could not have known. Since the prairie was one of the last biomes to be studied, there was little information to challenge the cultural stereotype of prairie as a deficient, monotonous wasteland. Nor could they have known the value, nay, the necessity of genetic, species, and ecosystem diversity. Wallace Stegner writes that most people in new environments were and are driven by "the compulsion to impose themselves and their needs, their old habits and new crops on new earth. They don't look to see what the new earth is doing naturally; they don't listen to its voice."

But I do hold accountable Morton and anyone else who refuses to become acquainted with the place they call home and who fights so hard against what is natural and right for a place. Nothing in Morton's writings indicates to me that he grew to appreciate the economy, productivity, diversity, and complexity of the tallgrass prairie that once covered eastern Nebraska or the mixed-grass prairie that he encountered on his political and business trips into central Nebraska. Nor have I found evidence that he grew to see the beauty of the grasslands. No accounts of bronze-purple stalks of big bluestem or the golden plumes of Indian grass nodding in the wind. No accounts of finding pleasure and solace in the seam where sky and land meet. No mention of the leadplant with its silver-green leaflets and its cones of purple blossoms and gold stamens or the abundance of orchids (lady's tresses, prairie fringed, showy orchis, bracted) or the scent of prairie roses or the brilliant red-orange of the Illinois bundleflower. It appears to me that the high spot near the Missouri River where Morton lived, worked, and dreamed remained for him an estranging-place. In his efforts to fill the emptiness that he projected onto the land with what did not belong there, he squandered his time, energy, intelligence, and prosperity. If Morton had not had such contrary designs on the land, he might have experienced the freedom and discipline that comes from living in and with nature.

In one respect, Morton and the other forest people were a magnificent failure. Despite their tree-planting zeal, despite Morton's legacy of 128 years of tree-planting incentives, at the turn of the millennium, only about 3 percent of Nebraska is forested—the same percentage as was forested a couple of hundred years ago. What has changed, however, is where one is likely to find trees. The native deciduous forest on the west bank of the Missouri has been cleared for agriculture and the expansion of such Missouri River cities as Omaha, Bellevue, Papillion, Plattsmouth, and Nebraska City. Native red cedars have moved out of the river valleys and onto range and woodlands. Dams and reservoirs have reduced floodplain forests; yet flood control has permitted trees to clog rivers and streams, robbing sandhill cranes and migrating waterfowl of their preferred habitat. At the same time, tree planting in cities— the only tree-planting efforts on the Great Plains that I support, since trees reduce the heat island effect, clean the air, and create the rather sheltered, rather private, outdoor enclosures that we want near our living spaces—is far below what it should be. According to Assistant Nebraska State Forester Dave Mooter, Nebraska's urban forest is less than 50 percent stocked.

But in another respect, Morton and the other forest people were a magnificent success. A recent *National Wildlife* report states that only .2 percent of the prairie remains, making it the rarest and most fragmented ecosystem in the United States, the one in gravest danger of disappearing altogether. John Madson observes that "[t]oday, it is easier to find virgin groves of redwoods than virgin stands of tallgrass prairie." Even when one does find a stand of never-broken prairie, it is usually but a fenced-off plot, a museum piece, too tiny and isolated to accommodate those species with large territorial needs, too tiny and isolated to even suggest its former range and glory. Now we can only imagine what once lay outside the Mortons' back door—dark bison moving through bright, seemingly endless acres of big bluestem, golden sunflowers, white asters, and purple gayfeather.

Alien and Native

Say the word *alien* (from the Latin *alienus*, "of or belonging to another person or place") and most people picture something strange, foreign, not like them. Big-headed, big-eyed, tiny-bodied, androgynous creatures from other parts of the cosmos. Dark and taciturn or dark and fast-talking people with unpronounceable names who come from far cities. Borrowed words that reassert their place of origin with each utterance. Tête-à-tête. Quid pro quo. Jihad. Zeitgeist. Nisei. El Niño. Prickly or angular ideas that you just can't wrap your mind around.

But then, some aliens have been here so long and in such abundance that they seem native. Soybeans, lilac bushes, measles, sparrows, people from Europe and Africa, zebra mussels, black and brown rats, democracy, purple loosestrife, Holsteins, Christianity, tumbleweeds. And some natives (from the Latin *nasci*, "to be born"; hence, innate, indigenous, aboriginal, natural), such as pure prairie, nature worship, bison burgers, the brown people who work in Nebraska meatpacking plants for eight dollars an hour, and so on, seem exotic and Other. Borrowed words become so adapted to the uses of the borrowing language (hence, they are *naturalized*), that only etymologists or lovers of lexicons know their origin. In truth, you can't tell the natives from the aliens just by looking.

Aliens can become naturalized. For plants and animals, that means becoming adapted, habituated, or acclimated to the new environment. In the case of humans, that means being given the rights and privileges of the members of the dominant group. And natives can become alienated. In most cases this means giving the native's home territory to another organism or group of organisms—as if it were yours to give away.

3. The Memory of Trees

During the night of October 26, 1997, thirteen inches of wet, heavy snow snapped tree limbs already weighted with ice and fall foliage. My neighbor said that he couldn't sleep on the night of this great storm because each snapping branch sounded like a gun being fired. The next morning, the city looked like a war zone. Big limbs had pulled down power lines, making some streets impassable, leaving 150,000 eastern Nebraskans in the dark and cold. Schools and some businesses were closed for more than a week. The more lasting consequence is that the Great Storm killed approximately one hundred thousand trees in eastern Nebraska, six thousand city-owned trees in Lincoln alone. Many more trees were injured.

At the time of the Great Storm, I was still living in the estranging-place. I was glad to have missed the storm that damaged so many of the silver maples, Siberian elms, green ashes, oaks, sycamores, cottonwoods, hackberries, red buds, and various ornamentals that form Lincoln's urban forest. These trees are remarkable because they would not occur naturally in such large numbers in this place. A Nebraska State Historical Society photograph of Lincoln in 1871 shows the first university building, a many-storied, brick structure, surrounded by several dozen houses, barns, sheds, and streets, but not a single tree. Since that time Lincolnites have planted many thousands of trees, converting the vast, bright prairie into a comfortably shaded, cityscape.

These trees are also dear to me because they remind me of people. The scars where limbs have been removed from the trunk of my pin oak form a distorted face: two eyes, one higher than the other, each cocked in different directions, a round nose, six gaping mouths. When I look out my living room window, my attention is pulled toward this humanesque face. Ovid's description of Daphne's metamorphosis, from lovely hunter and disinterested object of Apollo's attentions to laurel tree, details the other physical resemblances that we humans have long recognized between our bodies and the arboreal forms: "Scarce had she thus prayed when a down-dragging numbness seized her limbs, and her soft sides were begirt with thin bark. Her hair was changed to leaves, her arms to branches. Her feet, but now so swift, grew fast in sluggish roots, and her head was not but a tree's top. Her gleaming beauty alone remained."

Perhaps the similarities between trees and humans are what led ancient peoples to believe that trees had souls and so were living, conscious beings. The tree gods provided sun and rain, made crops grow, herds multiply, women reproduce, and oracles speak. Because the tree and the god were one, a person who killed a tree had to offer his or her life in exchange; reciprocal penalties existed for those who injured a tree god. Scottish anthropologist James Frazer said that under old German law, one who skinned the bark of a living tree was punished by having his navel cut out and nailed to the injured party. The culprit was driven around the trunk until his guts provided a living substitute for the bark he had peeled.

Eventually, humans believed that their deities weren't the actual tree but only resided in trees and could leave their abodes at will. As soon as the tree spirits became mobile, they began to more closely resemble the human body. The Canaanite goddess Asherah is a transitional form in which the tree god as tree and the tree god as human coexisted. This benevolent, enduring goddess, the mother of seventy gods, was worshipped in the temples as an unshaped piece of wood. But, in private devotions, she was a simple, woman-shaped clay figurine. In time, Asherah became less treelike and more human until finally she appeared as a naked, curly headed goddess riding a sacred lion and holding lilies and serpents in her upraised hands. I find this tree goddess' goodness and power deeply appealing. I can see why the Hebrews' version of the Great Spirit was so threatened by Asherah that he ordered Moses and his followers to destroy her altars, break her images, and cut down the groves where she was worshipped (Exodus 34:13).

Although the followers of abstract, patriarchal gods may have prohibited the outright worship of trees, the links between trees and deities persisted. Yahweh spoke to Moses from a burning bush. While sitting beneath the oak of Mamre, Abraham beheld a flash of light, a sweet odor, and he turned and saw Death approaching in great glory and beauty. Buddha found enlightenment beneath a bo tree; just prior to his death, the Blessed One asked that his head be placed between two trees. In response, the trees burst into bloom and scattered their blossoms over his body even though their bloom time was long past. Anne, the mother of Mary, received the news of her Immaculate Conception while sitting beneath a laurel tree. Jesus was crucified on the holm oak or ilex. In the cabalistic teachings of the medieval Jews, the process of creation was represented as emanations from the branches of a cosmic tree, hanging upside down and rooted in the "inscrutable heights." Three hundred years ago in Rajasthan, India, 350 women and men, members of the Bishbios sect that held trees sacred, allowed themselves to be slaughtered as they resisted the axmen who came to take their trees for the maharajah's new palace. In 1917, Our Lady of Fatima appeared over a small oak in Portugal. In the early 1960s, two thousand Marian apparitions occurred in a pine grove at Garabandal, Spain. In 1992, an image of the Virgin of Guadalupe appeared in an oak trunk at Watsonville, California. And so on. Even those people who do not pledge their allegiances to a deity still claim to feel "more spiritual" when in a grove of trees. Even those of us who find the treeless horizon of the grasslands heart expanding, soul liberating, and more utterly beautiful than any other landscape, sometimes yearn for the enclosed, chapel-like atmosphere of a wood or neighborhood streets so thick with trees that they seem to be porticos or galleries.

It is of little wonder, then, that people so easily project their feelings onto trees. Venerable oaks. Majestic elms. Ancestral sequoias. Weeping willows. Gay maples. Laughing cottonwoods. Isaiah said that in praise of the creator, "All the trees of the field shall clap their hands." William Carlos Williams's trees "thrash and scream/ guffaw and curse—/ wholly abandoned/ damning the race of men." Louise Erdrich wrote that trees in a forest on a windy day seem passionate, "as though they were flung to-gether in an eager embrace, caressing each other, branch to branch. . . . There must be great rejoicing out there on windy days, ecstasy, for trees move so slowly on calm days." Even scientists impose human characteristics on trees. Botanist Donald Culross Peattie advised people to emulate the pines who "suffer bodily pain and know weariness" yet never "toss with insomnia, or doubt till they [can] no longer act." People who emulate pine trees can "hardly be small," said Peattie, and they "might, sometimes, have a noble thought."

When I gratefully came home to the grasslands of Nebraska in July 1998, I moved into the little house in which I had lived six years earlier. I walked the neighborhood I once knew so well with my eyes on the ragged edge where sky and treetops meet. But instead of being surrounded by the familiar, I felt that I was in an eerie sculpture garden. Big chunks had been ripped off some trees, transforming spheres into clumps of tufts. The ways in which the outlines of many trees departed from the field guide descriptions were more apparent when I sketched them and their shadows on paper. Instead of widely spreading branches, some large trunks were topped with close leafy caps. One hackberry had the customary lateral spread in its lower limbs, but no upward thrust—an empty bowl. Some red cedars had lost their peaks. One linden formed a V instead of a pyramid. New growth sprouted defiantly from branchless trunks. Dead limbs dangled. Young trees seemed old and decrepit in their sparseness and brokenness.

I especially noticed the difference in my front yard. Once my house had been shaded by a pine across the street, three pin oaks (one in my yard, one across the street, one in the yard just south of mine), and an elm, also in the yard south of mine. But now my neighbor's elm and pin oak are gone, the pine is stripped of many of its middle branches, the top two-thirds of the pin oak across the street has been lopped off, and my pin oak is not only missing its top but a middle chunk big enough to drive a pickup truck through. The measurable effect of these losses on me is that my living room and my daughter's bedroom receive full sun in the afternoon and early evening and so are sun-broiled in July and August. In autumn, there is less rustle and color from starving leaves. In the winter, there are fewer layers of dark, moldering foliage.

And too, the loss of trees and parts of trees interferes with the picture of home that I carry in my head. In this picture, my house is safe, cozy, and protected because of the full trees surrounding it. But when I behold my house as if it weren't my own, the broken and missing trees make it appear small, seedy, and exposed. I'm struck by how the loss of trees and parts of trees violates my innate sense of form. Although I do not expect trees to exhibit the precise symmetry I find in animals, I do expect them to grow symmetrically. Such balance is practical. When branches extend in all directions, the foliage can absorb the maximum amount of light, both direct and reflected. When the branches are evenly distributed on all sides the tree is stable; when the tree is not evenly weighted, say, if it has one or more major limbs on one side only, it is more likely to topple in high winds. I see precariousness but remember balance. Time and again my memory and the reality do not match.

We more willingly integrate changes in our bodies, our environment, and our philosophies when they occur gradually rather than suddenly. The slow swelling of my abdomen during my pregnancies gradually repositioned my center of balance, gradually limited my range of movements. But the first quick or balancing movement, the first forward bend following childbirth was disorienting because I had to compensate for the sudden loss of a heavy, round weight. The step-by-step movement of housing subdivisions into the country can be more easily overlooked or absorbed by those who live near that edge, but to those of us who haven't seen the area for many months, the change is unsettling because it appears to have happened overnight, without our permission or participation.

So, too, the arrival of a new paradigm. After almost four centuries of dominance, the mechanistic model of the human body (that is, the body as a machine whose parts occasionally break or malfunction usually because of some factor beyond one's control—germs or genetics, for instance) is gently being nudged aside by a model that is more dynamic, more holistic, more participatory. If this radical shift arrived at once and fully formed, its accompanying changes would overwhelm us. But because the signs of change have arrived gradually—midwives in hospitals, the coverage of acupuncture by some insurance companies, a growing number of allopathic doctors who inquire about emotional well-being as well as physical symptoms—we can rather smoothly integrate an old philosophy that for many is new.

The trees in my neighborhood literally changed overnight. But I am not able to make such sudden revisions in the map of my home terrain that I carry within me. I am not able to forget what my memory has prepared me to see. Months after I first laid eyes on the damaged trees, I still expect symmetry. Perhaps in time my eyes will anticipate the now truncated forms of familiar trees. Perhaps in time my skin will anticipate greater warmth and light, less shade and coolness, as I walk familiar streets. Perhaps in time I will see, know, remember, and imagine the trees as they are instead of as they were. But for now I am bewildered, a bit unhinged that trees, deliberately chosen, planted and tended, like humans in so many ways, are no longer part of the steady, unwavering background but are brief, susceptible objects in the inconstant, changeable, foreground.

Though trees lack what most of us consider a mind/brain, it is hard to conceive of them as senseless objects. "A head, a heart, a central organization of any sort, nerves, and consciousness, a tree does not own," observed Peattie. "But something runs in it that is vital, that, when it disintegrates, leaves the great body untenanted, a corpse."

In the late 1960s and early 1970s a number of questionable scientific experiments suggested the presence of memory and intelligence in plants. One study published in the winter 1968 *International Journal of Parapsychology* set out to prove a primary perception in plant life. Cleve Backster, an American expert on the use of the lie detector, arranged for one of his students to uproot and stamp on one of two plants in a room. The crime was committed in secret; neither Backster nor any of the other students knew the identity of the "plant-assassin"; only the surviving plant "knew" who the murderer was. Backster attached a polygraph to the witness plant and led his students past it one by one. Whenever the killer approached, the witness plant made the needle of the galvanometer go wild. Backster concluded that this plant, and by extension, all plants, are aware of their surroundings and are capable of remembering.

Likewise, A. Merkulov published a study in 1972 that postulated the presence of at least a short-term and possibly a long-term memory in plants in the Soviet publication *Science and Religion*, a journal that at the same time presented the latest scientific findings and set out to refute religious beliefs. Merkulov explained that after proper instruction, beans, potatoes, wheat, and crowfoot "remembered" the frequency of flashes from a xenon-hydrogen lamp. The plants repeated the pulsations with what Merkulov called "exceptional accuracy." (Unfortunately, the account I read of this study does not explain *how* this accurate imitation was achieved—through a movement? An utterance? An excretion?) Merkulov concluded that because crowfoot was able to repeat a given frequency as long as eighteen hours after it was last emitted, it was possible to speak of a long-term memory in plants. In another experiment, Merkulov administered an electrical shock to a philodendron each time he sat a mineralized rock next to it. Eventually, the plant became so conditioned that it could distinguish between mineralized and barren rock and became "upset" when ore was placed next to it. (Neither does the account I read of this experiment explain how the scientist knew that the plant was distraught, whether, say, it shuddered, blanched, wilted, dropped leaves, or whether Merkulov also relied on a galvanometer.) Despite my questions about the protocol of these experiments, the contention by Backster, Merkulov, and some other unconventional scientists that plants possess a consciousness on the cellular level is plausible and worthy of careful, controlled investigation, not so that plants can be put on the witness stand or used in mineral prospecting but because some of us want to know just who else lives at our address.

Even those scientists who reject the notion that plants possess thoughts, emotions, and sensations acknowledge remarkable powers and sensitivities in the plant kingdom such as inter-plant communication, achieved not telepathically but chemically. Tree care expert John M. Haller says that once "inducible defenses" are developed in a victimized plant, they can be communicated to nearby plants of the same species. For instance, when the Sitka willow (*Salix sitchensis*) is attacked by insects, it responds not only by making itself unpalatable or indigestible but also by transmitting a "warning" to those willows in the area who have not been attacked. In response, those willows also begin to modify their chemistry, chiefly by producing greater quantities of tannins and phenolics. These chemical messages travel from plant to plant, via root grafts in most cases, yet some studies indicate that the signals may also be wafted through the air. Perhaps on the night of the Great Storm, the wind carried shrieks, snarls, wails, warnings, and farewells.

If plants possess some level of awareness, perhaps they, too, are troubled by sensory ghosts or phantom pains in their amputated limbs long after the site has physically healed. Some people who have lost an arm claim that they can wriggle missing fingers or reach out and grab objects within an arm's length. Amputated legs still dance, run, pedal, kick. Amputated breasts still swell to tenderness for a few days each month or tingle in anticipation of touch. If the sensation of life's processes continue in a tree's missing part, perhaps the tree still feels the pull of an elongating and thickening growing tip, the hot pressure of leaves, stems, and flowers breaking through the tough bud scales; the irresistible unclenching of leaves in autumn.

Even when the whole crown is destroyed, the new growth tends to reshape the tree along its original lines, as if there is an intelligence— perhaps from within, perhaps from without, or both—guiding the process. A broken elm will attempt to produce several arching limbs that end in pendulous branchlets. A broken sycamore will attempt to recover a crown that is open and spreading. In time, my pin oak will no longer contain a broken mast and a huge triangular gap between the bottom and the topmost branches. From the coniferlike, strong, central leader will sprout many slender spurs, the "pins" from which the tree gets its common name. Active growth will continue until this particular tree fulfills the law or organization of pin oaks.

I did not realize how deeply I was affected by the disruption in the patterns of the trees in my neighborhood until one morning, after I had been back in Nebraska but a week. I awakened facing the south window in my bedroom; the blind was partially raised. My first thought was that something was wrong. My bedroom should not be so light-filled; I should not be able to see so much sky through my window. Then, I remembered. My neighbor's Siberian elm and pin oak were no longer there. That one of the trees was an elm made its absence particularly poignant. Graceful American elms once formed a Gothic arch over Marietta Street, the street against which most of my childhood memories are set. By the time I was eight, all of the diseased elms had been removed, leaving our street shaven and bright. Even now, the elm's vase or feather-duster-shaped crown, its heavy, swinging branches form the template against which I compare all other trees; its doubly serrated elliptical leaf—lopsided at the base, rough and deeply veined below, smooth above—is the prototypical form against which I compare all other leaves. I know the sugar maple by the five non-elmlike lobes on its leaves and the way it compacts the elm's fountainlike arches into an oval.

Still, I wonder why my first thought upon waking would be about an elm that is no longer there. When I slept in this bedroom before, the bed had not been flush against the south wall, and so I had never seen the elm-that-is-no-longer-there from this position. Even if I had, would I have so internalized the quantity and quality of leaf-light falling through my window or remember the manner in which a nearby tree had once chipped the sky into pieces? What I was experiencing was not image- and language-bound headmemory but mute, sensation-bound bodymemory. I possess other such memories—the crackling, tawny edginess of September on the grasslands; the shoulder joint, left biceps, planted feet, steamy, soapy slam of a tray full of glass dishes into an institutional dish washer; the pleasant pain of hard milk moving down my breasts and out the tips in floral sprays when my babies cried; the skull tingle and spinal plunge that deepens my deepest prayers, which says that whereas the idea of God is known in the head, the presence of God is known in the bones, organs, tissues, plasma, cells. When William Faulkner wrote that memory believes before knowing remembers, I believe that he was speaking of recollections such as these experienced first and most profoundly in the body. Although I do not remember the particulars of the trees in my neighborhood—I cannot, say, sketch their once-unbroken forms from memory—broadly, diffusely, bodily, I remember their thrust and spread, their rough and smooth colors, the shelter and shade they made, the communities they hosted, the way they dignified my home. I miss the trees often and deeply.

Perhaps other organisms remember the absence of trees and parts of trees in their bodies, too. In the weeks following the Great Storm, birds may have dodged branches that were no longer there. Squirrels may have instinctively leapt for branches that existed only in memory, a memory stored as much in the paws and strong hind legs as in the brain. Some of the beetles, lichens, fungi, moths, cicadas, and blue jays that once found habitat in my pin oak may have left because they felt crowded and hungry in the now smaller tree. The grasses may remember their once-thin, shaded growth as that time before they saw the light. Thick, exterior leaves may remember a thin, interior position. Shoots from dormant tree buds, now elongating and leafing out, may still remember their long sleep. Perhaps the trees are as haunted as I am by memories of their unbroken forms. Perhaps the trees haven't yet been able to replace their memories of their whole forms with images of their new forms. Perhaps those memories have worn deep, permanent tracks, laid down like growth rings, memories forever borne in the body of the tree.

Some memories wear deep, permanent tracks in the human brain. Yet, some memories erode with each passing year. In time, they are but dust. I wonder if I could intentionally cause the wearing away of a memory, say, by pushing it down so that it is never foremost in my mind or by confusing the images each time they surface (not a pearl but a coffee pot; not heavy and musky but acrid and penetrating; not gracefully tapered but wildly skewed) so that they're hopelessly scrambled. Or would that only serve to strengthen the link between the stimulus and the data encoded and stored in the memory circuits?

I read that forgetting happens as more and more memories with similar meanings or associations pile up without enough clues to single them out. In time, it is difficult if not impossible to recall the original material, not because the storehouse is overcrowded with memories but because new experiences and changed habits of thought break the connections or cues that help distinguish one memory from another, cues that are critical if one is to retrieve a memory trace. Perhaps if I fill my head with images of the trees as they now are my memories of the trees as they once were will fade or become indistinguishable from my other memory traces. Not an easy task since old memories can be sturdy enough to withstand any meddling short of brain damage, and new memories can be as fragile as moth wings.

Nonetheless, I walk my neighborhood with my eye on the rough edge where sky and treetops meet. I take in the new forms of familiar trees. I guard a single image with single-pointed concentration until it lands on fertile ground. I wait for it to unfurl its tiny white thread, root tip at one end, a bud and a pair of bright leaves at the other. I wait for this seedling to grow with and against gravity's pull. I wait for its roots to lengthen and rebranch. I wait for the branches to lengthen and rebranch, to clothe themselves with leaves, to reach until they fill the empty spaces.

Creative

When I was working on a master's degree in composition and rhetoric in the mid-1980s, I had a vague idea that I wanted to find ways to help first-year college composition students be "more creative." I delved into the writings of Plato, Aristotle, Abraham Maslow, Peter Elbow, James Moffitt, and others for ideas as to how to accomplish this. When I told the professor of cognitive psychology who was a member of my thesis committee about my project, he said that he refused to use the word "creative," since he didn't know what it meant. "People think that anything a kid does with a box of crayons is 'creative,'" he explained. "Some even think it's 'creative' if my dog runs across the kitchen floor with muddy feet and leaves behind beautiful patterns." I dropped the cognitive psychologist from my committee and replaced him with a professor from the education department whose only concern with my thesis was that I had used the first person singular (he circled each "I" with an orange magic marker) instead of the less engaged and engaging third person. The thesis that I submitted in fulfillment of my degree requirements, *A Study of Audience in Two Classes of College Freshmen*, was utterly practical and utterly lacking in the imaginative leaps and new solutions that I recognize as *creative*. (*Create* is derived from the Latin *creare* and the Sanskrit *kar*, meaning "to make," and the Greek *krainein*, meaning "to accomplish.")

In time, I realized that the cognitive psychologist was correct. Most of what a child does with a box of crayons is neither original nor innovative. The toddler may be scribbling on the wall just because it feels good to move her arm back and forth. The first grader drawing lollipop-shaped trees and round yellow suns encircled with evenly spaced, yellow bristles is reproducing what first graders have been drawing at least since I was one. Not creative in the godly, prime mover sense of bringing into being something from nothing. Not creative in the human sense of making something else from what is already there. Rather these are expressive or imitative acts. Meanwhile, the dog is running, instinctively running, unaware of the tracks that she's leaving behind.

The act of making something else from what is already there always involves a simultaneous creation and destruction. While breaking the land and planting it with the seeds of Eastern Hemisphere grains resulted in a beautiful sea of amber waves, this act vanquished the native prairie plants. While the creation of the State of Israel provided a homeland for the Jews, it meant the destruction of Palestine as a geopolitical entity and homeland for those Palestinians whose families have dwelt there for several millennia. While Korczak Ziolkowski's statue of Crazy Horse on his horse might well be a worthy tribute to this hero, it has ravaged the six-hundred-foot-high granite mountain near Custer, South Dakota, into which it is being carved. In 1998, five hundred tons of granite were blasted from the mountain so that work could begin on Crazy Horse's horse, whose head was twenty-two stories high. Even what seems like the purest, most self-contained type of creativity—turning the events, images, and ideas of one's life into a written story—is a destroyer. Writing about one's memories, trimming, padding, moving them around, reshaping them until they fit a readable or "tellable" form, changes those memories in great or small ways. What the writer remembers after her act of creation is not her memory of the event that is the subject of her essay or story, but the written account of her memory.

4. Affinity

On September 18, 1999, Meredith and I are at the Edgerton Explorit Center in Aurora, Nebraska. This science center is a tribute to Dr. Harold Edgerton (1903–90) from Fremont, Nebraska, who developed techniques of high-speed and stroboscopic photography. During World War II, he invented an electronic flash bright enough to permit aerial photographs to be taken at night at an altitude of more than one mile. After the war, he photographed U.S. nuclear explosions and ocean depths. I study reprints of Edgerton photographs: a bat in flight, a tennis racket hitting a ball, bullets impacting a steel plate, a drop of milk hitting a hard surface.

The Explorit Center is filled with hands-on activities, just as Edgerton, a professor at the Massachusetts Institute of Technology, would have wanted. Meredith and I whisper in the echo dome, inject "poisons" into a cross section of the water table, take turns pedaling a stationery bicycle fast enough that we illuminate a light bulb. About one-quarter of the museum is devoted to an interactive display about Nebraska agriculture. There we size chicken eggs, compare different types of dry beans and seed corns, don a beekeeper's protective gear, and slide packages of cereal, shampoo, and photographic film past a cash register scanner that lists the Nebraska agricultural products in each item. And we examine a section of a center-pivot irrigation pipe. I had only seen one of these from afar: enormous insectlike contraptions that spray water on corn and bean fields. While I appreciate Edgerton's photographs of things too small or fast for my unaided eye to perceive, I fail to see the utility of his invention. Yet I am certain of the effects of center-pivot irrigation on the lives of many Nebraskans. In part this technology was responsible for the surge in irrigated farm acreage in Nebraska, from fewer than nine hundred thousand acres in 1950 to over six million in 1982, much of that on land once considered too arid for anything but grazing (U.S. Bureau of the Census 1952, 1982). By 1981, almost twenty-seven thousand pivots were operating in Nebraska (Sheffield and Rundquist 132). Now, only California has more irrigated acres than Nebraska. Meanwhile, the production of center-pivot systems has affected more than just our farmers. In 1983, the manufacture of the systems represented about 6 percent of Nebraska's industrial work force. In other words, nearly one out of every hundred paychecks in the state was bankrolled by the center-pivot industry (Swinton B2, B5). I photograph Meredith standing before the aluminum tube and nozzles.

After we leave the Explorit Center, I drive south on Highway 14. Farm workers are cutting swaths of stubble around or through their fields and filling their trucks with mounds of gold. The center-pivot irrigators traversing most fields are dry, still, and waiting.

To understand how the center-pivot irrigator was able to so alter the landscape of Nebraska, one must know something of the climate of the state and the expectations of most of those who farm here. In eastern Nebraska, mean annual precipitation is 27.8 inches; in central Nebraska, 22.3 inches; in western Nebraska, 17.9 inches, though some parts of the Panhandle average fewer than 10 inches of rain per year. Those who came to the Great Plains from places with at least 30 inches of precipitation per year were bound to fail if they tried to raise the same crops with the same methods that had worked in Illinois, Pennsylvania, Georgia, or England.

In 1878 Major John Wesley Powell (1834–1902), a geologist with the U.S. Geological Survey, issued his *Report on the Land of the Arid Regions of the United States* in which he stated that nonirrigable farming could not be carried on west of the area beyond the hundredth meridian, roughly the western half of Nebraska, because that area receives fewer than twenty inches of precipitation per year. Land receiving between twenty and twenty-eight inches of annual precipitation was marginal, in Powell's judgment. With a half century more of precipitation records at his disposal than Powell, Texas historian Walter Prescott Webb placed the dividing line between conventional and irrigated farming at the ninety-eighth meridian, meaning that crops must be irrigated in all but the eastern third of Nebraska (Webb 5).

Powell recommended that people in arid and semiarid places dwell near rivers and streams; that land be divided not into the squares of the Jeffersonian grid or into proscribed amounts of the Homestead Act and related legislation, but according to the lay of the land; that because of the expense and labor involved, farmers who had to irrigate be limited to tracts of no more than 80 acres; that those who grazed cattle should work tracts of 2,560 acres, sixteen times the size of plots provided by the Homestead Act; and that land and water be used cooperatively and communally, with the Hidatsa and Arikara villages on the upper Missouri, the métis settlements of southern Alberta, the Mormon communities in the Great Basin, and the ejido villages of Mexico serving as models (Manning 108).

Powell, the director of the Bureau of American Ethnology and the U.S. Geological Survey, saw his ideas debated, ridiculed, or ignored. He saw people heed the ideas of Professors Samuel Aughey and Charles Wilber of the University of Nebraska, who claimed that precipitation would increase as "civilization" extended westward. He saw people heed the ideas of those who claimed that the arid plains were undermined by artesian wells that would spout water to the surface as soon as the grasslands were broken and cultivated, and the ideas of J. Sterling Morton, who believed that almost anything—orchards, eastern forests, and tobacco—could flourish on Nebraska soils.

Until the end of the nineteenth century, those farmers who irrigated their fields did so through trenches. By 1889, there were 214 irrigated farms in Nebraska, averaging fifty-five acres each. But the low farm prices and droughts of the 1890s caused many people to leave the land. During this time, my father's paternal grandparents left south-central Nebraska just a few years after their arrival there for southeastern Iowa, where precipitation averaged thirty-two to thirty-six inches per year and the Mississippi flooded the bottomlands most springs. Of those who remained on the land in Nebraska, many began irrigating in earnest. By 1898 about two thousand windmills, most of which were homemade, were hoisting underground water onto fields (Sageser 113).

Some farmers living in regions where the annual rainfall was between eight and twenty inches per year avoided irrigating through dryland farming techniques. To conserve every drop of moisture, they covered the soil with a blanket of dust mulch after plowing. They ran furrows across instead of up and down the hillsides, forming a series of rain-holding troughs, one above the other. They tilled the soil to kill moisture- and nutrient-stealing weeds. They planted fewer seeds on bigger spreads and idled the land every other year, so it could store moisture, and they planted crops adapted to semiarid regions—alfalfa, sorghum, potatoes, beets, and varieties of Russian wheat.

Following the droughts of the 1930s, farmers began pumping water laid down over three million years ago in the High Plains (Ogallala) Aquifer, as well as water from rivers. They applied this water to their fields through siphon tubes or "gated" pipes, with multiple controllable outlets. Both methods required intensive labor. Next, irrigators watered their fields with sprinklers—first by hand-moved pipes, then with pipes towed by tractors, then with rotating boom sprinklers, then with self-propelled center-pivot systems (Sheffield, "Economic Analysis" 9).

The center pivot is a long aluminum or plastic pipe mounted on wheels and attached by a swivel connection to a well in the middle of a field. The nozzle size increases from the part of the pipe nearest to that farthest from the well, so that water can be applied uniformly. Adjustable water cocks allow the sprinkling of three-tenths to four inches of water per application (Dick 415). The 1,200-foot pipe moves in a giant circle like a clock hand, spraying water, pesticides, and insecticides to 130 out of 160 acres—all but the corners. In *Grasslands*, Richard Manning writes that when viewed from the air, these sprinklers create a distinctive pattern on the land: "big circles like markers on a filled bingo card" (226).

Through irrigation pipes, the water came to the farmer instead of the farmer to the water. Through irrigation pipes, lands of little rain became lands of instant rain.

The center-pivot irrigator is the creation of Columbus native Frank Zybach (Zee-bok). I first learned of him when I read a brief profile, "Inventor Created Instant Rain for Farmers," by Al J. Laukitis in the July 1999 *Lincoln Journal Star* special section, "Twentieth-Century Legacy: 100 People Who Helped Build Nebraska." In the photograph accompanying the article, Zybach is sitting on what might be the front porch of his house, his sleeves rolled up, his hands age-spotted, his belt buckle off-center, his shirt pocket filled with pens, his jowls falling, his hairline receding, his glasses' frame dark above his eyes and clear below, his expression neutral. He looks as comfortable as an old shoe. What fostered this common man's inventiveness? I wondered. And why was he so unheralded? In terms of directly measurable effects,

Zybach's invention has touched the lives of more people who reside in Nebraska and certainly has had a more profound effect upon the land and economy than the contributions of such widely recognized Nebraskans as Willa Cather, Buffalo Bill, Warren Buffett, Bob Kerrey, and the more notorious members of the Cornhusker football team. Yet, I had never heard of Zyback until July 1999.

Apparently, most other Nebraskans knew little or nothing about him, too. After several days of research at the state historical society and the university libraries, after numerous long distance telephone calls to the Platte County Historical Society, to the *Columbus Telegram*, to the grandson of Zybach's business partner, to people who had known Zybach (each described him as nice, common, pleasant, humble, full of good ideas; none offered illuminating anecdotes), and a day in Columbus at the Columbus Public Library, the Columbus Catholic cemetery, and the streets where Zybach had lived, I had little more than the basic outline of this influential but obscure man's life. What I've pieced together about him is this.

Frank's parents—Edward Zybach, the son of Swiss immigrants who settled in Duncan, Nebraska, and Lena Liebengut, also of Platte County—had moved to Oregon where Edward was employed as a logger. Frank L. Zybach was born in Lafayette, Oregon, on July 10, 1894, the second of four children, the first boy. When Frank was three months old, the Zybachs returned home, settling on a farm four miles north of Duncan, a tiny Swiss and Polish community seven miles west of Columbus. All that I know of Frank's formative years is that his formal education ended following the seventh grade, but his education in metals continued in his father's blacksmith shop. Frank may have learned how to court and bring forth ideas from his father, who was also an inventor. Edward patented a device that could transfer power from a car engine either to a corn sheller or sawmill (Thorson 119). When Frank was thirteen he built his first invention: a cart with a seat and two swivel wheels that could be attached to a harrow, a drawn device that levels the land and breaks clods. "That saved me from walking," he told Thorson. This, like most of Frank's inventions, was practical and labor saving.

On October 21, 1914, Frank Zybach and Elizabeth Kozlowski (1894– 1974) married. All that I know of Elizabeth is that she also lived in Duncan and was the daughter of Prussian (Polish) immigrants. In March of 1919, Frank's parents and later, his brother, Edward Jr., moved to a farm near Strasburg, Colorado, where the elder Zybachs remained until the 1940s when they moved into Strasburg, a tiny railroad town just east of Denver. I found nothing suggesting the reason for this move. Edward Sr. died in Strasburg in 1946; I do not know where or when Lena Zybach died. At some point, Frank moved to Strasburg, too. One source says that he was farming near Strasburg by 1947 (Sheffield, "Economic Analysis" 5). He may have moved there around the time of his father's death so that he could be near his newly widowed mother, but, too, his parents may have followed him to Colorado where he was engaged in work other than farming until 1947. Most years, precipitation in eastern Colorado totals twelve to twenty inches per year. There Frank Zybach was a dryland wheat tenant farmer.

And he continued inventing. Zybach, who was really "more a blacksmith, metal worker and tinkerer than a farmer at heart," installed a forge and metal working tools in his farm shop (Thorson 119). His early years as an inventor are filled with stories of near successes. On October 8, 1920, Zybach filed for his first patent on an automatic tractor guide for steel-wheeled tractors. Once the farmer had plowed the outermost furrow, the tractor could plow the rest of the field by itself. Zybach sold the patent to the Chase Plow Company of Lincoln, Nebraska. "For a few years they did quite a business on them," he told *Lincoln-Journal Star* reporter Sam Thorson.

Another invention was a self-cleaning lug for steel tractor wheels, which was quickly outmoded by the appearance of the rubber tractor tire. "I didn't get much out of that," Zybach told Thorson. Another idea, a hydraulic drive system for an automobile, was too expensive for Zybach to build. When he approached the big auto companies with his idea, they told him that they were already working on something similar and ignored his invention. "I didn't go any farther with that," he told Thorson. Later Zybach built an automatic automobile transmission that he almost sold to Chrysler. He invented a walking doll from alarm clock parts. Several people invested in this invention, but the venture died when Zybach's partner was killed in a plane crash. I hope that Zybach's daughters, Angeline and Frances, both had walking dolls—the first in Strasburg, the first anywhere.

In 1947, Zybach and a neighbor attended an irrigation field day near either Prospect City or Hudson, Colorado, where they watched a demonstration of a sprinkler system. Zybach observed men struggling to disassemble twenty- to thirty-foot lengths of aluminum irrigation pipe while standing in mud after a watering. Then they carried the pipes by hand through the wheat to the next set of pipes and reconnected them. I imagine him wondering if there wasn't an easier, less labor-intensive way for his neighbors to irrigate their land. But, too, I imagine Frank being driven by less altruistic motives: he delighted in the stimulation and absorption of solving a mechanical problem. At any rate in 1948, he designed "a small, two-tower, experimental center pivot system" (Sheffield, "Technology" 93).

In 1952, Zybach patented his Self-Propelled Sprinkling Irrigation Apparatus (Sheffield, "Economic Analysis" 6). He told Thorson that he did not install the first system on his own land because he had scarcely enough well water to supply his house. Instead he installed it on the Ernest Engelbrecht farm north of Strasburg where it irrigated forty acres of alfalfa. This system remained in use on the Engelbrecht farm until the late 1960s or early 1970s. A photograph of Zybach's first center-pivot system shows low, graceful suspension lines leading from five, **A**-shaped towers. Each tower rests on what looks to be a bicycle (Sheffield, "Economic Analysis" 8).

Since Zybach hadn't the money to mass-produce his invention, he contacted Albert E. Trowbridge, a Pontiac GMC dealer in Columbus. This was a logical move since Trowbridge had helped fund some of Zybach's earlier inventions. Even though none of them had paid off, Trowbridge continued to believe in Zybach's creative genius, and Trowbridge knew how to sell a product. His grandson, William Curry, told me that his grandfather was "a wheeler and a dealer . . . an old-fashioned guy who drove around selling things: a plunger." During the summer of 1952, Zybach invited Trowbridge to come to Colorado to see his just-patented irrigation system. Trowbridge ended up buying 49 percent of the patent rights for fifty thousand dollars. In the fall of 1952 Frank, and I suppose Elizabeth too, moved back to Columbus. Zybach and Trowbridge rented a machine shop, hired a few workers, and began producing center pivots (Sheffield, "Technology" 94). I wonder what the neighbors thought of this endeavor—or if they even knew about it. I wonder what Zybach's daughters told their friends about their father's curious occupation.

Zybach had designed the center pivot for use on shorter crops—sugar beets, alfalfa, and melons. He and Trowbridge raised the pipeline several feet for use on taller, row crops—specifically, corn. Each pivot Zybach made was an improvement on the last, which meant there was no continuity in parts or timing. Trowbridge's duty, says Curry, was to bring "a little discipline to Frank. He told Frank to stick to one design." During the first two years of their partnership, they built nineteen pivots, which sold for about seven thousand dollars a piece (Sheffield, "Economic Analysis" 9).

At first it was difficult to sell the pivots. Curry says that in those days, farmers believed that "water from the earth wasn't as good as water from the sky." But Zybach's theory was that "the farmer just wasn't used to having something running around on his farm without him being there" (Thorson 119). At any rate, the partners sold their exclusive manufacturing rights to Robert Daughtery, owner of Valley Manufacturing Company (later, Valmont Industries) in Valley, Nebraska, in 1954. Sheffield offers different explanations for this move. In his 1971 dissertation he says that the partners realized that they couldn't fund "the marketing, distribution, sales, and service of the new system." But twenty-two years later, Sheffield writes that they sold "out of mutual frustration. . . . It became clear that a deep conflict existed regarding how the new venture should be managed" ("Technology" 94). In exchange for the sale, the partners received 5 percent royalties for each unit sold before the patent expired in 1969. (I do not know if each partner received 5 percent or if they split that total.) Eventually, Zybach and Trowbridge both earned over one million dollars in royalties— more than enough money to enjoy many years of financial security and comfort in Columbus, Nebraska. But they could have earned more. Four years after Zybach and Trowbridge's patent expired, the Soviets began buying large quantities of corn and wheat from the United States. Prices for these commodities surged. In response, farmers invested in center-pivot systems so they could put even more acreage into crop production. If Zybach and Trowbridge had retained their patent, they might have been among Nebraska's wealthiest entrepreneurs. "The Wizards of Columbus," we might have called them, just as we refer to Warren Buffett, the second richest person in the United States, as "The Wizard of Omaha."

Most of what I know about how Zybach spent his later years comes from Thorson's 1973 interview with him: "Now retired and living unostentatiously—but comfortably—in Columbus, Zybach tends to his ailing wife and has little time for inventing. 'I do slip away and go to the races once in a while,' he admits." Elizabeth died in 1974. The 1979 *Columbus City Directory* lists Zybach with a new address and phone number and living with Nora S. Zybach. In 1980, Zybach and Trowbridge both died at eighty-six. I do not know whether the two men spent time together in their final years or not. According to some reports, they were best of friends; according to other reports, they didn't like each other at all. Frank and Elizabeth are buried in Columbus's Catholic cemetery, row 17, set 2. Nora was present at the 1982 ceremony when her late, new husband was inducted posthumously into the Nebraska Hall of Agricultural Achievement ("Frank").

My brief biography of Zybach raises more questions about what matters most to me (Zybach's creativity and inventiveness) than it answers. I wonder, for instance, if Frank was the classic, solitary genius or if he consulted with others. Did he, like Edison, create through repeated try-anything, trial and error or did he, like Nikola Tesla, whose inventions include the alternating-current induction motor, work in abstractions, the invention appearing in his head, full-fledged? Was Frank driven to create for pleasure, necessity or, like Edison and Ford, primarily for profit? How did he stimulate his creativity?

Did he encourage inventiveness in his daughters, perhaps as his father had in him, or was he so involved with his inventions that he was distant or detached from his family or only intermittently involved with them? Was he a conformist in lifestyle or did he also live inventively? How did he earn his living during his most inventive years? Is Zybach unheralded because he was not affiliated with a university or big corporation, because he wasn't formally educated, or because he preferred it that way? Is he unheralded because his invention isn't glamorous or widely coveted? Did he not leave an "explorit" center filled with invention apparatus or written records, photographs, sketches, a scrapbook bulging with acceptance and rejection letters, patent documents, and newspaper clippings at a historical society, library, or museum, because of stinginess, humility, lack of a promoter, lack of foresight or a hunger for privacy? What would he think of me, writing about him, uninvited?

J. Robert Oppenheimer, the physicist credited with inventing "the bomb," resigned from his job within two months after witnessing the first successful A-bomb explosion. Thereafter he worked for legislation to control the use of nuclear power. Did Zybach also come to regret the changes wrought by his invention? Marty Strange, former codirector of the Center for Rural Affairs in Walthill, Nebraska, writes that because center-pivot systems are so expensive to purchase and maintain (indeed, throughout the 1970s, the pivot, wells, pumps, and related equipment cost more than the land itself for some farmers), they have contributed to the demise of the family farm. Strange says that "more than a third of the land taken over by lenders to satisfy uncollectable debts is irrigated by the rotary systems" (118).

At the same time, the ease of watering vast areas of marginal land with few employees has contributed to the rise of highly specialized "mega-farms," vast acres of monoculture crops covering an area that once supported several family farms. So, too, the center-pivot irrigators have contributed to the fall of the water level in the High Plains Aquifer (which some experts predict will be exhausted by 2020) and the decline in the channel width and peak flows of the Platte River. During the extreme drought of 2000, the Nebraska Department of Water Resources shut off seventeen junior irrigators along parched Turkey Creek in Fillmore County, while the fields and bank accounts of those with older water rights remained green (Hicks A1, A8). The money that Nebraska won in an expensive, protracted court battle with Colorado over the water in the South Platte is now funding our battle with Kansas over the water in the Republican. Our sixty-four-year battle with Wyoming over North Platte River water is being settled out of court, a process that precludes public input. Perhaps Kansas historian Donald Worster was correct when he said that the American West is an oligarchy, a hydraulic society, where supreme power is concentrated in the hands of those with water rights. Had Zybach foreseen any of this? And if he did, is that why he didn't promote himself, writing a weekly "ask-the-expert" column in the newspaper, lending his support to an annual, irrigation day festival in Duncan or Columbus (a parade, a queen contest, a sweet-corn feed, a speech by the inventor of the center-pivot irrigator), or establishing a fund in his name to provide capitol for other inventors?

What is it that drew Zybach back from Colorado? Did the astonishing number of agricultural inventors working in the Columbus area in the 1940s and 1950s create something akin to a magnetic field, whose pull Zybach could not resist? "Young men, faced with carving futures else-where, have devised more than 100 improvements for use on the robots that elbowed them off the farms," writes William S. Dutton of the dozen or so farm inventors from Columbus in the March 1955 issue of *Popular Science*. Zybach, then sixty, was no longer a young man, and so not included in the article. But like most of the other Columbus inventors, he was farm-bred, handy with tools, and had never been to college.

Did Zybach choose to stay in Columbus, a town of about thirteen thousand in the early 1960s, because everyone knew him and thought him pleasant and common or did he stay in spite of this? Did he stay because he didn't like change? Did he stay because he couldn't persuade either of his wives to move to a window-filled, A-frame house in the Colorado mountains? Did he stay because of a commitment to the land, community, and home? Did he stay because he needed to live near the Loup, a few miles before the spot where it loses its name and separate identity by entering the Platte?

"Biography," writes André Maurois, "is a means of expression when the author has chosen his subject in order to respond to a secret need in his own nature" (Edel 68). Maurois said that he wrote the life of Percy Bysshe Shelley because of the similarities between his own and the poet's youthful romanticism and indulgences. "Yes, in very truth I felt that to tell the story of his life would be in some measure a deliverance for myself. . . . I wanted to kill the romantic in me; in order to do so I scoffed at it in Shelley, but I loved it while I scoffed" (Edel 69–70).

So, too, his choice of British Prime Minister Benjamin Disraeli as the subject of a biography. Maurois, a Jew who grew up in Dreyfus-era France, was drawn to Disraeli, because he was a Jew who defied the bigotry he encountered in nineteenth-century England. "Being unable, for very many reasons, to lead a life of political activity myself," Maurois said, "I took a passionate pleasure in joining in the struggle by donning the mask of a face that appealed to me." When one has such feelings for his subject, what one writes is "to a certain extent . . . autobiography disguised as biography."

While it is pretentious for me to speak of Maurois's biographies of Shelley and Disraeli and my brief profile of Zybach on the same page, our motives are one: we were drawn to our subjects by an affinity, by a spark of recognition, perhaps in the surface details, perhaps in the deep story, perhaps in both. What Zybach and I might have in common is this.

Inspiration comes through common acts at common places (attending an irrigation show, reading the local newspaper). The demands of the task seem modest (an easier way to move sprinkler pipes, portraying a person about whom one knows so little). But they require repeated trial and error (years of tinkering in the garage, four different attempts at this essay and dozens of revisions of those attempts). Then, the breakthrough arrives. I do not know when or how this occurred for Zybach, but for me, it occurred when I took a moment to scribble about small daily details in my notebook while Meredith drew on the chalkboard at the Edgerton Explorit Center. Then I asked myself the right question: "Why do I have no desire to write about Edgerton?" Certainly researching Edgerton would have been easier than researching Zybach. Edgerton was the subject of a biography and a 1985 *Nova* television documentary. Because of his affiliation with a university, he probably left papers, students, and colleagues who could reveal his creative processes. However, Edgerton's well-funded research in a far part of the country did not spark my imagination. Then I wrote for several pages in my notebook about my personal connections with Zybach. Eureka! After several weeks of research and writing I had finally found my way in.

I am drawn to Zybach because I suspect that financial security eluded him for most of his life. William Curry described his grandfather's partner as "an inventor with not much money." Zybach told Thorson, "I was always monkeying with something to make some extra money. But never got much out of anything until this sprinkler came along." Perhaps inventors, like many artists and writers, struggle with the need to be both the one who earns and the one who creates. For many of us that means alternating between periods of working only or mostly for ourselves—in which we create to our heart's content, but eat too cheaply and are uninsured—and periods in which we work primarily for others, which pays the rent and stocks the kitchen cupboards, but precludes what Henry James calls the "depth and continuity of attention and meditation" that creation requires (Olson 12).

I am drawn to Zybach because his manner of living called little attention to itself. I suspect that people in Columbus could not believe that one who lived among them and appeared so common, who attended mass at St. Bonaventure, who bought metal things at the hardware store, who was always puttering in a garage that was so like everyone else's garage, could think so creatively, could find such passionate pleasure in bringing forth ideas, could be so *interiorly* different from them, could have such a profound effect on the economy, agriculture, water, and land.

Several years ago upon reading something I had written, a friend said to me, "I can't believe that you're the same person I eat pancakes with at Village Inn." I was stunned to learn that my friend found the persona in my essays so at odds with the me who chauffeured children to lessons and appointments, who shopped with coupons at Super Saver, who talked too often about trite, silly things, who spent weekends reading student essays, who was this woman's friend and who ate chocolate-chip pancakes with her at Village Inn. And I was stunned to learn that my friend, herself a budding essayist, would find essays written mostly while my children slept, such an impossible, incongruent achievement for me or for her. Perhaps there was something inauthentic or disconnected in my writing or living, between my projected and my actual existence, or both. Or perhaps these two expressions of my inner self are simply different. Michel de Montaigne observed that "[t]here is as much difference between us and ourselves, as between us and others" (Frame 244). Certainly this is true for the essayist. The self she presents in her writing is a smarter, more sensitive, clever and articulate version of the self who attends to small, daily details. Perhaps it is true for other types of inventors, too. I imagine Zybach musing upon the incongruities in his life.

But an even stronger link between Zybach and me is based entirely on speculation: that the land itself holds the key to his inventiveness. More precisely, I hope that he knew that for many of us, creativity at home is profoundly different from creativity at a place that is not home, because at home it is rooted in a place and a past, because at home one's energies can be single and pure in the absence of the fragmenting force that is homesickness and the disruptive unfamiliarity of a place that is not one's own. During the three years that I lived away from Nebraska in a part of the country where the soil was too poor, hilly, and rocky for row crops, where the average of forty-four to forty-eight inches of precipitation per year precluded any need for irrigation or the presence of tallgrass or mixed-grass prairie remnants, where there was no chance of seeing hundreds of thousands of migrating sandhill cranes each spring, where there were no braided river channels, I wrote little that mattered to me. But my return home was met with a burst of new writing that mattered deeply. Clearly, if I want to continue to create, I need to stay home. I hope that Zybach, with several decades of brilliant and almost timely inventions to his credit knew that all he lacked in bringing to fruition his most important work was being in the right place.

Citizen

Once, the people of the United States were referred to as "citizens," from the Latin *civitatis*, "a state city." A citizen was a member of a state or nation, especially one with a republican form of government, who owed allegiance to it by birth or naturalization and was entitled to full civil rights. Not so long ago, the media, economists, politicians, and others who comprise the powerful, impersonal "they," to whom we so frequently refer, began speaking of the American people as consumers instead of citizens. Being a consumer is good, we are told, because consumerism, a progressively greater and greater consumption of material goods, is the heart and soul of the American economic system, the very foundation of our freedom.

This new label reflected or initiated a forfeiting of responsibilities. While a citizen would question how to balance wants and resources (after all, to consume is to destroy something else), a consumer would not. While a citizen is charged with a sense of mutual responsibilities (civic and political duties in exchange for civic and political privileges and protections), a consumer is not. In a nation where most people aspire to be greater and greater consumers, to be little more than one's preoccupation with the getting of things is considered fruitless or aberrant only by the radical fringe—those who are consumed by a passion for self-reliance, deep community, God, or the life of the mind.

5. A Salt Marsh Reclamation

I. How to Get There from Here

I cross Cornhusker Highway and drive north on North 27th Street. Ten years ago this spring, I bought worms in a dark fish-bait shop at this intersection. Beyond the shop were fields. Now, the site of the former bait shop is occupied by a Super K-Mart, where the father of one of my daughter's friends works third shift.

I follow North 27th past a dazzling, mega-hardware store, over Salt Creek, past another hardware store, a furniture warehouse, Wal-Mart, a grocery, Payless Shoes, Jumbo Sport, the various fast-food franchises, office buildings, drive-through banks, an industrial park, and the farthest strip mall, where the major tenants are Toys 'R Us, Petsmart, and Slumberland.

Farms do not begin where the businesses thin out. Rather, this is land adjacent to Interstate 80 and Highway 77, a place of new apartment complexes and motels and signs announcing the future construction of more motels. Backhoes wait across the street from the Cracker Barrel Restaurant and a new Phillips 66 station. Behind the restaurant, a new road traces a wetland. Here even soggy land commands high prices. I follow North 27th over the interstate. On the right side of the road is Arbor Lake, a wildlife area, a salt marsh managed by the Nebraska Game and Parks Commission.

Once about sixteen thousand acres of saline wetlands were included within Nebraska's borders, most of which were in Lancaster and Saunders Counties. Now about one thousand acres remain. Thus Arbor Lake, located only one mile north of Lincoln's present city limit, represents the rarest and most endangered natural community in the entire Great

Plains. While this particular salt marsh is safe from destruction for the time being, it is too close to the edge to provide the sanctuary it did even five years ago.

I climb the steps to the observation platform. In the winter, all but the center of the marsh is dry. Where the marsh is crusted with salt, vegetation is sparse. But following the spring rains, most of the twenty-acre depression is a watery patchwork of greens: tall dark circles of slough grass, short, pale inland salt grass, bright wavy blades of pondweed. To the left of the marsh is a farmhouse where a chained chow dog watches and barks from the other side of a fence. To the right of the marsh is a cornfield. Ahead, Lincoln Electric Service's white fiberglass windmills spin and blink above Interstate 80.

I filter out the rumble of semitrucks, the farm dog's barking, and the rolling, sky-scraping roar of a plane preparing to land at the airport just a few miles west of the marsh. The sounds of the marsh move through me. The bubbling kon-ka-lee of red-winged blackbirds. The barking of Canada geese. The rasp and falling buzz of yellow-headed blackbirds. The grunts and cackles of American coots, as ungraceful as their lobed toes. The buzz and rattle of marsh wrens. The tsu-wee of plovers. The wing snap-snap of a bathing grackle. The high scream of a red-tailed hawk. The swelling of male frogs' vocal sacks: the earth's pulse.

As I watch wind bend the light-filled salt grass, as I watch black terns rise and fall, I believe that I have dreamed this place where everything is moving toward me. But when the wind that ripples the water surface, that bends the salt grasses, that ruffles the terns' feathers, moves around but not through me, I know that this place is real.

II. Other Oceans
Dakota sandstone lies beneath much of eastern Nebraska. The porous, rust-colored layers of sand and clay are visible around the base of some of the steeper slopes on the Salt Creek's west bank and some road cuts. Water made salty by deposits from the continental seas that once covered southeastern Nebraska spring up or seep out of this sandstone.

Gravity decrees that the brine flow into the shallow, wind-hollowed basins in the flood plain. In "Nebraska Salt Marshes: Last of the Least," John Farrar and Richard Gersib explain that where the soil does not drain, the evaporating water leaves behind salty compounds. As the cycle of seepage and evaporation is repeated, a white crust accumulates, "concentr[ating] salt in flood-plain soils, setting the stage for the formation of saline wetlands."

Just as coastal salt marshes are ocean fed, so too are inland salt marshes.

III. The Recent History of Salt in This Place

"The discovery of salt deposits west of the Appalachian Mountains was one the most important factors in the westward advance of the American frontier," writes Agnes Horton in her 1959 study of the history of Nebraska's saline land grant. In the absence of inland salt deposits, people from earlier centuries would have been limited to coastal areas by their need for salt to preserve meat, antisepticize wounds, tan leather, make soap, regulate the water balance, maintain normal heart rhythms, conduct nerve impulses, contract muscles, and achieve the correct acid-base balance in their own bodies and that of their livestock.

The absence of trees and the presence of salt were the first things that Euro-Americans noticed when they came to what is now Lancaster County, Nebraska. Of his arrival at the salt basin stretching along the west side of Salt Creek in 1861, William Cox wrote: "There was something enchanting about the scene that met our eyes. The fresh breeze sweeping over the salt basins reminded us of the morning breezes at the ocean beach. This basin was as smooth as glass, and resembled a slab of highly polished, cloudy, marble." Augustus F. Harvey, who made the first survey and plat of the town site of Lincoln, reported that "twice a day, like clockwork, the basin flooded with brine to a depth of two to three inches. When the 'tide' receded, the brine would disappear into the cracks, leaving a white crystalline film behind from solar evaporation. Over the course of days or weeks, this would accumulate to a depth of three to four inches and could simply be scraped up and used without further refinement."

When some saw the salt lake, they dreamed of fortunes to be made. Indeed people from as far away as Iowa, Kansas, and Missouri were willing to trade meat, eggs, butter, fruit, potatoes, equivalent amounts of flour, new sets of clothes, live chickens, cast-iron stoves, sorghum pans, and money for Lancaster County salt. By 1860, several salt manufacturers were established in the area of what is now Lincoln. In 1864, J. S. Gregory Jr. manufactured salt to sell to the Indians and those traversing the Overland Trail.

But the dreamers did not foresee the difficulties they would encounter in extracting salt from water for large-scale use. In the mid-nineteenth century, the prairie was whole and vital enough to prevent the encroachment of trees. In *Lincoln: The Prairie Capital*, James McKee writes that those in the salt business couldn't find enough fuel to feed the fires beneath the big kettles where they had hoped to boil the water from the salts. The solar method—pumping brine into a system of wooden vats or reservoirs and allowing the sun and wind to evaporate the water—was too slow. J. Sterling Morton of Nebraska City believed that these methods were unnecessary since "the best and finest article of table salt" could simply be scrapped from the banks of the Salt Creek. However Sterling's son, Joy, founder of the Morton Salt Company, made his fortune, not from Lancaster County salt but from salt caves in Kansas and Michigan where he found the mineral to be more easily extracted. By the late 1880s, all efforts at making a living directly from salt production in Lancaster County ended.

Yet there was money to be made indirectly from salt. The Lloyd Mineral Well of Union, Nebraska, bottled and sold salt water. The sulpho-saline baths in the basement of the Lincoln Sanitorium were, according to Erwin Hinckley Barbour, who was the Nebraska state geologist from 1891–1921, "deservedly popular and enjoyed a local reputation, especially among those afflicted with rheumatism." In 1895 a pair of entrepreneurs dammed the east end of the salt basin and rerouted Oak Creek so that its waters created a permanent lake, then called Burlington Beach since the Burlington Railroad shuttled customers from Lincoln and the surrounding areas there and back. An 1897 photograph of the lake shows still waters, two sailboats, a man in a rowboat, and a strip of beach in the foreground. In the background is a pillared structure—the dam, I guess. At the end of a long pier is a pavilion, perhaps for refreshments or dancing or bathing in the supposedly medicinal waters. In 1906, the new owner named the lake Capital Beach (later Capitol Beach). For the next several decades it continued to offer swimming and a midway. Now the lake is rimmed with private residences on streets named Surfside, Sailside, and Lakeside Drive.

More recently Lancaster County salt marshes have become the sites of several garbage dumps, have been drained for the construction of Interstate 80, for industrial parks, car dealerships, the Capitol Parkway West bypass, a hemorrhage of housing subdivisions, and one of two new high schools to be completed by 2003.

In the absence of salt, Lancaster County probably would not have been chosen as the site of the state capital and now be home to almost a quarter of a million people, making it the second most populous county in Nebraska. Nor would it have suffered such rapid and violent changes in the natural environment.

In the yellow heat of a late May afternoon at the salt marsh, I remove my black sun hat. A white ring marks the inside brim. I bend down and take a pinch of the gray clay. The salt in the soil stings my tongue.

IV. TRANSIENTS

I spend the afternoon at Arbor Lake watching the black terns through my binoculars. At first I thought the birds were swallows because of their deeply forked tails. But the black terns are larger, less colorful birds, and instead of twittering like swallows, they utter calls similar to the sound made by rubber squeak toys. Nor do they dive toward the water surface from great heights like swallows. Rather, they erratically drop to the water, rise, hang in the air, then drop again. What they are doing is hovering, then swooping down to peck insects from the water surface. Occasionally one hawks an insect in mid air.

Perhaps these terns can use any salt marsh as a motel, campground, nursery or wayside eatery upon their vernal return from the tropics. Or perhaps their presence here is deliberate. The same black terns and their offspring return to Arbor Lake because it is their place of origin and the site of several millennia-worth of annual family reunions. For these birds there is no other cattail stand in which to build their nest.

V. WHO CAN'T LIVE WITHOUT IT

Red-winged blackbirds, great blue herons, and red-tailed hawks are year-round residents at Arbor Lake. I know that coyote hunt here because I've seen their scat. In the cold part of the year, frogs, snakes, salamanders, newts, and turtles sleep in the mud. The eggs of other permanent residents—dragonflies, grasshoppers, spiders, beetles, flies, mosquitoes, and ticks—are everywhere. Thousands of single-celled protozoa, fungi, and bacteria dwell in a single handful of soil. Last winter, near a stand of sedges, I found a skull, perhaps of a white-footed mouse, which from the orange tip of its two top incisors to the back of its skull is the length of my thumb, tip to first joint. I keep this relic, a representative of the millions of organisms who call Arbor Lake their one and only home, nestled in a bed of gauze in an earring box on my altar.

That pondweed, marsh elder, spearscale, foxtail barley, cattails, bulrushes, cordgrasses, and sedges can grow on such seemingly hostile, poisonous soils is remarkable. Gerry Steinauer, wetland biologist for the Nebraska Game and Parks Commission, writes that because many halophytes (plants adapted to grow on salty soils) "concentrate salts in their cell sap, [they] can draw soil water into their roots, since water generally flows from areas of low salt concentration to areas of higher salt concentration." Other adaptations include a shallow root system, which allows plants to exploit the less saline water found in upper soil layers after a rain, and special glands in the leaves that excrete salts before they reach toxic levels. Some halophytes—saltwort, sea blite, and saltmarsh aster—are reported in Nebraska only on the salt marshes. But other species such as inland salt grass is found throughout the Great Plains. On the dry, salt-encrusted outer rim of the salt flat, the salt grass might only reach a few inches in height and be sparsely spaced. But at the less saline salt flat-prairie transition zone, it grows in thick clumps, reaching eight to ten inches in height. What I like best about this wiry grass is that it crunches when I walk on it.

After a June evening at the salt marsh, I dream that I am searching for the tiny yellow corollas and pastel disks of the saltmarsh aster. I look in the pavement cracks in the island in the middle of the street, on the banks of a concrete-lined creek, beneath a colony of billboards, along the chain-link fence separating this parking lot from that one. My anxiety deepens. I run hard, searching for the edge where the asphalt ends and the grasses begin.

VI. A Reckoning

Shortly after Arbor Lake was set aside as a protected place in 1992, my children and I stopped along the margin for a look. Though I had read about what a unique ecosystem this was, honestly, I saw nothing but straw-colored grass, dried cattails, a few crows, shotgun shell casings, and a "Closed to Hunting" sign. I couldn't yet see why Thoreau called wetlands "tender places on the earth's surface." But after six years spent hiking in Iowa, Illinois, Nebraska, and Kansas with field guides and people who know and see more than I do, I returned to Arbor Lake. Now I spend entire afternoons at the salt marsh, absorbed in the birds, the grasses, the dragonflies and beetles, the complicated webs of interdependencies, the nearness of the Cretaceous Period and the as yet unnamed geologic periods that will follow our own.

Some people see nothing of value in a marsh. For them, "reclaiming" wetlands means draining them, filling them, and turning them toward human ends. In the twentieth century in the Rainwater Basin of south-central Nebraska, a critical stopover on the mid-continental spring migration route for seven to nine million ducks and geese and a half million sandhill cranes, over 80 percent of the original wetlands have been "reclaimed" primarily for the irrigated, mechanized, chemically controlled production of soy beans, corn, sorghum, and wheat.

In March of 1999 the Lincoln City Council rezoned a salt marsh from agricultural to highway commercial, despite objections from the Lincoln Planning Department. Speaking for the majority, Councilman Curt Donaldson said that Lincoln did not need to add another layer of wetland protection to guidelines established by the federal government. But city planner Nicole Fleck-Tooze said that federal restrictions did not preclude the marsh from being filled in. For the majority of the city council members, immediate economic gain outweighed long-term ecological stability. "To build a road is much simpler than to think about what the country really needs," Aldo Leopold observed over a half century ago.

The loudest opposition to the March 17, 2000, inclusion of the Salt Creek tiger beetle on Nebraska's endangered species list came from David Thompson, attorney for the Home Builders Association of Lincoln. Of the plan to protect this beetle, that has experienced a 90 percent loss of habitat in recent years and whose total population fluctuates between one hundred and six hundred individuals, making it the most endangered insect in the United States, Thompson said: "There's a concern that it can lead to tying up land. It can prevent landowners from using their land the way they want." Thompson and the 532 house builders that he represents appear to be motivated by the same philosophy as the nineteenth-century salt-boilers: the land and the biotic community are there for them to use any way they want.

The only objections I've heard voiced against plans to build a new high school on a salt marsh north of the city is that this particular parcel of land is more costly than other available land in the area. The irony in this situation infuriates me. Over the years, my children have received numerous lessons in the public schools about the threatened tropical rain forests; yet those who make decisions on behalf of the local public schools demonstrate no awareness of or regard for the threatened ecological communities in and near their own city.

Perhaps some can so easily alter wild landscapes because they believe that temporary homes aren't as valuable or as necessary as permanent homes. One day they visit the marsh and it's aflutter with black terns, sandpipers, avocets, shovelers, and snow geese. They come back in January and no one is home but the crows. "Preserve this?" they ask of a place that seems the same as any other soggy field. And, too, salt marshes are neither permanent nor stable. As salinity and moisture levels fluctuate, plant zones widen or narrow and blend. During the extreme drought of 2000, Arbor Lake was dry, a pool of pale green grass occupying the usually submerged center, and not a tern, shorebird, or waterfowl in sight. Farrar and Gersib write that some salt marshes are on their way to becoming solid ground; others have became so diluted by freshwater that they are no longer saline. Salt marshes are always on their way to becoming something else.

But for those of us who find beauty, complexity, and a sustaining body of metaphors at the marsh, reclamation means returning the land to a condition in which it hosts a greater diversity of life forms. On the west bank of the Salt Creek this means plugging drainage tiles, filling ditches and dugout pits, ripping up asphalt and concrete, and enforcing limits on the growth of our cities, towns, suburbs, and, most importantly, our human population. Because of agricultural runoff, invading plant species, silt deposition, and alteration of watersheds, the marsh cannot return to what it was when the Pawnee journeyed there to scrape salt or when bison herds paused there to lick the white crust. But it can become healthier, wilder, more alive. Thus reclamation is an act of redemption.

Such reclamation will not happen with any frequency until there is a shift in our collective mind-set. I cannot say how this shift will occur, but I can say that it will move us to see the consumption of place as an act of deep disrespect, even violence, since it renders homeless countless organisms who have fewer and fewer places to go—if they can go. This shift will move us to accept radical changes in what we eat, where we live, how we travel and spend our leisure time, and who we vote into and out of public office, so that these fragments of biodiversity are less vulnerable, so that there are near places where we can observe and pay homage to what Gary Snyder calls "the pathless world of wild nature."

Some have already made the shift. Capitol Beach resident Rich Wiese, a seventy-one-year-old retired pipe fitter, dreamed of buying 117 acres of salt marsh near Capitol Beach Lake from the housing developer who had planned to drain it, build houses upon it, and dig canals linking the houses with the lake. In the early 1990s, Wiese, who had no experience with conservation work, and two of his neighbors, Richard Powell and Sue Kuck, each donated $2,500 of their own money to initiate a project to purchase the marsh. When they couldn't get support from county, state, or federal governments, they appealed to local businesses, residents, and developers who contributed a total of $260,000. The U.S. Fish and Wildlife Service donated an additional $75,000. Wiese and his partners bought the land and immediately transferred the ownership of it to the Lower Platte South Natural Resources District in perpetuity. Since then the local Audubon chapter has identified about two hundred bird species on this marsh and two of Nebraska's endangered species, saltwort and the Salt Creek tiger beetle.

Of course, there are compelling reasons not to make the shift from disregard to respect. In a culture in which happiness is sought through the consumption of more and more material things, knowing and loving a wild place demands a counter-culture philosophy and lifestyle. It demands, in Bill McKibben's words, "an all-out drive for deep thrift, for self-restraint, for smaller families . . . smaller homes, more food grown locally, repair instead of replacement." It demands knowing how much is enough.

Knowing and loving a wild place also means living with an, at times, uncomfortable range and depth of emotions. To love a salt marsh, for instance, is to live with sadness. I am mindful of the fifteen thousand acres of salt marsh that no longer exist and the fragility of the approximately one thousand acres that do exist. Each year more and more non-native plants assume spots once held by the native marsh plants. Each year more and more birds descend upon Arbor Lake because other wetlands in the area have been drained. Even though Arbor Lake lacks trees, restrooms, water fountains, wood-chip paths, and picnic tables, more and more people use it as a park. Sometimes I share the marsh with people eating their lunches on the observation deck, or exercising their dogs, or drinking beer in cars or trucks, thumping and rattling from the volume of the stereo. Always I find evidence of human use—broken glass and cigarette butts at the edge of the marsh, fireworks, fast-food and condom wrappers in the parking lot. Given the current rate at which the cornfields, pastures, and salt marshes north of Lincoln are being paved over or planted in bluegrass or fescue, I predict that within the next decade, a two-lane street will replace the gravel road near the marsh; power lines will be strung overhead; and landscaped, half-acre backyards, three-car garages and houses the size of small castles will surround Arbor Lake on culs-de-sac and winding streets named Salt Marsh Circle and Avocet Lane. Then, will migrating birds still come to Arbor Lake? If I can't find birds and solitude, will I?

To love the marsh is to live with hope. I hope that those office and retail sales workers who eat their lunches at the marsh see the birds and other creatures that dwell there. I hope that they know something of the human and natural history of this place. I hope that they yearn to see one of the agile, long-legged, and elusive Salt Creek tiger beetles. I hope that they consider which extravagances they can forego in order to protect wild places for those who dwell there and for those of us who can't live without them. I hope that one day they'll initiate or support a grass-roots reclamation or preservation project of an inland salt marsh or a native grassland or a stretch along the Niobrara or Platte Rivers. Above all, I hope that this place and those who dwell there will be permitted to endure.

But also, to love the salt marsh is to be overwhelmed by joy. In the absence of water in the fall and winter, I find a nest, perhaps a black tern's, anchored near the base of a cattail stand. On a late afternoon in winter, I follow the silent flight of a short-eared owl above the winter-killed, wind-bent tufts of salt grass. In the spring and summer, I watch dark-headed, adult black terns and the white-headed juveniles, rise and fall from the water surface. As the wind ripples the water and the inland salt grasses, as the wind flutters the delicate, awl-shaped leaves and pale lavender rays of the saltmarsh asters, as the wind bends the ribbonlike cattail leaves, my heart and throat open with love and gratitude for the rich and fragile beauty before me.

Body

The Germanic tribes that settled in England fifteen to sixteen centuries ago had various names for the body: *bodig*, *feorgbold*, *feorhhus*, *flæsgchama*, *lic*, and *lichama*. But their most provocative name is also a metaphor: *banhus*, "bone-house." And by extension, the mind is personified in the Old English narrative of the biblical Exodus, as *banhuses weard*, "the guardian of the bone-house."

Obvious physical similarities exist between a house and a body: the skeleton of a body corresponds to the frame of a house, bodily cavities to rooms, the various bodily orifices to windows, doors, chimneys, and other points of ingress and egress. To enter a body or house without the owner's permission is an act of aggression, a violation of private, inner space. Yet, this metaphor breaks down rather quickly. A house is a shell or container that becomes inhabitable space when one adds furniture and a source of heat and light. Bodies, however, arrive as inhabited space, possessing all or most of the essentials, even if small, undeveloped, or defective.

While the shape of the houses we inhabit influences how we perceive space, the shape of the body determines how we perceive everything. The body is, in Anne E. Berthoff's words, "our primordial speculative instrument" as well as the source of the images by which we "represent our recognitions." Try to imagine how an earthworm, spider, crane, or cow perceives the world based purely on the number, position, or lack of limbs or eyes.

Yet people have long conceived of the body as the temporary and earthly abode of the soul or mind. In *Gorgias*, Plato wrote that the body is the prison of the soul. The unknown author of 2 Peter conceives of his body as a shelter or outer covering: "I think it right, as long as I am in this body [tent, in the Greek], to arouse you by way of reminder, since I know that putting off of my body [tent] will be soon."

At the turn of the millennium we are as convinced of the split between body and mind as were the ancient Greeks, the early Christians, the old Anglo-Saxons. When we fail to meet our own expectations, we say that our spirit is willing but our flesh is weak. When we encounter hard times, we say that it takes everything we've got to keep body and soul together. "Posthuman" artists, extreme body-mind dichotomists, believe that through technology they can transcend the "wet sack" that is the body. Sterlac, an Australian performance artist, had wires inserted into his limbs and organs by which his audience could manipulate his body via the Internet and then watch his responses. *Ping Body* is what he calls this piece of work. (His other works include *Evolving URL Body*, *Metabody*, and *Extra Ear*.) Sterlac says that through his art, "the body becomes hollow, with no meaningful distinctions between public, private, and physiological spaces. . . . One no longer looks at art, nor performs as art, but contains art. The hollow body becomes a host, not for a self or a soul but simply for a sculpture."

Even people who know better have a hard time letting go of the body-mind dichotomy. Candace Pert, the biochemist who discovered opiate receptors and other peptides that are the biochemical units of emotions, says that the peptides and their receptors "float around on the surface of the cells." Yet she confesses that it took her fifteen years before she could believe the deep story in her research: that mind is not just in the brain but "part of a communications network throughout the brain and body." In other words, mind, emotion, and body are in our every cell. The body is at once the guest and the host, the dweller and the dwelling place.

6. Staples

I. RABBIT STEW

When Ian came in the front door from his first hunting trip, I could see a bulge in his hunting vest. "It's a rabbit," he said. "I shot its head clean off. All I have to do to prepare it for supper is skin and gut it." When I was a child, we ate rabbit and squirrel like chicken—cut into legs, back, breast, and then fried. But I would cook this rabbit whole.

The next day I bring down the crock-pot from a high shelf and wedge the cottontail's long, lean body inside the pot. Meredith slices carrots; I chop potatoes and onions. We add a couple of cups of water, frozen green beans, salt, pepper, and dried basil from our garden. All afternoon the stew bubbles, filling our house with a thick, meaty fragrance. Just before supper, Meredith and I bake a pan of biscuits.

I ladle a full bowl of stew for Ian. Because Meredith thinks that eating rabbit is gross, even if it does smell good, I give her just a taste. I had planned to eat biscuits and a salad for my supper, but I feel moved to partake of the stew. So, I fork out chunks of potatoes and carrots cooked in the rabbit's juices.

We bow our heads, and I pray. "Great Giver and Taker of Life, bless these plants and this animal who died so that we might eat. And bless our time here together, Lord." Our forks clink against our bowls.

"This is some good rabbit," Ian says.

"Yeah, it's okay," Meredith says as she holds her bowl up for more.

As they eat, my children drop little bones from their forks onto the table. The purpose of some bones is a mystery, yet the purpose of others—tibia, femur, humerus, radius, ulna, scapula, vertebrae, rib—is obvious. I wipe off one of the powerful leg bones that just yesterday carried our young rabbit lightly and quickly through winter-killed fields. The bone is brown and bowed, the surface so smooth that it feels oily. One end is complicated and irregularly shaped, but the other end is four-pronged and chalky white like an enamel-less molar.

"I'll keep this bone to remind of us of the first time you provided game," I tell Ian. The bone still rests on the windowsill above the sink where we can look upon it when we wash dishes.

After we eat all of the stew in our bowls that our forks can reach, we sop the juices with chunks of biscuits. It would be wicked to waste a single drop.

II. BEET JUICE

I grab a tasseled top and pull firmly until the beet root releases its hold on the earth and life. In just a few minutes, I've pulled up my entire beet patch. Some beets are fat and shaped like a child's top; some are skinny and carrotlike. A line of eight holes remains in the earth.

At my kitchen sink, I wash off the crumbs of dirt and cut away the root tips and leaves. I would like to cook and eat the leaves but because the rabbits and insects got to them first, they are more purple stems and main veins than greens. I return the trimmings to the garden and place the beets in a water-filled pan. Even before I turn on the burner, the beets bleed into the water. I wish I had bleached flour sacks to dip in this beautiful, red-purple water. But instead of making luscious, beet-pink dishtowels, I pour the water down the drain. Then I slice the beets. Such a curious texture for a vegetable. Not grainy or mushy like cooked potatoes or carrots. The knife slices cleanly through the firm beet layers, some lighter, some darker than others: fleshy remembrances of dry or wet, hot or cool weather, and the pack and composition of the soil.

I shake a couple of jiggers of white vinegar over the slices, sprinkle them with sugar, and cover them with water. This small bowl of beets could be enough for a half-dozen people to have just a taste with their supper or for me to have plenty. Next summer, there will be more. Now I know that I should have weeded the seedlings until the remaining plants were four inches apart. Then all of my beets would be plump and top-shaped. Now I know to sow beet seeds three or four weeks before the average date of the last killing frost and every two weeks thereafter until early September. Then I'd have fresh beets all summer and into the fall. But how many plants would be enough? I read that one should plant one five-to-ten-foot row of beets per person or ten-to-twenty-foot root per person for canning, though instead of canning I'd store the surplus in a box of leaves in the laundry room. My children won't touch beets, yet I can eat beets every day. Perhaps three or four ten-foot rows are what I need.

That evening, I take the bowl of beets from the refrigerator. I spear a slice with a fork and eat. It is firm and tangy and dripping with red-violet juice. I eat one slice after another. I'm disappointed that the beets are gone so soon. As I start to pour the sharp, sweet juice down the drain, I remember the hard black beet seeds that I soaked and planted last spring. I didn't have to guess if the leaves that eventually poked through the bare soil were weeds or beets. In remembrance of their genetic code, those hard black seeds converted soil, sunlight, rain, and water from my garden hose into red-streaked green leaves. Nearby, other seeds converted the same soil, the same light, the same water into the solid green leaves of tomato, pepper, squash, okra, lamb's quarters, or hollyhock plants. I lift the bowl to my lips and drink the dark, beautiful memory.

III. Soy

Once I surprised a pair of Saline County farmers, the sister and brother-in-law of a former friend, when I told them that I bought soybeans at the natural food co-op to use in casseroles and soups. They knew that their soybeans were processed into soybean oil or high-protein cattle feed or used as a ground-beef stretcher in institutional food. But they'd never known anyone who ate the "raw" beans. The next day, just before my friend and I returned to Omaha, the brother-in-law said, "Come back when the beans are ripe, and you can pick all you want." I accepted the invitation. But my companion and I soon went our separate ways, and I never returned to that farm. To this day, I've never had the pleasure of sitting on my back step and shelling soybeans that I'd picked myself.

Soy was not a food of my childhood; but it has been a staple for most of my adult life. While I no longer put soybeans in my soup (now I prefer black or garbanzo beans), I buy plenty of soy flour and soybean curd. In part, I cook with soy flour because I am mildly allergic to wheat; but in part I replace some of the wheat in pancakes, bread, or muffins with soy because I like the robust, nutty flavor of that grain. In recent months, I've appreciated the ability of soy to prevent hot flashes—those sudden, brief, always surprising flushes of warmth in my face, neck, and chest that I experience when I've been without tofu—or, more specifically, the phytoestrogens in soy—for more than a week.

Not so long ago, eating tofu was considered weird. "What do you do with this stuff?" more than one grocery-store cashier asked me as she examined with curiosity and/or disgust the water-packed tofu that I was buying. Then, the many medical benefits of this wonder food weren't widely known in this country. Then, few people knew that isoflavone, a phytochemical in soy, reduces "bad" cholesterol and thus the risk of coronary heart disease; the phytoestrogens in soy protect men from prostate cancer and women from breast cancer, uterine fibroid tumors, fibrocystic breast disease, endometriosis, and other estrogen-driven diseases. Then, few people knew that soy is rich in protein, calcium, lecithin, vitamins, minerals, and acids. In the early 1980s I tried to explain this to the Omaha physician who told me that a vegetarian could not be well-nourished and healthy no matter how much soy she consumed. Consequently, he sent me to the University of Nebraska Medical Center for blood tests that he believed would reveal the deficiencies in my diet. The tests revealed exactly what I expected them to—that I was well-nourished and in need of a new physician. A few years later, my obstetrician recommended that I consume many servings of dairy products each day to make up for the protein that I wasn't getting from meat and that he believed I could only get from other animal products. I quietly ignored his advice. Instead, each week I bought and ate four blocks of fresh, homemade soybean curd from a Korean restaurant and grocery near 84th Street and West Center Road in Omaha. It was the finest tofu I've ever eaten and the best raw material I knew of for making a baby's brain, bones, heart, and flesh.

When driving through the countryside, I take pleasure at the sight of Black Angus in yellow fields. But I do not feel the same affinity toward grazing beef cattle as I do toward a field of burnt orange and green leaves and seed pods, lumpy with ripe soybeans. Perhaps we look more lovingly, more yearningly, more tenderly upon those aspects of the landscape that fuel our thoughts, our words, our deeds, that have become our bodyminds.

IV. CHOCOLATE

Even though my children usually find devious hiding places for their Halloween, Christmas, or Easter chocolates, I eventually ferret out their caches. But once the location of the Easter loot eluded me for so long that I forgot about it until gravity made me remember. As I was getting dressed in my bedroom, I heard a "thunk." Not a loud heavy thunk, but the thunk of something small and solid falling a short distance. There on the hardwood floor beneath my dresser lay a foil-wrapped chocolate coin. I dropped and rolled as if I was on fire. Beneath my dresser, my children had taped their foil-wrapped chocolate coins and eggs. I swooned. O, dear confection! O, sweet, exotic indulgence! O, Hershey, you hushed secret, you whispered seduction.

I could be seized and held rapt by more dangerous vices, like a hankering for raw seafood; impulsive men; wine with dinner, one glass after another and another and another; the stingingly good, hand-rolled cigarettes that I enjoyed at twenty; world-softening sedatives; stock-car racing. At worst, my passion for chocolate provides me with a few more calories each day than my middle-aged body can burn.

Of greater concern to me is that my chocolate consumption keeps me from treading lightly upon the earth. The best climate for raising cacao trees is within a twenty-degree latitude north and south of the equator. Even though cacao and coffee trees are part of the forest understory, accustomed to growing in shade or partial sunlight, people are leveling the dense, tropical forests so that the trees can grow in full sunlight and, with the aid of more chemicals, produce more abundantly. The loss of forests has drastically reduced the diversity of the flora and fauna in that region as well as the number of migratory songbirds that I can spot on my jaunts through Midwestern woodlands. And too, many poor, equatorial countries pay their debts to wealthy lender nations and institutions by exporting cash crops—chocolate, coffee, sugar, cotton, bananas—instead of growing food for their own people.

Yet I am powerless to resist chocolate's luscious lure. The chocolate kiss that I melt in my mouth after a sip of hot coffee in turn melts the crankiness and frustration of an entire afternoon spent replying to work-related E-mail messages when I'd rather have been writing. Neat wedges of quadruple-chocolate cheesecake (crumbly chocolate crust; chocolate cream cheese filling; chocolate icing; tiny, chocolate chips sprinkled on top) sustained me through my divorce. The handful of chocolate chips that sweetened my morning bowl of oatmeal gave me something to get up for in the morning when I lived in the estranging-place. I reward my children and myself for our great and small triumphs with double scoops of ice cream from Goodrich or Baskin-Robbins ice cream shops. My children, who don't yet appreciate the mood-altering properties of chocolate, choose from a rainbow of flavors—raspberry sherbet, dinosaur crunch, apple pie, mocha, strawberry cheesecake. But for me, nothing satisfies like Chocolate Caramel Crunch or Fudge Swirl or Brownie Nut Fudge. Then, God's in her heaven—all's right with the world!

Satisfying or attempting to satisfy a craving takes us out of ourselves and our circumstances in the ritual act of sipping coffee and melting chocolate kisses, sipping coffee and melting kisses. And the object of our craving and the associations that it conjures takes us home. As I lick and swirl German chocolate ice cream, I remember the Brach's chocolate cremes that I found in my stocking each Christmas morning as a child. I remember the boxes of chocolate-covered cherries that Grandpa Parris often brought me for no special reason. I remember the yellow cakes with glossy, milk chocolate frosting that my mother made for my birthdays, at my request. I remember the seemingly endless supply of Oreos and Chips-Ahoy! chocolate chip cookies in my parents' cookie jar. I remember the Tootsie Rolls among the lemon drops in Grandma Knopp's candy dish. I remember my mother's homemade Christmas fudge.

Yet there's more driving my craving for chocolate than the desire to forget myself. I can achieve that in meditation, in reading a good book or writing an essay, in provocative conversation. Other food memories are just as likely to take me home: remembering my dad's fried egg sandwiches, my mother's homemade dill pickles or butterhorn yeast rolls spread with thin white icing or Hungry Jack instant potatoes, yellow with Blue Bonnet Margarine. When meditation, imagination, human companionship, and memory take me away, it is because I allow them to. But chocolate's polysyllabic chemical soup (anandamine, an endogenous cannabinoid; phenylethylamine, the "love chemical"; and tryptophan, which is involved in the production of serotonin) alters my mood and creates a warm, happy inner glow—with or without my permission. Thus, chocolate reminds me of what I would rather forget: that while I am seized by emotional, intellectual, spiritual, and altruistic hungers, I am also a collection of chemicals under the command of a genetic code. Only through teeth-clenching, nail-digging will power can I resist my keenest appetites.

Consume

Mason and Folkert's pyramid of energy, biomass, and numbers shows how usable energy decreases as it moves from a lower to a higher trophic or nourishment level. For instance, plants, the wide band at the base of the pyramid, are producers, since they nourish themselves not by consuming other life forms but through photosynthesis. These plants nourish the next band on the pyramid—the primary consumer—say, a Holstein steer. The steer in turn nourishes the next band—the secondary consumer—say, a human, who is at the peak of this comparatively simple pyramid. When the human consumes the cow in the form of a beef burrito, she takes the cow (as well as corn meal, cheese, and seasonings) into herself. Thus, the corn, sorghum, alfalfa, and red clover that the cow ate, becomes part of every cell of the burrito-eater. ("Everything Miss T. eats becomes Miss T," begins the nursery rhyme I once knew by heart.) Union is always the result of consuming or of being consumed (derived from the Latin *consumere*—*con*, "together"; *sumere*, "to take"; *sub*, "under"; and *emere*, "to buy, take"; thus to consume is to take up completely, make away with, burn up, devour, waste, spend). To be consumed, say, by a passion, a disease, a beloved, or despised other is to be taken into the "body" of the other. Before the days of cement-incased, steel coffins, the consumer of the beef burrito became a producer by entering that final earthly union of which Whitman sings in *Leaves of Grass*: "I bequeath myself to the dirt to grow from the grass I love. If you want me again look for me under your bootsoles."

7. Braided

A soft braid doesn't hold; an uneven braid doesn't please the eye. A good flat braid is uniform, the rug yarn or bread dough or hairs divided into three equal sections. It is firm, with no equivocation, no change in the tension as one makes one diagonal pass after another, stacking a neat, slightly tilted row of v's.

Since I was twenty-one, my hair has been past my waist. If I wear it loose it catches on doorknobs, buttons, or wrist watches and mats so badly near my neck that I have to cut the snarls. So for the past two decades, I have braided my hair first thing in the morning and whenever it becomes loose and wispy during the day. I start the braid in the back of my head, both hands raised and working where I can't see them; after I've made five or six v's—enough that the braid feels really started—I swing my hair over my left shoulder and braid within a few inches of the end. Done in about two minutes. At the top my braid is almost as thick as my wrist; at the bottom where it is bound with a coated rubber band, it is the diameter of my thumb. I suppose that from a distance, my braid looks like an utterly supple, external spine.

I do not remember when I first learned to braid or who, if anyone, taught me. But I remember that when my own hair was too short to braid (my mother insisted that I wear a pixie cut until I was nine), I braided everything else—my doll's yellow yarn hair, the fringe on chenille bedspreads or woolen scarves, slick stems of white clover, Christmas tree tinsel, twisted threads of drapery tassels.

Perhaps I was drawn to braiding because it produces a whole that is stronger than the sum of its parts. Or perhaps because a braid is more than it appears to be: two criss-crossed strands.

Driven by rain and snowstorms in the Rocky Mountains, the turbulent sediment-laden waters of the North and South Platte Rivers flow toward the adjacent high plains of Wyoming, Colorado, and western Nebraska. The North and South Plattes meet in a dramatic moment in the city of North Platte, Nebraska, in a spot uncommemorated by either a plaque or a park, and continue as a single body toward the Missouri River: a total journey of nine hundred miles. Like almost every other river on the Great Plains, the Plattes flow east, a liquid link between the Rockies and the Midwest. An astronaut's view of the region reveals that the North and the South Platte Rivers are the extended arms of a great, wavy Y, of which the Platte River is the stem. But I think of the Platte as a spinal column, arching, rounding, straightening across the entire 450-mile width of Nebraska.

The eastern quarter of the Platte from its confluence with the Loup to its confluence with the Missouri, is one wide, flowing stream, like the Mississippi, the Des Moines, the Missouri, and other rivers I have known. But from the confluence of the two branches at North Platte to Grand Island, the river winds through tree-lined, creeklike channels.

Because of these several shifting channels that intersect and part again and again, the central Platte is referred to as "braided." The development of the braid is fairly simple. Because the land has a low, steady gradient and because the river lacks the volume to flush out the silt, a midstream bar of sediment forms. This obstruction parts the water. More deposition occurs and many sandbars form, dividing the river into even smaller channels.

An aerial view of the central Platte shows that the erratic parting, looping, and reuniting of the streams, the disappearing islands, the shifting shore lines, the channels leading nowhere, create a braid that is neither firm nor even in its weaving of light-filled water and land, but a wild vascular snarl.

Other than myself, only three people have braided my hair. One, a beautician whom I paid for a trim, asked if she could French-braid it just to see how it looked, no charge. She began with three clumps of hair near my crown. As she plaited, she picked up strands of hair along the sides, not only vertically stacking the tilted v's but basting v's along each side of the braid through the continual additions of hair. When she was no longer working near my scalp, she worked in a plain, flat braid. Her creation was beautiful, but I was afraid that the interlacing wouldn't come out. After I left the beauty shop, I spent a terror-filled ten minutes unplaiting.

When I was in my early twenties, I tended bar in a smoky tavern. So that my hair would not absorb as much of the stink of the cigarette smoke and would stay firm through an eight- or ten-hour shift, my mother braided it so tightly that I couldn't drop my eyebrows. When I combed out my hair after work, it fell in yellow ripples like those of the angels and Madonnas in fifteenth-century Flemish paintings—the closest thing to curls that my hair has ever known.

Now my mother says that whenever she can't sleep, which is often, she imagines an endless length of hair, that she braids tightly and evenly, what was outside moving inside, what was inside moving outside, until she drops her work and sleeps.

While we're standing in line at the grocery store or library, Meredith removes the coated rubber band and unravels my hair almost to the top of my braid. Then she rebraids it all the way to the tip and so loosely that she can wiggle a few fingers between the v's. "It looks longer that way," she says, and it does. It touches the top of my thighs. I imagine that when I am old, forgetful, and too stiff to reach behind my head, Meredith will braid my hair into a long, white queue, at the top, the diameter of my thumb, at the bottom, the diameter of a pencil.

A trinity is a braid of sorts, binding three parts into an indivisible whole.

The ancient Hindus conceived of the deity as having one body with three heads, each facing in a different direction. Vishnu, the preserver, appears on the right; Siva, the destroyer, on the left; Brahma, the creator, in the middle. Each aspect of this triune god plays an essential role in the cycle of life and the workings of the universe. Each aspect is indispensable.

The ancient Hebrews also might have conceived of God as a plurality, perhaps even a trinity. Elohim, the frequently used name for God in the Hebrew scriptures, is the plural form of Eloah. In some passages the verb that follows Elohim is plural, but more often it is singular. Thus, some say that rather than referring to the plurality of God, Elohim is "an intensive plural," used to denote God's greatness and majesty. Others, however, argue that a plural noun is a plural noun no matter what follows it, and so it denotes more than one. When three visitors (men in some translations, angels in others) appeared at Abraham's tent to announce that, within the next year, Sarah would bear the son that she and Abraham were long past even hoping for, Abraham bowed before them and called them Elohim, the great, majestic God that is at once singular and plural.

Many centuries later, the Christian doctrine of the trinity was developed as a rebuttal to Arius, the heretic priest of Alexandria, Egypt, who believed that while Jesus was a superior being, he was not equal to God. The Nicene Council of 325 said that God, who sends Jesus, and Jesus, who sends the Holy Spirit, are one. *Mia ousia, treis hupostaseis.* God is three persons in one nature, and the Trinitarian symbol refers to the three ways in which the one God is humanly known: as creator, as transformer, as inner spirit.

Most thinking, contemporary Christians find this doctrine of the deity's plurality to be overly abstract, patriarchal, largely extrabiblical and just downright uninspiring. Mostly we ignore it. Yet once I liberate this old symbol from the mass of dogmas that have developed over the centuries and reconceive it in terms of my experiences with God, it is meaningful. For instance, Trinitarian theology reminds me that the god I live with and love is not a flat, cutout figure, nor is the deity an unknowable abstraction. Rather God is three-dimensional and a someone rather than a something. And this god is one of relationships: Motherfather god in the sky; daughterson god of the earth; all-encompassing, transforming, genderless spirit. Not three separate centers of consciousness and will, but one great spirit that exists through the relationship of the parts, just as I exist only through the boundedness of my three parts—spirit, body, mind.

Meditating on this koan that is the Trinity teaches me that when I focus on the parts, I perceive the grass flower instead of the prairie, the historical event instead of the historical pattern, the individual notes instead of the melody. By surrendering control over the process of seeing, I see more. Try it. When you blur the eye and allow all of the parts to exist at once, you behold the landscape, the meaning of the story, the essence of the other, something of God's depth and breadth. Be there as long as you can.

Prior to the construction of a series of dams and reservoirs, the central Platte flooded each spring in response to melting snowpack in the Rockies, the greatest part of the river's annual discharge. During the spring the central Platte was more than a mile wide. During the rest of the year, the river might be just a thin trickle. Or it might dry up altogether. Paul J. Currier, deputy director of the Platte River Whooping Crane Maintenance Trust, reports that since the turn of the century, flood flows and mean annual flows have declined more than 70 percent. Likewise channel widths have declined 50 to 90 percent.

Where does the water go? In 1990, one million acres in Nebraska were irrigated through surface water, seven million by ground water. Most of the surface water was drawn from the Platte and its tributaries. The river also has been manipulated for flood control, power generation, and the growing urban centers that demand water for showers, dishwashers, washing machines, green lawns, and golf courses. In short, eastern Nebraskans use an average of two hundred gallons of water per capita per day; Nebraskans from the semiarid western half of the state use more than double that amount.

One effect of the reduced flow and speed of the river is that it can no longer scour the flood plains, banks, and sandbars clean of the cottonwoods, willows, alders, and Russian olives that germinate in the wet soil. Without the discipline imposed by annual floodwaters, the river appears to be a creek threading its way through dense, flood-plain forests.

While some native species—wild turkeys and white-tailed deer, for instance—have benefited from the increased vegetation, most have not. The Big Bend, the eighty-mile stretch between Overton and Grand Island, the tightly corseted waist on the hourglass that is the central flyway, hosts millions of migrating birds, including seven to nine million waterfowl, one-half million sandhill cranes, five endangered species— whooping cranes, least terns, piping plovers, Eskimo curlews, peregrine falcons—as well as bald eagles, who were recently removed from the endangered species list. Late each winter these and many other avian species leave their winter feeding grounds in Texas, New Mexico, and Mexico. Sandhill cranes, for instance, stop along the Platte for several weeks to rest, fatten up, perform their courtship rituals, and mate before continuing their journey to their summer nesting grounds in the Arctic. They prefer broad channels and shallow water because there they are protected from such nighttime predators as coyotes, dogs, and foxes and not so long ago, wolves and cougars. They prefer wet meadows to woodlands because of the greater food supply. If the river becomes too loosely braided, more land than water, more trees than light, the birds will go elsewhere—though I don't know where that might be.

When Meredith was three, she twisted her doll's long hair into a coil. She called it "braiding." But the moment she released her hold, the cord sprang loose. "Teach me to braid," she said.

We combed the doll's hair, then divided it into three equal sections. I showed her the simple over-and-over-and-over motion. But she could not duplicate it. Instead she wanted to pull strands under as well as over, creating a more complicated, nay, impossible design. When the rather cross-stitched pattern did not emerge, she gave up.

Now Meredith is nine. She says that her hair is brown, red, black, gold—every color. The texture is somewhere between the thick kinked strands of her father's Negroid hair and the thin, straight strands of my Caucasian hair. She likes to wear her hair, which has never been cut, free—only held by a headband or pulled into a high ponytail so that her curls form a billowing crown of glory. But since she does not like having her hair combed out, she only has two choices: very short and natural or always braided.

Before I begin braiding Meredith's hair, I oil her scalp with Blue Magic Bergamot Hair and Scalp Conditioner and work a wide-toothed comb through snarls that make us both scream. Then I draw clean parts and begin braiding, my hands slick with the blue grease. While tight braids make my hair look shorter, they work against Meredith's curls, creating a longer look. Conversely, by braiding her hair loosely I can create a shorter, thicker look since a softer braid permits the curl. Finally, I decorate her braids with bright pairs of interlocking plastic beads. Sometimes Meredith's father's wife or his sister braids her hair. Then corn rows radiate from Meredith's crown. Or liana-like braids frame her face. Or braids coiled like snails are bobby-pinned in the center of neat squares. Or braids swirl and rise into a cluster of beads and spill out like water from a fountain. When a former neighbor of mine, a black man with the same birthday as the writer Richard Wright and me, saw one of these intricate, imaginative creations that my daughter was wearing, he said to me, "You've learned to braid."

Ephemeral objects of beauty—an ice craving chiseled in finest detail; a room aglow with the light of scores of candles; a celebration cake piled with sugary roses, bows, and scalloped moldings—are shot through with preciousness and urgency, qualities lacking in more durable works of art, say, animal-shaped bronze bells from the Shang Dynasty (1500–1027 B.C.), a Michelangelo fresco, a Georgia O'Keeffe painting. The artist who worked three dozen braids and hundreds of beads into my daughter's hair was not seeking to leave a lasting testimony to her skills. Rather she brought forth an extravagant yet functional beauty to be savored now or tomorrow because next week would be too late. Meredith tries to preserve her stepmother's or aunt's short-lived works of art as long as possible by wearing a pair of pink tights that she has outgrown over her braids, the legs tied in a roselike knot above her forehead when she sleeps.

But when she only has one, two, or three braids—one of her or my simple creations—she skips the pink cap and replaits her hair in the morning. As I watch her hands, I am delightfully confused: it is my mother's hands, my hands, my daughter's hands, fluidly, automatically pulling the hair over and over and over; mother, daughter-mother, daughter; heavenly parent, earthly child, boundless, permeating spirit; meandering channels, dividing and joining, water, land, and light.

One blessed trinity flowing into the next.

Beauty

Some say that beauty is a quality inherent in the object, completely independent of the perceiver. The eighteenth-century British philosopher Edmund Burke believed that beauty is "some quality in bodies acting mechanically upon the human mind by the intervention of the senses." Plato believed that the form or essence of beauty is knowable, exact, rational, and measurable. Thus for many centuries philosophers and aestheticians have tried to verify and analyze the existence of beauty in terms of proportion, unity, variety, symmetry, simplicity, grace, aptness, suggestiveness, intricacy, and so on.

As proof of beauty's freestanding nature, Mortimer Adler says that if you remove from an admirable work of art "those traits which, when present, make them objectively excellent and admirable" you will spoil that work. Let's say that I were to revise Sandro Botticelli's *The Birth of Venus* (1485–86) by tampering with the clear rhythmic lines, the delicate color, the artist's sophisticated understanding of perspective or the suggestion of motion from Venus's coy right foot, which is just beginning to lift from the lovely, scalloped shell toward the Cyprian shore. Surely, it would be a less beautiful painting. Even what is anatomically incorrect in this painting—the unnatural length of Venus's neck, her rounded shoulders, the odd way in which her left arm is attached to her body—all serve to create a more graceful outline than would have been achieved by more normally proportioned body parts. Remove anything from the painting—the flowering orange grove in the background, Chloris and Zephyr's rose-strewn exhalations that pushed Venus's shell shoreward, the diaphanously clothed nymph who is about to receive Venus with a purple cloak—and the integrity or harmony of the work is destroyed.

Or, let's say that I were to revise Peter Paul Rubens's *The Judgment of Paris* (1635–38) by tampering with the radiant colors, the glowing light, the exquisite rendering of the nudes, the glowing, shaded landscape. Of course, my revisions would result in a less admirable and excellent creation. Yet something in the painting involving neither Rubens's technique nor his aesthetic vision detracts from his technique and aesthetic vision. Paris, who has been asked to select the most beautiful goddess, eyes Hera, the goddess of home and hearth, Athena, the goddess of war and wisdom, and Aphrodite or Venus, the personification of beauty, with such an innocent eye. I suppose that the average, seventeenth-century Fleming would have delighted in that pregnant moment before the decision is made. Why not behold these utterly desirable, utterly voluptuous, thick-bodied beauties as long as possible? What mortal could choose among them? Yet many viewers in the early twenty-first century would first like to "fix" the goddesses' billowing buttocks, rippling midriffs, and ungraspably thick upper arms before picking a winner. In *The Judgment of Paris*, the results of Adler's test prove that beauty is, in the words of the eighteenth-century Scottish philosopher Francis Hutcheson, an "idea raised in us." What this means is that we shouldn't judge those who find opera arias more beautiful and soul-expanding than bluegrass ballads as existing at some lower rung on the evolutionary ladder, where the ideal of the beautiful hasn't yet been fully realized. In truth people see beauty where and how they've been taught to see beauty. And what is beauty? That which gives us pleasure when we behold it.

8. Inherent Value

The pallid sturgeon is an odd-looking fish. Its long slender, practically scaleless, body is pale gray blue or tan above and white below. The head ends in a long snout, as pointed and triangular as a pie server and slightly upturned like an oversized clown's shoe. From the bottom of the head dangle four fringed barbels, extremely sensitive whiskerlike growths. When the barbels detect something edible (insects, fish eggs, mollusks, crustaceans), the elephant-trunklike jaws drop down and suck up the prey. Like most bottom feeders, the pallid sturgeon's belly is smooth. Bony plates covering the rest of the body provoke one of this creature's common names: hackleback. Its sharkish tail is upturned. The fins are fanned, veined, and as wavy-edged as ginkgo leaves. Field guides differ widely on the age of sexual maturity in female pallid sturgeon, three to twenty years, though all agree that this fish matures slowly. Spawning occurs infrequently (once every three to ten years) in the spring, when the water levels are highest. And this fish lives a long time—150 years in some cases.

Or so I've read. I've never seen a pallid sturgeon or any other sturgeon as far as I know. Actually, I haven't paid much attention to any fish. I am more drawn to flocking starlings than shimmering schools of shiners, to overlapping leaf bud scales than winter rings on fish scales. In fact, watching swordtails gliding through aquarium water or imagining pallid sturgeons vacuuming food from the river bottom leaves me gasping for air.

My chances of seeing a pallid sturgeon are pretty slim. The October 1993 NEBRASKA*land Magazine* reports that: "According to commercial fisherman who began fishing the Missouri River in 1927, 15-to-20-

pound pallid sturgeons were commonly caught as recently as the 1950s between the mouth of the Niobrara River and Greenwood, South Dakota." Yet since 1970, only seventeen pallid sturgeons have been reported in Nebraska and most of those near the mouths of the Niobrara, Platte, Elkhorn, and Little Nemaha Rivers, all Missouri River tributaries. Moreover, "No larvae or young-of-the-year pallid sturgeon have been collected in Nebraska to date." Either this fish is very secretive or very rare.

There are good reasons to believe that human-caused changes in the river are responsible for this fish's place on both the state and federal endangered species lists. In his fine essay, "The Return of Beaver to the Missouri River," Conger Beasley describes watching this river's "last great flood" from a bluff in his hometown of St. Joseph, Missouri, in 1953. "Levees crumbled, dikes collapsed, water swept across wheat and alfalfa fields, carrying houses, cattle, barns, and automobiles with it. From bluff to bluff between the two states [Kansas and Missouri], a distance maybe of five miles, the river was stippled with foamy whirlpools and entire trees."

Now, the Missouri is no longer so wild, free, and robust, nor is it as long or as wide. Several massive dams on the Upper Missouri have resulted in greatly reduced river flows. To render the river even less flood-prone and more accessible to barge traffic, the Army Corps of Engineers has straightened the channel (at a loss of 127 miles between Sioux City and St. Louis) and deepened it (at a loss in width of more than 75 percent in some places). Banks lined with rock riprap no longer support vegetation; silt buildup behind the wing dikes further narrows the channel. Beasley says that the Army Corps has reduced the Missouri River from Gavin's Point Dam near Yankton, South Dakota, to the river's confluence with the Mississippi just north of St. Louis "to a tawny ribbon whose least impulse can be carefully monitored." He quotes one old timer who says that now the river is nothing but "an irrigation ditch."

These alterations have affected the pallid sturgeon's ability to reproduce. Cold water released from reservoirs changes the flow and temperature of river water, two factors believed to trigger spawning. The presence of dams not only interferes with the passage of spawning sturgeons, but releases from dams can cause fluctuations in the water level that leave the eggs and larvae dry and exposed. In addition, alterations in the river reduce the number of wetlands, which trap pollutants that would otherwise enter the river and sever links in the food chain.

Thus, on the infrequent occasion that our few pallid sturgeons do spawn, they are most likely to do so in the mouths of Missouri River tributaries where the waters more closely match what the Missouri was before it was tamed.

A precarious situation. Yet I can't say that I care deeply for a creature so seldom seen that I sometimes wonder if it even exists. And too, I find this fish, well . . . ugly. Certainly it's less endearing than some of Nebraska's other endangered species—playful black-footed ferrets, sweet-faced piping plovers, or blowout penstemons, with their luscious lavender bells.

Still, there are good reasons for protecting even unlovely creatures. The biodiversity argument posits that the continued stability of the food web—so intricately complicated that no one can predict all of the ramifications of a single extinction—depends upon its integrity. The indicator-species argument holds that if populations of extremely hardy fish, like carp, rise and populations of the more sensitive fish, like pallid sturgeons, fall, then the river is out of balance. The knowledge argument contends that if we lose pallid sturgeons, relicts of the palaeoniscoids, "dinosaur fish" that flourished from Devonian to Jurassic times, we lose crucial information about the evolution of the species, both piscine and primate. And finally, the ethical argument insists that all creatures are worthy of respect and consideration. "The other beings—four-legged, winged, six-legged, rooted, flowing, etc.—have just as much right to be in that place as we do, they are their own justification for being, they have inherent value, value completely apart from whatever worth they have for . . . humans," writes Dave Foreman, founder of Earth First!, an organization that consistently places the welfare of the ecosystem ahead of economics.

On my more faithless days, I question if the web of life is as fragile and interlaced as ecologists say it is. I question if dams, deep channels, and pollutants have caused pallid sturgeon numbers to dwindle or if other factors are to blame. And I question if the pallid sturgeon has been around for two hundred to three hundred million years. Or if anything has, for that matter. But what I can't argue with on any day of the week is the justness of extending the right to life and habitat to all creatures, with exceptions made for dangerous bacteria or viruses that might invade our bodies, food, or water supply, or insect and rodent infestations of human habitations. If I act in accordance with this belief, I must do whatever is in my power to protect the land and rivers. This means living as simply and as unintrusively as possible. This means fighting efforts to weaken, defy, or overturn the Endangered Species Act, one of our nation's most enlightened pieces of legislation. This means supporting efforts to protect or restore habitats. If one day I learn that there are no pallid sturgeons, my efforts will not have been in vain. I'll have made the rivers, indeed the entire ecosystem, safer for other organisms.

Pallid sturgeons have responded favorably to habitat restoration. In August 1999, biologists working in a restored section of the Missouri River at the Big Muddy National Fish and Wildlife Refuge near Columbia, Missouri, found pallid sturgeon hatchlings in the wild. Prior to this finding, the only pallid sturgeon hatchlings any of these biologists had ever seen were the result of spawning operations at hatcheries. The sturgeons were thriving in this stretch of the river because higher-than-usual river levels in the mid-1990s had created a backwater where they could breed.

Some Nebraskans seek to balance the needs of the river's human and nonhuman residents. They advocate higher water levels in the central Platte, which would create more hospitable conditions for whooping and sandhill cranes, piping plovers, interior least terns, and other migratory bird species as well as for the pallid sturgeons in the lower Platte. But others, such as members of the irrigator group Nebraskans First and Governor Mike Johanns, who has vowed to "aggressively" defend the interests of irrigators against environmental needs, refuse to share the river.

I do not know what enables people to recognize the inherent value in another living creature or how to engender respect for life. But certainly, knowledge of the Other is an apt starting point. After studying the many sketches, the two photographs and the half-dozen articles I found about the pallid sturgeon, I've grown to find this fish's scutes and barbels, its sensitivity and elusiveness, quite endearing. With a little more time and knowledge, I might even find it beautiful.

Faith

Faith, from the Latin *fidem* meaning "to trust," is a belief in something despite a lack of supporting evidence or despite the evidence against it. For instance, I proceed into the busy intersection as soon as the traffic light facing me turns green, assuming that the lights facing the cars on my left and right have turned red and that the drivers have stopped or will stop. Such faith is ill-founded. Dozens of times, I have entered an intersection after my light turned green only to slam on my brakes because those other motorists in whom I had placed my faith did not stop when their light turned from yellow to red. Once, after the light flashed WALK and I'd just entered an intersection on my bicycle, a man making a right turn on red ran over my front bike tire. My son, who was in the child's seat, suffered a concussion, and I was sore and bruised from my irrational efforts to hold the bike up against the weight of the car. On two different occasions in recent months, I was so distracted, once by a tragedy, once by a story that my daughter was telling me, that I drove through a red light.

My faithfulness knows no bounds. I believe that the pills that the pharmacist hands me will kill the infection in my sinuses instead of, say, trigger seizures, despite the fact that the last time I bought a prescription drug, the bottle contained two different types of yellow oval pills. I believe that when my children go out into the world without me that they will return to me in the same condition, even though I have evidence that children are abducted, shot by their classmates, killed or injured in traffic accidents, or taught things that will change them forever. I believe that when I haul a trunk-load of newspapers, tin cans, plastic detergent bottles, junk mail, and flattened cardboard to the recycling center, that it will be converted into new newspapers, cans, bottles, junk mail, and boxes rather than hauled to the dump. I believe in the reliability and accuracy of the credit union computers and employees with such conviction that I toss my monthly statements into the recycling bin unopened.

The infidel spends most of her days collecting empirical data or only trusting life's few provens. But we faithful live at relative ease, only seeking evidence when the object of our faith fails us—say, when the flick of a switch or the turn of a knob fails to bring immediate light or heat or sound or when our loved ones appear to us as strangers.

9. In the Air

The woman who lived in my house before me claims that she has been struck by lightning. She is not old, but her hair is gray and frazzled. Her eyes are steady and icy blue. She speaks haltingly, as if her circuits have been broken.

I've read that lightning bolts can follow telephone wires or water pipes into houses: electrified messages that seek entrance into our lives any way they can. Though the spasm may kill the conversing or showering recipient (one stroke of lightning measures more than 15,000,000 volts; 2,350 volts shot four separate times kills a man completely dead in Nebraska's electric chair), the strike and the electrical charge are brief: you may start CPR at once. But most lightning stories I hear are of near hits. In *The Kingdom of Grass*, Nebraska Sandhills native Bob Ross, a friend of mine, writes that during one of the summers he spent working at his Uncle Oz's ranch, he hung a radio above his bunk in the old schoolhouse and plugged it into two hundred feet of buried extension cord. One weekend while Ross was in town, a storm hit. His bunkhouse mate reported that a little ball of fire came out of Ross's radio and floated to the foot of his bed. "When I opened the radio," Ross writes, "there were some burned-out components and the smell of plastic, but it continued to work fine. Only the tone had changed; it seemed scratchier, or maybe just a little tense."

I believe the eerie stories that people tell me about what lightning has done to them. What I doubt are the explanations I read about what causes lightning. Scientists say that the conditions for lightning occur when water droplets in a cloud freeze. The lighter, positively charged ice crystals rise to the top of the cloud; heavier, negatively charged water droplets fall toward the bottom; scattered positive areas exist at the base of the cloud. Due to the concentration of electrons, the ground, which usually is negatively charged, becomes positively charged in the area beneath the cloud. When the charge gradient between positive and negative areas becomes unbearably great, energy is discharged and lightning flashes. The average cloud-to-ground lightning bolt begins as a zigzagging stream of negative electrons, a "leader stroke" that flows from the negatively charged region of a cloud toward the positively charged ground. As the stream of negative electrons nears the earth, it pulls a stream of positive electrons upward: the "return stroke." The meeting of the leader and the return stroke creates a channel for the electrical flow. The visible lightning bolt is created by the massive downward flow of negative electrons to the ground. The surrounding air expands as it superheats to tens of thousands of degrees, then contracts as it cools. We know the resulting shock waves as thunder.

Or so I've read. According to Richard A. Keen in *Skywatch: The Western Weather Guide*, even the National Oceanic and Atmospheric Administration, the United States' largest weather research organization, admits that "no completely acceptable theory explaining the complex process of thunderstorm electrification has yet been advanced." I have no more evidence of upward and downward moving streams of electrons than I do of wicked Loki forging the lightning bolts that Thor pitches earthward. In the absence of observable evidence both theories must be taken on faith.

I can list in one paragraph all that I know with certainty about lightning. Lightning bolts meander and branch like rivers, nerves and dendrites, trees and family trees, blood vessels, knowledge. Lightning moves so fast between a cloud and the earth that our language makers dropped the *e* from "lightening," so that the word hits, pauses, and falls just as lightning jabs, paralyzes, then shakes the sky. Lightning strikes from out of the blue or the black with the sudden, unexpectedness of disaster, miracle, or one of those history book moments that is gone before you are even aware of it. Lightning is the stitch that for a quivering, fiery moment bastes the heavens and earth together.

II. Dog Days

In this heat, I float just beneath the surface of sleep. My thoughts drift from torrid Ethel Waters's rendition of "Heat Wave" to the feverish long-range forecast of melting glaciers, warming oceans, sprawling deserts, and skies dark with the smoke of forest and range fires; to ancient peoples who hung wet mats over their doorways and hoped for breezes; to Venus's volcano-studded surface, an acidic inferno at 869 degrees; to India where bride-burning has increased in frequency and has spread from Hindu to Muslim to Christian; to a searing heat that vaporizes senseless people the moment they say, "It's not the heat that's so bad but the humidity."

Each summer those of us who refuse the expensive, gray isolation of air-conditioned air must endure at least one extended period of sweltering heat. The dog days. The ancient Greeks applied this name to the period when Sirius, the Dog Star, rose and set with the sun, a period of about forty days beginning in early July and ending near mid-August. I carry jugs of water to the drooping basil growing in pots on my porch. Wilted leaves hang close to the stalks. When I return a few hours later, the leaves are smooth and upright. Tomorrow morning, they'll be limp and folded again.

I read that as the temperature rises, molecules move faster and require more space in which to move. As a result, all gases and most solids and liquids expand when heated. In this heat, I hear and see this acceleration and expansion. The night chants of male tree frogs, the daylong chants of male cicadas, the strings on Meredith's violin, my breath in my flute all vibrate faster and with less effort. The steel bridge arching the Salt Creek expands. My cat rubs against my legs, rolls from side to side on the floor, presents herself, raised rear end, tail bent to one side, and cries her love song, "Do it, do it," with increasing urgency. Overnight, the sticky-hairy tendrils of the bur cucumber drag their heavy vines over trees, fences, other vines and unfurl their five-lobed leaves, each as big as a man's handkerchief. I blot calamine lotion on the rash festering on Ian's feet and ankles; I remove ticks, bloated and gray with hot blood, from Meredith's tummy. In this heat, petunias, sycamore leaves, dog poop, tomato vines, car exhaust, grilled beef, and sweat produce a brew of fast, piercing odors. I read that all molecular activity would cease if the temperature dropped to minus 460 degrees Fahrenheit, absolute zero. Nothing would bloom or decay. No creature would be there to smell it if it did. On this day I cannot believe in a place that is not hot, vibrating, and scent-drenched.

I lie on my living room floor. Odors, once slow and subtle, now fast and sharp, drift through my windows and hang in the air. I open myself to the scent of marigolds. Of the daddy-longlegs nimbling over the side of my house. Of concrete strips. Of iridescent scales, feathers, and petroleum stains. Of small, lost metal things. Of glyphs of mice trails. Of motes of dust drifting in shafts of light. Of the whims and intentions of the couple walking past my house. Of summer haze and Sirius's glow. Of the crow's hard bark. Of dreams of heat and cool relief.

III. METEOR SHOWERS

The newspaper reported that between November 15 and 19, Nebraskans could see six to ten meteors per hour in our night skies: the Leonid Meteor Shower, so named since the shooting stars appear to radiate out of the constellation Leo. These meteors, gatherings of comet dust, small pieces of asteroids, or chunks of planets blasted off by other meteors, have been orbiting the sun for millions of years. But this November, they were being flung earthward. As the meteors move through the earth's increasingly dense atmosphere, air friction heats them to two thousand, three thousand, four thousand degrees Fahrenheit, until they are white-hot streaks. In most cases, the meteors completely burn out or break up before reaching the ground.

But some smash into the earth. The encyclopedia says that when the Tunguska Meteorite struck ground in Siberia, people felt the blast fifty miles away and saw the flash hundreds of miles away. On the east side of the Hudson Bay is a four-hundred-mile-wide depression: the earth's largest known meteor crater. In 1990, a thirty-seven-ton meteorite, the second biggest in the world, struck in Argentina. The Willamette Meteorite, on display at the Hayden Planetarium in New York, weighs over fifteen tons and is heavily pocked on one side by rust and atmospheric friction. If I could thrust my hands into these holes I would believe in this rock. But even if I caught a falling star, what reason would I have to believe that it is burning cosmic debris, a spark shot from a flaming god, or anything else offered by imagination?

It wasn't a lack of interest, a lack of time, or disbelief that kept me from venturing into my front yard and counting the shooting stars last November. Rather I just didn't do it, and so the meteor showers came and went without me. Then I wondered, Does a meteor shower exist if I'm not there to see it?

A few days later in a dream, something called me to my front door. White sparks zinged through the dark sky. The streets were filled with clusters of people crying out loud as they pointed to the busy heavens.

I suppose they sought warnings, cures, and assurances. I stood behind my storm door. Sometimes the tail of a meteorite shone for several minutes. I clung to its fiery existence until it was extinguished. But most lights were gone before I could focus on them. I softened my eyes until everything in the sky was background. Though I could not isolate a single shooting star, I received a sky alive with bright, quick movements.

Scientists estimate that as many as two hundred million visible meteors enter our atmosphere each day—a number pulled out of the air, for all I know. Perhaps white-hot meteors streak our daytime as well as our nighttime skies. But because their presence is beyond our ken, we do not gather in the streets in anticipation of a direct hit or a near miss. Neither do we marvel at or hope upon what scientists estimate to be the one thousand tons of micrometeorites: specks of cosmic dust that fall each day, powdering our streets, our roofs, our heads, eyebrows, shoulders, shoes; each speck, a direct hit, too fine to be detected, too common to be hoped upon.

IV. Deep Freeze

Two days before Christmas, my friend and I head for the lake so we may survey the constellations from the high, artificial levee. Scientists say that nine thousand stars are visible without a telescope; city lights hide all but a few of the brightest stars. The Hubble Space Telescope reveals galaxies upon galaxies upon galaxies—at least 1,500 within a tiny slice of sky north of the Big Dipper's handle. On the way to the lake, we stop frequently to drop our heads back and gaze at what is brightest and what we have names for: the Big Dipper, Sirius, Cassiopeia, Canis Major, Betelgeuse, Rigel, Orion, Aldebaran, Taurus, Pleiades, Jupiter, and a sliver of the earth's moon.

In the warm times of the year, I am not drawn to the stars and galaxies. Then the space between molecules seems too narrow for my imagination to move through. But in winter's diminished heat, I'm drawn to the stars, the cold planets, and the wide spaces between them. The prevailing theory of origin in this time and place holds that perhaps fifteen billion years ago an explosion of such power occurred that the universe is still hurtling from it in all directions. Even now the spaces between galaxies continue to stretch, the void continues to widen. Some scientists predict that if there is too little matter to slow this expansion, immeasurable distances will develop between galaxies, spreading our universe far too thin. They call the resulting cold and emptiness the Big Chill.

My friend and I have stopped too often and for too long. Though I'm wearing two pairs of gloves beneath my mittens, my fingers are numb. I pull them out of my glove fingers and roll them into fists. Though I'm wearing a pair of tights beneath my blue jeans, two pairs of thick socks, and my cheap hiking boots, my toes feel fat and hard. I can no longer wriggle warmth into them. A half-mile from our destination we turn around and begin the two-mile walk home.

Earlier in the month, temperatures in parts of Nebraska reached an almost record-breaking seventy degrees and stayed near that point for several days. People wore shorts and T-shirts as they mowed grass and hung Christmas lights. Then, overnight, the temperatures plunged. According to Steve Bryd, a weather service meteorologist, this sudden and dramatic change of temperature occurred because the weather had been "so mild for so long" that the jet stream held large air masses high above Canada, away from the sunlight for an unusually long time. When the air masses finally descended upon the northern plains, they were colder than normal. On solstice the temperature in Lincoln dropped to four below. In Valentine twenty below. In Alliance thirty below. The rural areas were several degrees colder than the towns and cities, with their heat-radiating concrete and asphalt.

When my companion and I arrive home my toes are burning and I'm on the edge of screaming. I know about frostbite. The mammalian body is a container that must be filled and vibrating with a certain amount of heat, the most perishable of perishables. I know that the ice crystals that form inside the body's delicate cells can stab their way through the cell membranes like tiny daggers and burst them like balloons. I know that when the water in our cells freezes, the remaining salts become so concentrated that our life processes become dangerously unbalanced and the cells can die. This knowledge puts me even closer to screaming.

As my stargazing companion wraps his big hands first around one of my feet, then the other, he tells me about honeybees. They alone of all the insects do not hibernate through the winter or die at its onset. Instead, they form loose clusters of thousands over the honey cells. Because bees in the core of the cluster are loosely packed they can spread their wings, crawl around, raise young, and feed on the approximately forty pounds of stored honey that will support the colony for the winter. The bees at the core must maintain a temperature of at least sixty-four degrees Fahrenheit. But the bees in the densely packed, insulating outer layer have a harder task: they must maintain a minimum temperature of fifty degrees along this periphery. When they get cold, they rapidly kick their feet and flap their wings, until the other bees respond to their agitation. Soon the entire cluster is firing up their flight muscles, generating thoracic temperatures of up to 100 degrees. By constantly moving from the edge of the cluster into the core and then back out, all bees find warmth. A bee separated from the cluster dies in the cold, but a bee in a colony survives.

My companion opens the space between his thumbs and blows one stream of lung-warmed air after another into the space that encloses my toes.

V. Prevailing Winds

Almost five years ago tornadic winds split or ripped mature trees up and down the street where I once lived. In my former backyard, the winds toppled a stout white birch, and tipped a Russian olive ninety degrees to the north. A *Lincoln Journal-Star* photograph from the 1930s shows a Nebraska farmer climbing a gracefully scalloped mound of dust that has buried all but the top row of his barbed wire fence. "When all the loose Nebraska dust was blown away, it began to blow in from Kansas, Oklahoma, and Texas," writes Hallie Myers Nelson in *South of the Cottonwood Tree*. "In a short time, everything—building roofs, bushes, weeds, garden plants, and even the cat and dog were layered with the red dust of Oklahoma and Texas."

The ovules of corn, grasses, ragweed, cattails, and most common trees and shrubs are fertilized one wind-borne grain of pollen by one wind-borne grain of pollen. My wind- and sun-dried clothes are stiff and fragrant. Just north of Lincoln a 290-foot-tall white fiberglass wind turbine, a low, spinning star, generates enough energy to power about 175 homes per year.

On a wind-tossed day, a grocery-store parking lot evangelist tells me that God is like the wind: you can't see him, but you can see the results of his power and presence. This is a good analogy, I believe, because it acknowledges the creative and the destructive aspects of both the deity and the wind.

Scientists say that winds are caused by a number of factors. Of course air moves simply because the earth is spinning. But, too, the sun warms the earth's surface, which in turn heats the air, stirring it into motion.

Some places are heated more than others; there, rising warm air draws cooler air beneath it. Other places are heated less; there sinking cold air pushes warm air outward. So air circulates continually between warm and cold areas, carrying moisture with it and creating everything that we call weather: heat waves, cold snaps, wind, rain, snow, hail, fog, lightning, and thunder. The swirling clouds seen in satellite images of the earth show the constant motion of the restless, weather-making air.

Twentieth-century knowledge of how air moves transformed weather forecasting from the observation of the behaviors of weather-predicting plants and animals and the movement of mercury in thermometers and barometers into a mathematical analysis of cool, polar, and warm, tropical airstreams, of dry air masses over continents and moist ones over oceans. Still, a well-prepared-for winter storm veers off its predicted course; dew freezes, withering seedlings and delicate transplants long after the predicted frost-free date; an unforeseen shower soaks the guests and the cake at an outdoor wedding; tornadoes are upon us with little warning. In truth, sophisticated equipment and mathematical analysis have made us no more adept at predicting the weather for more than a week at a time. The close attention that the meteorologist for *The Old Farmer's Almanac* gives to solar activity still yields the most reliable forecast of the winter ahead (a 65–70 percent overall accuracy) that I know of.

Climate experts smell the wind and offer vastly different and usually dire prophecies as to what lies ahead. Some foresee global warming triggered by automobiles, industry, volcanoes, and nuclear bombs heating the earth not to record temperatures, but to high temperatures in record time. This, coupled with the predicted depletion of the High Plains (Ogallala) Aquifer around 2020, will leave most of Nebraska unfit for agriculture, towns, and cities, though quite fit for grama and buffalo grasses, pronghorn antelope, and herds of bison. Or the ice may descend again. The Yugoslavian astronomer Milutin Milankovitch says that glaciation comes in cycles determined by wobbles of the earth in its orbit. When the wobble increases the earth's distance from the sun, ice and snow accumulate. Each hundred-thousand-year-long Milankovitch cycle includes as many as ninety thousand or as few as sixty years of glaciation followed by forty to ten thousand years of warmer periods or interglacials. Or we may be buried in sand. Scientists at the University of Nebraska-Lincoln speculate that the Sandhills, which cover more than one-quarter of Nebraska and are the largest dune fields in the Western

Hemisphere, may be wind-borne again if the vegetation cover is too deeply damaged by the predicted warming and drying of the Great Plains over the next half-century. Brown blizzards will wear down the high places and fill in the low ones, creating a landscape more lunar than earthly.

Or perhaps the cause of climate change will come from beyond the earth. Luis Alvarez and three other scientists at the University of California-Berkeley conclude that a meteorite, whose impact conveyed a force greater than the detonation of all the nuclear weapons in the world, occurred at the end of the Mesozoic Era. The blast literally shook the earth, drastically changed its atmosphere, and caused the mass extinction of several species, including dinosaurs. "It is conceivable and even likely," writes entomologist and biodiversity expert Edward O. Wilson, "that a volcanic eruption or a meteorite strike of such magnitude occurs every ten million or one hundred million years." Given that range, we're due. Many astronomers concur that the sun will finish burning the hydrogen in its core in another five billion years. Then it will swell up to become a red giant. Eventually the core will collapse and a final thermonuclear reaction will blow off the outer layers. As a white dwarf, the sun's core will be too cool for fusion reactions to take place. Over the course of billions of years, our sun will radiate off its remaining energy and slowly dim. Finally only a black cinder of degenerate matter will remain. Then the place I know as Nebraska will be cast into breathless darkness and cold.

But in the absence of evidence, these theories, forecasts, and hearsay are nothing I'd stake my future on. Rather I'll know what the weather is when it's upon me.

Adaptation

Adapt is comprised of the Latin *ad*, meaning "to," and *aptare* meaning "to fit." To adapt is to change, accommodate, adjust, suit, arrange, fit or conform something about oneself (behavior, attitude, structure, and so on) to new or changed circumstances. The modification that results from such a change is an *adaptation*.

I understand the purpose of some adaptations. The pronghorn antelope, the fastest mammal in North America (she can reach speeds of sixty to seventy miles per hour), is well adapted to the once vast, almost obstruction-free grasslands. Two adaptations account for her endurance and speed. First, her large leg muscles are attached near her body so she doesn't waste energy by lifting her body up and down (that is, galloping). Rather she runs in an economical, almost straight, line. Second, she runs with her tongue hanging out and her mouth open ("as if drinking in the space," writes Gretel Ehrlich), which allows her to take more air into her large trachea. This large-capacity respiratory system accounts for her ability to run at about forty miles per hour for as far as fifteen miles. Thus, wolves and coyotes, who wear down their prey by running relays (another excellent adaptation), can't keep up with the pronghorn. Now, fences, highways, and human habitations pose more of a problem to the pronghorn than do her ancient enemies.

I fail to understand the purpose of those adaptations that result in a narrow and utter dependency. The female pronuba moth cannot lay her eggs anyplace but on a yucca (soapweed) plant. The pregnant moth uses her specially adapted mouthparts to roll the sticky pollen of the yucca flower into a mass. She carries this golden ball to another yucca flower where she inserts a few of her eggs into the flower ovary and then presses the pollen into the cup-shaped stigma. There the sperm-bearing pollen tubes fertilize hundreds of ovules. The moth's larvae feed on some of the hundreds of black seeds, but most seeds are dispersed in the fall. In the absence of yucca moths, the yucca cannot set seeds (its pollen is beyond the reach of the wind) and can only reproduce by root offshoots, a method that does not allow for geographical expansion and that results in plants that are identical to the parent. Apparently, this method works well. I see yuccas and yucca moths thriving in my urban neighborhood and in the Sandhills. Yet I wouldn't want my well-being or that of my offspring dependent on the continued presence of a particular species or set of environmental conditions. If either the yucca or the yucca moth can't be found at the right time and place, both will fail to reproduce. Both species would either adapt or vanish forever.

It is the adaptability of the European starling of which I am the most envious. In 1880, Eugene Schieffelin, who hoped to create a garden that included every bird and plant mentioned by Shakespeare, released eighty pairs of European starlings in New York City's Central Park. Starlings easily multiplied and filled most of North America because they are true omnivores, feasting upon anything, from the finest fare of the field or bird feeder to garbage and sewage. They willingly settle anyplace, from the most desolate urban environments to the most bountiful cornfields. They willingly nest in any hole in the wall: a hollow tree trunk, rotted eaves, gutters, drainage pipes, the openings where wiring or plumbing enter a building, barn rafters, attic vents, or a hole used, or once used, by another bird. And starlings ignore, outsmart, or outmultiply the various scaring devices, repellents, and avicides designed to kill them or drive them away. Starlings may very well inherit the earth.

10. Necessary, Honorable Work

I walk through the woods with an eye for late autumn beauties—crimson bittersweet berries, rattling seedpods, bare branches veining the lower sky, migrating geese and fungi. I pause to admire clusters of leathery half circles extending from the sides of an old stump. These are bracket fungi, so named because they cling to a branch or stump like a shelf on which to set a vase, a clock, a marble bust.

Seen from above, the fungi are composed of graduated annual growth rings rising from the point of attachment like tiers of seats in an amphitheater. The center ring of the specimen I hold in my hand is covered with pale green fuzz and is encircled by rings of ash gray, nut brown, bronze, pale yellow and dun. The oldest rings, which form the rippled outer margin, are a dirty eggshell white. Such stratified patterns are common in nature: I have seen them in the growth rings on turtle and mollusk shells, cut tree trunks, and exposed sedimentary rock.

Seen from below, the brackets present plainer faces. Through my magnifying glass I can see that the underside is pierced with hundreds of pinholes, so tiny that they are barely visible to the naked eye.

I place my foot on a large branch knobbed with fungi and pull on the narrower end with my hand. The spongy wood breaks easily. The three-foot chunk that I carry home is all ears. I am pleased with my quarry.

Since most people's interest in fungi is limited to learning what is and isn't edible, the few field guides I find in libraries and bookstores are devoted primarily to mushrooms, with few pages for those who want to differentiate one bracket fungi, one slime mold, from the next.

In part this omission is due to the disgust most people feel toward those members of the plant kingdom that neither flower nor produce chlorophyll. "Fungaphobia," the nineteenth-century British mycologist William Delisle Hay called this widespread antipathy. What eventually caused me to overcome my antipathy to the fungi was my desire to understand *why* I found this life form so alien, so impenetrable, so repulsive. That meant learning what roles fungi play in the ecosystem.

The ringed fungi clustered on the branch I brought home from the woods are polypores, so named because of the presence of pores on the underside of the fruiting bodies. The pores are the openings of downwardly directed tubes, the inner surface of which are lined with basidia, club-shaped cells that bear the spores, or microscopic seeds. More specifically, my segment of tree branch is host to *Coriolus versicolor*, the many-colored polypore, one of the most common fungi in the world.

Coriolus spores can enter healthy trees through any opening—wounds left by wind or lightning-torn branches, woodpecker drillings, hearts and initials carved by lovers, the egg slits made by the narrow-winged cricket. Arising from the spore are the hyphae—microscopic, tubular threads. They form the mycelium—the vegetative body of the fungus—a tangled, subterranean network, usually hidden from our sight within the host tree or in the soil. The mycelium feeds on the protein portions of dead organic matter in the host or soil, reducing it to ammonia or other compounds that bacteria can convert into the nitrogenous material that green plants need for their new growth. A beneficial arrangement, for the most part.

Yet at first glance there are good reasons for feeling aversion toward this fungus. Trees infested by *Coriolus* mycelium eventually fall to "white rot," a type of heart-rot decay that destroys cellulose and lignin, the organic substances that form the essential part of the woody fiber. Once these cell-wall components are destroyed, the wood is softer, whiter, and spongier than healthy wood. According to one lumber industry estimate, more than 90 percent of the wood-rotting diseases in the United States are caused by bracket fungi, rendering 15 to 20 percent of our standing timber defective or unusable. But as ecologist and ethicist Aldo Leopold observed, the diseased oaks and basswoods on his Wisconsin wood lot made it "a mighty fortress" for raccoons, ruffed grouse, barred owls, wood ducks, woodpeckers, and prothonotary warblers. Diseased yet serviceable.

And, like many other fungi, *Coriolus versicolor* is most conspicuous and abundant in the autumn, the dying time of the year. At first glance, we find the death of summer's fertility beautiful and seek the fiery or radiant leaves of maples and oaks, ashes and cottonwoods. But our attitude changes when we meditate on the reason for the sizzling colors of Nebraska's woodlands: The leaves are brilliant because they are too undernourished to produce green pigment. They are in their death throes.

Nor are the woods so lovely if we concentrate on absences: the aerial parts of most plants have dried, browned, and stiffened; songbirds have departed for greener forests; my favorite insects—water darters, praying mantises, dragonflies, butterflies, moths, and daddy-longlegs— have vanished from the woods and the water's edge. Nor are the autumn woods so lovely if we focus on the fungi, which defy our classifications with their plantlike immobility and their animal-like means of nourishment; fungi, which grow as wild and as uninvited as age spots, goiters, tumors, warts, and melanomata; fungi, which led the English poet Percy Bysshe Shelley to wonder if the decaying dead had become animated with a spirit of growth. Under such scrutiny, the autumn woods lose their appeal.

But to feel gratitude for the fungi, one has only to imagine what the woods and forests would be like in their absence. Each autumn, in temperate zones, most trees would continue to shed their leaves. But without fungi, each year's leaves would fall on leaves from the year before and the year before and the year before. Branches would drop; entire trees would topple from old age or the damage caused by wind, lightning, insects, and bacteria. In the absence of fungi—bloated tan balls, soft and moist as frosting; cream-colored scales; crowded tiers of rubbery, red brown domes; yellow white pimples; waxy-capped mushrooms too fragile to pick; smoke-belching puffballs; and rings upon rings of polypores—the accumulation of dead plant materials would so overwhelm the rate of decomposition that a stagnant, acidic, oxygen-starved, nutrient-poor ecosystem would result. Wildflowers, vines, saplings, shrubs, and mature trees would be smothered from above by their own unmoldering substance and starved from below by a lack of nutrients for their roots. In time, the forests would be so choked with pieces of trees and layer upon layer of dead stems, stalks, and leaves that they would be impenetrable to hikers, loggers, logging protesters, and mycologists alike. No other agent of dissolution—insects, cycles of freezing and thawing, water, or heat—is as efficient as the fungi. That is why biologist Scott Camazine calls them "the planet's decomposers and cleanup crew, breaking down and recycling every type of organic material."

And trees can benefit directly from fungal associations. The roots of pines, willows, poplars, oaks, birches, hickories, and beeches are wrapped in external fungal nets, permitting them to obtain soil nutrients through mycelium surrounding their roots. In addition to extending the host plant's capacity to absorb nutrients from the soil, fungal filaments can provide a kind of external immune system for a tree by blocking viruses and pathogenic bacteria. Many native orchids host mycelium within their roots because the hyphae, which comprise the mycelium, are more efficient at absorbing nutrients from the soil than are the orchid's own root hairs. In the absence of fungi, I could not return to the woods each spring to find yellow lady's slipper orchids, Dutchman's breeches, Jack-in-the pulpit, columbine, tender new leaves, and the clouds of redbud and dogwood blossoms I so eagerly await.

The broken branch supporting clusters of many-colored polypores rests in the corner of my bedroom atop my dresser. The brackish, autumnal smell of wood, so damp and crumbling that it is almost humus, reminds me that without the destruction of once-living bodies, energy cannot move up and down the food chain. This branch and the earthy odor it exudes remind me that destruction and conversion, parts of the complete life cycle, is necessary, honorable work.

Niche

To the ecologist a *niche* (from *nidus*, Latin for "nest") is not just the passive receptacle into which eggs are laid and the young sheltered but a statement of dynamic relationship. In *Animal Ecology*, Charles Elton wrote that the word *niche* is used to describe "the status of an animal in its community, to indicate what it is doing and not merely what it looks like." *Habitat* is an organism's address; *niche* is its profession, the job it performs in the ecological system.

Figuratively speaking, a niche is "a place or position adapted to the character or capabilities, or suited to the merits of a person or thing." Sometimes one finds her niche ready and waiting; sometimes she must carve it out for herself. What is lacking in this dictionary definition is the mutual adaptation stressed by the ecological definition. If one is to live harmoniously, she must not only consider if the alcove she enters is tall, deep, and wide enough, but if she will complement the contents of other niches, and how she stands in respect to the main events— feasting, dancing, governing, worshipping, passing to and fro.

11. Backdrop

On August 20, 2000, I toured the University of Nebraska State Museum in Morrill Hall not to marvel at the age, size, and durability of the hard remains of the ancient beasts that once roamed the northern Great Plains, but to notice the murals behind their remains. I suppose that on other visits to the museum, I had been dimly aware of a setting and a brightness behind the mammoths, oreodonts, ancient rhinoceroses, and saber-toothed cats, but had never considered the source of that brightness or the appropriateness of that setting. What pulled these backgrounds into the foreground for me was a comment made by an acquaintance of mine that someone ought to write something about Elizabeth Dolan, the muralist whose work graces the walls of Morrill Hall and many other public buildings in Lincoln, Nebraska. I wondered how a woman got such commissions in the early years of the twentieth century. I wondered why an artist chose to create background instead of the objects on display. Was she so ill at ease with herself and others that she preferred background? Was she so self-assured that she did not feel diminished or upstaged when in the background? Was she so captivating that even when painting background, she herself was foregrounded?

Rigorous training and auspicious timing resulted in Dolan's employment as museum muralist. In 1912 she left Lincoln for study at the Art Institute of Chicago. Once there she won two scholarships, which provided free tuition for her studies at the institute in 1913 and 1914. From 1915 to 1919, she studied at the Art Students' League in New York City with draftsman George Bridgman, illustrator Thomas Fogarty, and others. From 1919 to 1924, she lived in Greenwich Village and paid her bills by designing stained glass windows for Louis Tiffany and by freelancing as a painter of miniatures and portraits, mostly of children. In 1924, she entered the École des Beaux-Arts in Fontainbleau, France, as a scholarship student to study *buon* (true) *fresco*, the art of painting with watercolors on wet plaster. Dolan told *Omaha Weekly Bee* reporter Mary Pollard Hull that she had always been interested in murals and frescoes and that she "love[d] the breadth of a big canvas, and the freedom that such space allows." I wonder about the origin of Dolan's interest in this ancient technique. In *The Artist's Handbook of Materials and Techniques*, Ralph Mayer says that by the end of the nineteenth century, fresco had fallen into such bad repute, in part, because those attempting to work in this medium hadn't attained a complete mastery of the materials and methods. Just a few years prior to Dolan's arrival in France, the École des Beaux-Arts established a school of fresco—the only one in the world—in response to a revival in that technique. Dolan was one of only three students to receive a diploma in frescoing in 1925. Her devotion to fresco suggests that she was either on the cutting edge or more at home in the late fourteenth and fifteenth centuries, when the art of European fresco was at its zenith.

After graduation Dolan was commissioned to paint two frescos on the walls of the École des Beaux-Arts: a Madonna and Child and an enlarged copy of *Saint Genevieve Watching over Paris*, by Pierre Puvis de Chavannes, the most popular frescoist of nineteenth-century Europe. Dolan's later works reveal Puvis de Chavannes' influence. Pale greens and yellows dominate several murals by both artists, serving to brighten the room or corridor. But, too, the choice of a subdued or "blond" palette may simply have been a personal preference on Dolan's part. She told Hull that it made her "shudder to see raw colors in a mural."

In 1926 Dolan came home to Lincoln in response to a sister's illness. Also in 1926, Morrill Hall, named for philanthropist Charles Morrill, who donated over one hundred thousand dollars to the state museum, mostly for paleontological expeditions, was under construction. I do not know how Dolan came to the attention of the remarkable Erwin Hinckley Barbour, then museum director and chair of the Department of Geology and Geography at the University of Nebraska, and a man with diverse artistic abilities. Perhaps a one-inch article had appeared in one of the local newspapers about Dolan's European success and Barbour contacted her after reading it. Perhaps Dolan approached him and told him that she knew exactly what the new museum needed: frescoes done in her bright, expansive, suggestive style. Until shortly before he hired Dolan, Barbour had planned to execute the murals himself. His charcoal sketches for the backgrounds show reconstructions of the animals whose skeletons were on display in the appropriate habitat. C. Bertrand Schultz, who directed the Nebraska State Museum following Barbour's retirement in 1941, wrote: "Dr. Barbour wanted 'impression-istic art' nothing distinct or detailed, but pleasing colors so that the skeletons would be the *main attractions* with pleasant backgrounds." Perhaps Barbour realized that his own detailed sketches would compete with the fossils for the viewer's attention. Perhaps he hadn't time for the demanding job of painting all four walls in Elephant Hall and eight alcoves in the corridors as well as continuing to teach, provide direction for museum employees, to coordinate museum programs, conduct field work, and publish his findings. For whatever reason, Barbour commis-sioned Dolan to work as a "decorator" in the new museum building for $100 per week. The only thing that Dolan wrote about her encounter with Barbour was that he "gave me my first big chance. . . . I believe I did not fail him" (Dolan).

In April 1927, Dolan went to work filling blank walls with images of a younger earth. To familiarize herself with the landscapes where important specimens had been excavated, she traveled five hundred miles, some of which were covered by rough, dirt roads, to the badlands of Sioux and Dawes Counties and about two hundred miles east of there to Devil's Gulch in Brown County. But the early-twentieth-century landscapes in northwestern and north-central Nebraska could not re-veal what those locales were like millions of years ago. Instead, Dolan had to rely on science, her imagination, and divine inspiration. For the thirty-seven-million-year-old skeleton of titanothere, the "Titanic Beast," she created lavender, green, and pink-orange hills and cliffs cut with bright blue vertical lines. The left and bottom center of the mural is covered with a chalky pink wash, which Dolan allowed to run. The sign next to the exhibit says that the mural represents the Chadron Formation, which Michael R. Voorhies, curator of vertebrate paleontology at the museum, describes as "a thick layer of multicolored mudstone and sandstone capped by a thirty-four-million-year-old ash bed." Not only is this formation Nebraska's oldest deposit containing abundant fossil mammals, but it is the only time and place that the rhinoceroslike titanothere or "Thunder Horse" lived. Dolan's eroded or lava-streaked landforms remind me of pictures I have seen of the canyon-cut, volcano-studded surface of Mars. But, too, these landforms suggest to me how our earth might have looked before the arrival of plants and animals or of some future time when heat, ice, or toxins have killed all visible life. Part of a red-flecked, yellow-orange orb glows above Dolan's surreal, lifeless hills in an almost cloudless sky. "I have tried to picture an early morning of very early creation," she explained to *Sunday World-Herald Magazine* reporter Eva Mahoney. "I worked in pure color, and kept my murals free from darkness. I hoped they would have something of a spiritual quality and I prayed earnestly each day that God might speak through my works. If they have any worth it is because He has guided me" (3).

Dolan intended for all of the Morrill Hall murals to be true frescoes. But because she feared that watercolors made in the United States might not be lasting, all but two of the murals are oil paints on dry plaster. *Lincoln Sunday Star* reporter Lulu Mae Coe, who witnessed Dolan's frescoing process, described Dolan penciling the small preliminary sketch for her frescoes, then drawing the cartoon or pattern, whose edges she perforated and placed onto the next-to-last layer of wet plaster. Coe reports that for a medium-sized panel, Dolan spent four days on the drawings, a week on the perforating and at least two weeks on the coloring. Dolan mixed and applied the plaster herself (perhaps three or four separate layers) and mixed her own paints, which she bought in powdered form. "In the telling it sounds rather simple," says Coe, "but it is a dexterous art, which requires quick, clear thinking, as the surface of the plaster is delicate and must not be overworked. The colors, too, become lighter as they dry, and the frescoer must take this into account" (1). If the frescoer makes a mistake, she can't simply paint over it. Rather, she cuts out the final coat of plaster with a sharp knife and trowel. Then she bevels the cut and replasters the area. When painting, she must be sensitive to the fact that paint is absorbed differently at the joins or seams. And she must work swiftly, since the paint must be applied before the plaster dries. Unpainted plaster is cut away; new plaster is reapplied the next day.

Dolan's two frescoes provide the background for two Miocene displays (the epoch twelve to twenty-seven million years ago). The alcove on the right includes the remains of a three-toed horse, four ancient pronghorns, four tortoises, and an oreodont, the most common plant-eating mammal on the Great Plains twenty to thirty-five million years ago. Behind this display is Dolan's most impressionistic background.

Ash-gray plaster has been slathered on the wall with a trowel or trowel-like tool to suggest rolling clouds and rocky cliffs, outlined and streaked with brown paints. The rocks to the left are chartreuse, blue-green, tan, and gray. Dolan's tortoise pauses on the crusty surface behind the horse skeleton on display.

The fresco in the adjacent alcove on the left creates the setting for the ten-million-year-old skeleton of a short-legged rhinoceros from Brown County. This large, hippopotamus-shaped specimen fills the entire alcove. Plaster built out as much as six inches from the wall forms a tree branch painted bright brown. On the upper left, thick plaster is grooved by fingertips or other tools; in the lower left corner, the plaster has been clumped and painted to look like leaves. Two red, white, and blue birds are perched on the thick branch; a white and red bird is perched on a twig in the lower left corner. The presence of these sweet birds jars me, and for good reason. George Corner, collection manager of the Department of Vertebrate Paleontology at the museum, says that when Dolan painted this mural, it provided the Southwestern setting for the glyptodont, an enormous, armadillolike creature whose armor-covered body was as tall as a washing machine and twice as wide. The glyptodont inhabited South America, but during the Ice Age dwelt as far north as Texas and Florida. Three of Dolan's glyptodonts were set in the center of the mural between rock formations, where blue patches suggest watering holes. Under Schultz's directorship the glyptodont was moved to a different display, and the short-legged rhinoceros was moved into the alcove where Dolan's Southwestern scene was no longer appropriate. Nathan Mohler, former exhibits designer at the museum, painted over Dolan's glyptodonts and added the little birds.

Dolan's largest murals are in Elephant Hall, the home of one of the most extensive collections of prehistoric elephants in the United States. When I stand near Dolan's seventy-foot-long, sixteen-foot-high African scene, it appears sloppy and haphazard. The plaster is course and craggy. The reflections on the water at the watering hole are created by running paint, which has dried over patches of color. Wide, wavy-edged lines of paint have been slapped down the wall. Outlines of elephants appear among these verticals, but I can't be certain if other shapes are tree branches, elephant tusks, or trunks.

Yet when I move back from the mural as far as the opposite wall permits, I no longer feel that I'm studying a drawing in a children's magazine captioned "How Many Elephants Are Hidden in This Picture?" Sloppy lines become reeds and grasses and fronds. Painted elephants near the Jefferson's Mammoth on display timidly emerge from the foliage near the water's edge to view the viewer. Bright foliage drips with condensation. Beneath the stomach of *Archidiskodon imperator maibeni* ("Archie")—the thirty-thousand-year-old Columbian Mammoth from Wellfleet, Nebraska, which Barbour obtained for the museum in 1922—Dolan's two small gray elephants move through tall grasses. My attention moves back and forth between the mural's soft greens, yellows, tans, and turquoises and the tan bones. My attention moves back and forth between Dolan's thatchwork of grasses, tree trunks, reflections in the water, and other vertical lines and the verticality of the fossil skeletons' legs, tails, ribs, and upward pointing tusks. Though I'm here to study backgrounds, I find myself absorbed by the mounted skeletons. Part of what is so right about this mural is its insistence on remaining in the background behind the items on display.

When followed in sequence, the Elephant Hall displays move through proboscidean evolution, from the four-tusked Prod Tusker, America's most ancient elephant, through the mastodons, then the mammoths and modern elephants set before the African mural. Posed before the latter are Jefferson's Mammoth found in Kewanee, Illinois; "Archie," the largest mounted elephant skeleton in the United States, perhaps the world; the thirteen-thousand-year-old pig-sized Dwarf Mammoth from Sicily, Italy; a contemporary Asian adult and baby elephant; a contemporary African elephant.

Once the ancestors of the modern elephant were found only in Africa. At some point, they spread through Asia, crossed the former Bering Land Bridge and ranged over the entire Western Hemisphere. Twenty million to ten thousand years ago elephants lived on every continent except Australia and Antarctica. In Nebraska, the remains of more than ten thousand elephants have been found in ninety of our ninety-three counties. "It is thought that no like area in the world contains as many fossil elephants as Nebraska," Barbour told Mahoney. I study the creatures' eye sockets, their tusks, which are but greatly extended incisor teeth, the vaulted ceiling created by the rafters of their rib cages, the five articulated toes on each of their feet. When Loren Eiseley, a member of the Morrill Paleontological Expedition, gazed upon the remains of ancient beasts like that of the twelve-million-year-old shovel-tusked mastodon that he helped excavate in Banner County in 1931, he was mindful of the similarities between its form and his own: "We are all potential fossils," he wrote in *The Immense Journey*, "still carrying within our bodies the crudities of former existences."

Once Dolan murals filled each wall in Elephant Hall. But the Niobrara River Valley bluffs and pine trees that she had painted on the south wall were replaced by Nathan Mohler's painting of an African savanna, an appropriate setting for the stuffed and mounted giraffe and the two elephants once exhibited before it. In 1992, Mohler's scene was replaced with Mark E. Marcuson's September 1992 painting of Imperial Mammoths, the modern elephant's Ice Age relative.

Marcuson's stunning floor-to-ceiling mural faces the entryway to Elephant Hall, so that the first thing one notices upon entering are his mammoths wading through the Platte River. Sandhill cranes and pheasantlike birds lift off in the background. A herd of elk has almost crested a hill. Five sandhill cranes wade in the water. I'm divided by my desire to step into the early spring landscape and to move out of the way of the lumbering mammoths. Marcuson's depiction is a sound addition to Elephant Hall, since it shows how the nearby skeletons might have looked when animated with life and the setting with which they interacted. But, at the same time, the almost photographic detail of the mural is distracting. When Corner mentioned the mammoth and mastodon skulls arranged on the sandbar display area onto which Marcuson's mammoths appear to be stepping, I could not picture what he was talking about. I returned to the museum to see what I had never seen before. There in front of the mural were the tusks and wisdom teeth of a Dannebrog Mammoth collected by Barbour in 1917 in Howard County and the skull and jaws of an adult Milford Mastodon collected by Eiseley and Schultz in Seward County in 1931. The impressionistic Dolan landscape that once covered this wall would have provided a less arresting setting for the hard-gotten, Pleistocene bones before it.

In this huge room that is Elephant Hall, I am mindful of the physical demands of mural painting. When Michelangelo painted the Sistine Chapel, a project taking four and one-half years, paint dripped on his face, plaster irritated his skin, and Pope Julius II pestered him mercilessly to finish. Dolan had kinder working circumstances. Still, there were challenges. The scaffolds were rickety and inconvenient; the display cases were so stuffy and hot that she directed a fan over a cake of ice to provide some relief from the late July heat ("Daemonelix"). But the greatest difficulty was the spectators. "It is so distracting to try to paint when people are watching you and making remarks," Dolan told *Daily Nebraskan* reporter Harriet Davis. "I put up big signs but people tear down the canvas and even cut holes in it." In a June 26, 1928, letter to Morrill, Barbour wrote, "Poor Miss Dolan who is so nearly done that she is trying conscientiously to finish has pinned on her back a big placard, to the effect that she would like to have her friends give her a chance to do her work." Apparently Dolan, who had to keep her awareness trained at once on the part and the whole, wasn't always patient when someone in the audience broke her concentration. One university student recalled Dolan jumping from her scaffold, running toward him, and pointing at the sign which forbade people from watching her work (Stevens 178).

Some muralists, such as Puvis de Chavannes, chose to do their work in the studio on a canvas, which they later affixed to the wall where it was to be viewed. Certainly the studio provided a more pleasant and distraction-free environment than did a hot, public museum with tall ceilings, cramped display cases, and spectators. Yet the studio production is contained by the edges of the easel and so is far less likely than the in situ mural to be of a piece with the surroundings. Nor can the studio production be as sensitive to the shape, color, and light of the particular place where the mural will be viewed. Nor can the artist working in an environment where her creations have always been primary, be mindful that it is background rather than foreground that she is painting.

Dolan signed most of her murals in the lower right-hand corner, her signature printed in all capital letters except for a lower case *i* in Elizabeth. The L in DOLAN formed a platform on which the A and the N rest. On several murals her name (either DOLAN or ELiZABETH DOLAN) was followed by the date 1927. The woman I imagine signing the murals is young, thin, and supple, with dark shoulder-length hair, deep-set, heavy-lidded eyes and a smile that is barely there, an image I know from the photograph of Dolan that accompanies most newspaper articles about her work. In this studio photograph she wears a low V-necked, black dress, a pearl necklace, a three-rose corsage, her smile is slight, she folds her hands before her. She appears to be in her late thirties or early forties. But the woman who executed the Morrill Hall murals was fifty-six and fifty-seven years old. A 1928 newspaper photograph of Dolan taken when she had almost completed her murals shows her standing sideways, her face turned toward the camera, a paint brush in one lifted hand, a palette in the other. She is wearing a white sailor shirt with a dark tie; the shirt is tucked into what appears to be light-colored, pocketed trousers. In the middle of her forehead hangs a single dark curl. This is the face of a mature woman, though she looks a full decade younger than she actually was at the time. If the Morrill Hall murals were Dolan's first "big chance," as she claims, then she waited almost her entire life for it to arrive. Yet in terms of where most artists and professional people are in the arc of their careers a decade after completing their formal training, the timing of Dolan's "big break" was more typical than not.

"My real life began when I entered the Chicago Art Institute enrolled as a student," Dolan said. "Beyond that time I have only vague memories of unhappiness, unfruitful struggles to acquire an art education in my effort to become a famous painter. That was then—and still is—my hope. October, 1912, life opened. Stepping off the train in Chicago, I faced a new world and a new life eagerly" (Dolan). On that October day when her life as an artist finally began, Dolan was forty-one years old, already middle-aged. She left no information that I have found about the difficulties she encountered in becoming the type of artist that she wanted to be. Certainly reactions to her gender slowed or complicated her entry into the art world. But were there other factors? Perhaps she was lazy and unambitious and so the difficulties were her own fault. Yet the documented part of her artistic life proves her to be ambitious, prolific, and hard-working (twelve hours per day on the Fontainbleau murals; nine hours per day on the Morrill Hall murals, according to Coe). Perhaps she was, as Tillie Olsen observes of some writers who have long periods in which they cannot create, "consumed in the hard, everyday essential work of maintaining human life." Perhaps laundry, cooking, and caring for family members (Dolan returned from Europe in response to a sister's illness; she went to Kansas for a prolonged stay in response to another sister's illness; while in Lincoln, she lived for a while with one of her brothers and for a while with one of her sisters—I do not know if she was a guest or live-in help in either of these circumstances) kept her from devoting herself as completely as she wanted to her art or education. Perhaps she accepted commissions that didn't interest her so that she could pay her bills. Perhaps the lack of information about Dolan's personal life (marriage? lovers? children? dear friends? domestic duties? domestic help?) means that like many female artists and writers, she accepted what Tillie Olsen calls "the patriarchal injunction," that a woman must choose between her art and her "fulfillment as a woman."

All that I know of the four decades in Dolan's life prior to that momentous day when she stepped off the train in Chicago is this. Elizabeth Honor Dolan was born in Fort Dodge, Iowa. Her parents, Mary O'Donnel Dolan and John Dolan, were Irish immigrants; she had five siblings. When Dolan was a baby, her family moved to a farm in the vicinity of Crab Orchard and Tecumseh, Nebraska, and a few years later to Lincoln. Dolan attended the University of Nebraska School of Fine Arts from 1891–92 and 1894–95. For one year prior to her departure for Chicago, she studied art in Des Moines.

For decades, Dolan's birth date was disputed, listed as early as 1875 on her University of Nebraska registration card and as late as 1890 in the 1953 edition of *Who's Who In American Art*. In June 1982 Connie Stevens, a University of Nebraska–Lincoln art student who was researching Dolan's work, received a letter from Dolan's niece, Margaret Cannell, of Menlo Park, California, who confirmed her aunt's birth date as May 1871. Perhaps Dolan provided more recent birth dates to match the age she felt herself to be and to coincide with her late start in life. Thus she did not feel forty-one when she stepped off the train in Chicago, but twenty-two, the approximate age when many men of the time were beginning to work in their chosen professions.

Georgia O'Keeffe (1887–1986), who also studied at the Art Institute of Chicago (1905–6) and at the Art Students' League of New York (1907–8), might have envied Dolan's privacy and secrecy. Toward the end of her life, O'Keeffe, who had long lived with an unwanted celebrity status, advised: "Where I was born and where and how I have lived is unimportant. It is what I have done with where I have been that should be of interest" (Didion 126). But Dolan, who was a nontraditional art student in age, gender, and geographical origin, might have envied O'Keeffe's privilege of entering art school when she was eighteen and having her first solo art show at Stieglitz's famous New York City gallery 291 when she was thirty. Dolan's first solo show, held at the Joslyn Memorial Art Gallery in Omaha, did not come until she was sixty-eight.

When Dolan climbed the scaffold to paint murals in Morrill Hall, her career as an artist was only a decade-and-a-half old, though she was in her mid-fifties. In 1930, her busiest year in terms of important local commissions (*Spirit of the Prairie* over the doorway of the Law Library in the State Capitol; a series of ten murals for the fiftieth anniversary of Miller & Paine, once a downtown Lincoln department store; a mural for the Lincoln Unitarian Church), she was fifty-eight and fifty-nine. In her sixtieth year, she was commissioned to paint four portraits for Founder's Hall in Morrill Hall (Morrill's will set aside four thousand dollars for the portraits of himself, his wife Harriet, his dear friend and museum director Barbour, and former chemistry professor and chancellor Samuel Avery). When she painted her curious, allegorical triptych, *World Peace*, for the first-floor women's lounge in the University of Nebraska Student Union, Dolan was sixty-one. At sixty-two, she painted a mural for the reception room of the new YWCA. At sixty-four, she painted ten murals for the Lincoln Masonic Temple. At sixty-seven, she painted *Hansel and Gretel* for the Children's Reading Room of Bennett Martin Public Library and the background for the Morrill Hall Daemonelix alcove, where fossilized corkscrew burrows, created by terrestrial, gopherlike Miocene beavers in western Nebraska, are displayed.

Throughout the 1920s and 1930s, Dolan received international attention for her work. In the January 1928 issue of *The American Magazine of Art*, Dolan's Morrill Hall murals received high praise, in spite of critic Lelia Mechlin's regional bias: "These paintings not only compare in quality with the best of the kind that have been done in our eastern museums but in some respects are superior. They are in high key, to an extent imaginative, and yet extremely accurate and effective. The rendering is broad and accomplished." In 1929, Dolan painted a fresco, a copy of Leonardo da Vinci's *Head of Christ*, in a thirteenth-century church in Fourqueux, France. In 1932, she was commissioned to paint a habitat mural of northwestern India for the Age of Man Hall at the American Museum of Natural History in New York City. In 1933 she was one of twenty-four, the only woman and the only artist from the West, invited to compete for the commission to paint the murals for the Theodore Roosevelt Memorial Building. Henry Fairfield Osborn, the curator in chief of the American Museum, wrote to Barbour that Dolan placed fifth or sixth out of a group that included "all the leading mural painters in the eastern part of America."

Unlike most writers, musicians, theatrical performers, and visual artists who take jobs unrelated or only somewhat related to their art in order to support themselves, Dolan lived entirely on her commissions. Coe reports that while employed in Morrill Hall, Dolan lived in Lincoln, dividing her time between her sister, Mrs. W. D. Cannell and her brother, Gorgonius Dolan. Later she lived in an apartment and studio above the former Liberty Theater Building just blocks from campus.

On May 27, 1948, at the age of seventy-seven, Dolan died in Lincoln of an unspecified illness. Her address at the time was 815 S. 13th, now a parking lot. Though I have found the headstone marking the graves of two of Dolan's siblings (John and Gorgonius) at Wyuka Cemetery in Lincoln, Elizabeth is not buried there.

"On looking back over the years," Dolan wrote, "I feel the same eager enthusiasm to plunge in, inviting beauty to leave even her shadow on walls where she has not passed before" (Dolan). I can't imagine what Dolan might have accomplished had she acquired the background she needed in materials and techniques in her twenties instead of her forties. Or perhaps she was so productive and so single in her focus *because* she had to wait so long for the opportunity to invite beauty to leave her shadow on walls. Interestingly, Dolan did not perceive the big break in her life to be her study abroad, her work for Louis Tiffany, or the cathedral in Fourqueux, France, but the murals in Morrill Hall. Perhaps this was a particularly triumphant commission because of the "unhappiness [and] unfruitful struggles to acquire an art education," during her earlier years in Lincoln, or perhaps hearing her work praised by people in her hometown mattered more to her than the praise she received from people far from home.

Over the three arched doorways leading from Elephant Hall to the museum information desk and entrance is Dolan's mural of a cave-dwelling family. The cave is dark in shades of green and brown; the opening to the cave is light-filled. A naked boy sits on a rock, holding what might be a blackened charcoal stick. He has paused in the execution of his mural, a drawing of a mammoth. The girl standing by the boy also holds something in her hand that I cannot identify. She does not look at the wall but at a sleeping dog and a man tending the fire. To the right of this scene, a woman sits on a rock holding a candle. A man is drawing mammoths on the illuminated portion of the wall with a charcoal stick. Before another day passes, I want to place a drawing utensil in the woman's hand. Before another day passes, I want to take the candle from her and ask someone else in the scene to illuminate the darkness while she creates.

Sojourner

At the heart of the Old Frisian *sojorner* or *sojourner* is the word *journey*. The Low or Late Latin root of this word is *diurnation*, "a day's travel or work." Generally, a journey refers to prolonged traveling; thus a sojourner is one who resides for a while in a place that is not her home among a people who see her as neither native nor alien. A sojourner is someone trying to go home again or trying to find a place and people that could become home.

In the Hebrew Scriptures a sojourner is one who lives in mutually responsible association with a community that is not one's own, trading faithfulness, obedience, and labor for protection and sustenance. The sojourner's status and privileges aren't due to kinship and birthplace but to the "bond of hospitality" between host and guest. "The stranger who sojourns among you" was exempt from the ban on eating the flesh of animals who died natural deaths, yet could participate in the assembly, was entitled to equal justice, and was required to celebrate the Sabbath, keep laws, observe festivals, and so on. Sojourners gathered wood and drew water for the Israelites.

In a literal sense, all humans were or are sojourners, since human history is essentially a travel narrative: the migration of one's people from that earliest home in East Africa or the Eden of the imagination to the other side of the river, ocean, plain, or mountain. In the Hebrew Scriptures, all of us are sojourners, just passing through, never completely at home on the earth or in our bodies. God is our good host who provides protection and companionship: "Hear my prayer, O Lord, and give ear to my cry; hold not thy peace at my tears! For I am thy passing guest, a sojourner, like all my fathers" (Psalm 39:12). We are to be good guests, helping with the supper dishes, not taking too long in the bathroom, accepting that our ways may not be the ways of our host, never completely unpacking our bags.

12. True Travel

It is a Sunday morning in October, and I am sitting on a rock slab near the foot of a trail in the Cibola National Forest, about seven hundred miles from home as the crow flies. Above me rise the Sandia Mountains; below me sprawls Albuquerque; through a distant brown haze waits Mount Taylor, an extinct volcano and the sacred mountain of the Navajo. I read that from the crest of the Sandia Mountains, one could see up to one hundred miles in each direction, a view that includes other mountain ranges. I planned to see that for myself. Along the way to the top, I hoped to find tree bark scarred with claw marks, berry-filled scats, seven-inch-long hind footprints: all evidence of the black bears that supposedly roam these mountains. If not a black bear, I at least hoped to glimpse the roadrunner's brown crest, red and blue eye patches, and long, white-tipped tail as it raced ahead of me. I read in an old book that, occasionally, hikers found prayer sticks near the former site of Oku Pin, a shrine once maintained by the Pueblo people at the Sandia Crest. If I found what I guessed to be one of these sticks, I would hold it and pray.

But after hiking a mere one-eighth of a mile, my heart was racing and I felt dizzy, a surprising reaction since I am accustomed to walking several brisk miles each day at home. At the Sandia Range Visitor's Center where I had bought a map of the mountains, I read the sign listing the stages of altitude sickness. The sign recommended that hikers not yet acclimated to higher altitudes exercise caution against overexertion. With this warning in mind, I chose to sit on a rock slab near the start of the trail, where I could observe and make notes—an equally valid, perhaps even better, way of encountering the mountain, since when one sits and watches, the world comes to her.

My trip to New Mexico was long overdue. Twelve years earlier, I had yearned to see this land. I had read D. H. Lawrence's observations about New Mexico: "In the magnificent fierce mornings of New Mexico one sprang awake, a new part of the soul woke up suddenly, and the old world gave way to the new." I had admired the red hills, sun-bleached skulls, and blooming jimson weed of Georgia O'Keeffe's New Mexican landscapes and I had read her observations about the place: "Perfectly mad looking country," she wrote to Stieglitz. "Hills and cliffs and washes too crazy to imagine all thrown up into the air by God and let tumble where they would." At night I dreamed feverishly about dry mountains and mesas, white gypsum sand and piñon pines. Twelve years ago, my desire to see New Mexico was born of a need for guidance. Then I hoped that if I placed myself in a high desert place and waited, I would receive a revelation. Though my yearning for a mountaintop vision is not as intense as it was when I was thirty (middle age has dulled the edges on many of my keenest desires, which I count as both a blessing and a curse), it has not died.

But could one receive enlightenment during a few hours on an unfamiliar mountain? The visions I knew about followed long periods of preparation. Elijah did not hear God speak in a still, small voice until after completing his forty-day trek to Sinai, the holy mountain. Muhammad did not receive a visit from the angel, Gabriel, until after he had meditated for several days in a cave on Mount Hira, a place he visited frequently. John Muir did not receive his baptism at nature's font, an experience in which he lost his sense of himself as a separate existence and "blend[ed] with the landscape . . . becom[ing] part and parcel of nature," until after he came to know Twenty Hill Hollow intimately. Perhaps the Pueblo people also made lengthy preparations before they received their revelations at Oku Pin. If I didn't have an afternoon flight to catch, if I didn't have duties and people to whom I must return, I, too, could stay on the mountain until I witnessed the old world give way to the new. In the absence of such an awakening, I could at least see as much of this magnificent, fierce New Mexican morning as possible.

Looking west from my position near the foot of the trail, I see that the land beyond Albuquerque does not bear the patchwork-quilt divisions of the Midwest and Great Plains. Other mountains in the Sandia Range are dotted with evergreens. At home, I would identify them as red cedars, but here I can't be certain. Junipers or piñon pines, perhaps.

A pale, three-quarter moon hangs above the mountains in the biggest, most intensely blue sky I've ever seen. Spider webs strung between weeds and low branches glisten. The Cibola National Forest is spacious and light-filled, lacking the dense, dark canopy of some eastern forests I have known. But I haven't the discriminating eye and precise vocabulary to describe such light: I can only say that it seems more brilliant, casts harder, darker shadows, and falls in a way that emphasizes absences as much as it does presences. In *American Southwest: People and Their Landscape*, Michael Grant writes that the light he knew in Texas is "horizontal . . . its principal property is distance." But Southwestern light is "vertical . . . its principal property is levitation." Perhaps so many painters and photographers of the Southwest choose plain objects in stark settings—an earthen jug on a bare table, the sky between bare cottonwood branches—so that they can focus on this light and its seeming ability to cancel the effects of gravity.

I am uneasy sitting alone on this New Mexican mountain. What if I develop congested lungs and pink sputum, the latter stages of altitude sickness, symptoms that demand prompt medical attention? What if I wander far from the trail, easy and tempting given the sparseness of the vegetation, or forget my way back or fall from a rock or meet a black bear face-to-face? The wild bear is reclusive and almost never acts aggressively toward people. Almost never. What if I am abducted, raped, or tortured, and left for dead in some remote part of the mountains where I won't be found for days? What if, in this land where I can name so little of what I see, I lose my ability to name or to remember names? What if the spirits who dwell in these mountains provide me with more of an encounter than I can survive?

From a half-dead, half-living cactus, I break off two, dry hollow stems—round, weathered lattices to place on my altar at home. From prickly pear leaves extend rows of red-purple thumbs. I want to pick one but don't. I know how easily the spines of this plant can work their way into flesh and how hard they are to remove. I move carefully. At the gift shop in the Albuquerque Museum, I browsed through *Poisonous Dwellers of the Desert: Description, Habitat, Prevention, Treatment*. I was not consoled that the book was so slim. One encounter with one brown recluse spider, one sculpted centroides scorpion, one western coral snake, one Gila monster, could make one's morning on the mountain pretty uncomfortable, if not one's last. Though I am in as much danger of being scared or bitten by poisonous snakes on my prairie or riverside hikes at home in Nebraska, I am more frightened of such a danger in this unfamiliar forest.

Something buzzes past my ear. At home I would say grasshopper, but here, I cannot be certain. A flying rattlesnake, perhaps. In the distance, two men whom I cannot see speak Spanish to each other, much too quickly for my ears to break their sentences into translatable units. I bend down to admire the iridescent abdomen of a crawling black beetle. What prey does it seek? What predator does it seek to escape? I realize that I have seen or heard surprisingly few birds this morning. Perhaps this forest is too thin, too brittle, too light-filled to provide food and shelter to any but the hardiest birds—jays, crows, ravens, sparrows, and road-runners, the latter of which I am still waiting to see.

The informational pamphlet that I picked up at the visitor's center says that one might see golden eagles soaring at the Sandia Crest. I face the rising sun and scan the sky for long, rounded wings. What I see instead is a patch of bristles at the crest. Giant prayer sticks, perhaps. More likely they are radio and television towers, transmitting messages over the eleven-thousand-foot mountains. I lay the hollow cactus branches at my feet, aim my camera, and shoot.

While still facing the sun, I close my eyes. The porous wood of the dead cactus unfolds, forming a maze against the bright orange of my eyelids. Like a scene from a nightmare, cactus branches unfold faster than I can run, faster than I can remember the labyrinth's design, the pores too small for me to squeeze through. I am trapped in a landscape where I am not on familiar terms with anything.

One reason I travel is to remove myself from familiar surroundings and entanglements and to immerse myself in what to me is foreign, exotic, Other. Such a change is wonder-filled and cleansing. But, too, I find it perilous.

In part my fear is understandable. True travel places me in unfamiliar contexts, where so many factors are beyond my control. But in part my fears are unfounded. I've never been attacked by a bear; I've never been bitten by a snake or insect or brushed against a plant whose juices have poisoned me; I've never been molested or raped by a stranger. Despite the discomforts and adjustments my fears cause (instead of lying on a warm rock ledge and allowing my attention to drift and scatter, I sit, listening and watching intently), I would not wish them away. In *Sunrise with Seamonsters*, Paul Theroux says that one must be willing to endure "a kind of alienation and panic in foreign parts for the aftertaste of having sampled new scenes." What Theroux calls "mock travel," or "Traveling as a Version of Being at Home," involves moving from one point on the globe to another with few if any deprivations, discomforts, anxieties, or dangers, and none of the insights of true travel. Likewise Albert Camus writes that we experience the chief benefit of travel when, far from home, we "are seized by a vague fear, and the instinctive desire to go back to the protection of old habits." At such a moment "we are feverish but also porous, so that the slightest touch makes us quiver to the depths of our being." Simply put, true travel unsettles as surely as it delights.

In *A Lady's Life in the Rocky Mountains* (1873), Isabella L. Bird explains how fear sharpened her senses and centered her in the present. Because Bird lacked the physical skills to ascend Longs Peak (altitude 14,700 feet), she says that her guide, Mountain Jim, literally "dragged me up, like a bale of goods, by sheer force of muscle. . . . Two thousand feet of solid rock towered above us, four thousand feet of broken rock shelved precipitously below; smooth granite ribs, with barely foothold, stood out here and there; melted snow refrozen several times, presented a more serious obstacle; many of the rocks were loose, and tumbled down when touched. To me it was a time of extreme terror." Yet Bird says that the "never-to-be-forgotten glories" she beheld at the peak—a dazzling sunrise, dense woods, mirrorlike lakes, the Grand River glinting like diamonds—were "burnt in upon my memory by six succeeding hours of terror." In the absence of such fear, Bird might have seen and remembered Longs Peak as just another mountain.

Once on a visit to my growing-up place of Burlington, Iowa, I took an afternoon drive in the hilly area north of town and west of the Mississippi River bottoms, because I was hungry for that terrain. I followed one gravel or dirt road onto another, delighting in the close gray skies and the early spring promises I sensed in every field and woodland. When the rain began, I enjoyed watching it from the warm, dry interior of my car. But when the shower became a torrent, my pleasure ended. I could barely see through my windshield, the roads, too long without fresh gravel, were soft and slippery, and I had not kept track of the way back. Though I wasn't truly lost as I might be if I wandered far from the trail in the Sandia Mountains, I was lost enough that I would have had to have made a series of lucky guesses if I were to find my way in the blinding rain to a paved road. Of course I could have turned into almost any driveway, knocked on almost any farmhouse door, and asked directions to Old or New Highway 61. When I told the person who answered the door my name, most likely she or he would have asked which Knopps I was related to. After I answered that I was Ruth and David's granddaughter, I am Patricia and Joseph's daughter, Jim and John's sister, Phyllis and Richard's niece, and some relation to Eva and all of the Georges, I probably would have been invited to wait out the storm at the kitchen table with a cup of coffee.

But I continued driving, imagining that I had left northern Des Moines County far behind and crossed into some terra incognita, where I truly was lost and had to live by my wits. I imagined foraging for wild foods, sleeping in a sheltered, matted-down place where deer had slept, and scheming ways to convince the locals that I was worth more alive then dead. Every moment was filled with hair-raising alertness to danger and opportunity.

Eventually the downpour became a shower. I turned onto a road that I recognized as Devil's Washboard, even though its steep hills had been leveled since I last saw it, and followed it to the highway. I realized that for the first time, I had seen the farms and farmhouses of northern Des Moines County—steeply banked creeks, concealing thickets, barns that looked warm and dry, barns that looked airy and leaky, houses with inviting front porches, houses where threatening dogs ran to the end of the driveway and snarled, houses that looked too broken-down and desolate for me to bother the inhabitants with my passing troubles.

"Travel," says Theroux, "has less to do with distance than with insight; it is, very often, a way of seeing."

Something rustles. Some sort of jay in some sort of shrub. Yellow flower heads on tall stalks grow in tufts near the trail. Goldenrod. The Albuquerque resident to whom I had put some of my botanical questions said that the plant was chamisa, or rabbitbrush, a weed. I leave my rock to pick a few blossoms. I inhale deeply. How shall I capture such a scent in my journal? I write: "First, the smell of sweaty feet; then something wild, rangy, good." Once I am home, I'll press these blossoms between the pages of my unabridged dictionary. Each time I look up a word and smell "sweaty feet; then something wild, rangy, good," I will be back in the Cibola National Forest.

I study a cactus whose branchlets form fleshy, yellow-green, ball-shaped "flowers" with orange star centers. The star cactus I name it. I gather the tiniest acorns I have ever seen from beneath a short tree whose holly-shaped leaves lack the holly leaf's dark, glossy green. I name it the holly nut tree. Near the tree, something familiar: tufts of grama grass, some of whose seed spikes are intensely curved like scimitars, others are slightly curved like eyelashes. The same buzz I heard earlier darts past my ear and lands. Oversized legs. Long, folded wings. Narrow head. Grasshopper. Just like the ones at home.

The sun has reached its zenith, and it's time for me to leave. I am relieved and regretful. I have not received glimpses of black bears, roadrunners, or of my future; nor have I been baptized in nature's font. Yet on this Sunday morning in the Sandia Mountains, my fear has split me open like a seam or a melon, revealing my essentially conservative, fearful nature as well as my tenacity. At the first sign of fear, I could have driven back to Albuquerque and spent my last hours in New Mexico reading a good book and drinking good coffee in the bagel shop near the motel or walking through the tourist shops in Old Town yet again. But I chose to spend my morning on the mountain, fearful and porous, unsettled by the dangers and delighted by new beauties. I chose to travel.

History

History is derived from the Latin *historia*, "an account or narrative of past events," and the Greek *iaropia*, which means "a learning or knowing by inquiry" as well as the account of one's inquiries. More than just the professedly true record of past human actions and affairs, a history is the process of gathering and interpreting information and turning it into story.

Sometimes the process of inquiry continues after the story has been crafted, calling into question the interpretation or patterning of facts. The Smithsonian Institution's 1995 exhibition of the Enola Gay, the B-29 from which the United States dropped the atomic bomb on the people of Hiroshima during World War II, raised vexing questions about whether this deed was necessary or not, the actual and the professed motives behind it, and whose interpretation of the deed and its consequences would be primary. During the controversy surrounding this exhibit, Senator Dianne Feinstein of California asked for the impossible. She proposed that public museums offer no interpretation of historical events. Present the facts without a point of view, she said.

But sometimes the facts themselves are called into question. In the 29 October 1999 cover story of *Ha'aretz*, an Israeli daily newspaper, Tel Aviv University archaeologist Ze'er Herzog was quoted as saying: "This is what archaeologists have learned from their excavations in the Land of Israel: the Israelites were never in Egypt, did not wander in the desert, did not conquer the land in a military campaign and did not pass it on to the 12 tribes of Israel. Perhaps even harder to swallow is the fact that the united monarchy of David and Solomon, which is described by the Bible as a regional power, was at most a small tribal kingdom." If

Herzog and his like-minded colleagues are correct, those biblical stories that have been used to establish Israel's national identity must be read as fictions. Some critics say that Herzog's position is post-Zionist and so dismiss his ideas. But I suppose that others shrug their shoulders and say, What difference does it make if the story is fiction or nonfiction as long as it presents truth? My solution to the surfacing of new facts or reinterpretations of the existing facts is utter honesty. Every historical account, every museum exhibition, every national monument should bear the following statement of fact: Here is an account of what I knew at a particular time and how I knew what I knew.

And, too, once we've reopened one of the stories that we've lived by or under or above, the challenge is to resist the impulse to close it too soon, too easily. "Always someone forcing the scattered timbers of history into a sensible bridge," writes Albert Goldbarth. The same timbers that were used to construct a sensible bridge to support the ideologies of our times can also be used to build a school, sweatshop, temple, recital hall, hospital, library, prison, or café.

13. Trail's End

One of Nebraska's most written about, taught, and celebrated historical events is the mid-nineteenth-century passage of one-quarter to one-half-million immigrants on the Overland Trail, variously known as the Mormon, the Oregon, or the California Trail. Every Nebraska history text that I've seen devotes at least a full chapter to details of life on the trail and the political, economic, and cultural forces that brought the trail into being. All summer long, pieces of this history are reenacted or commemorated at festivals on or near the trail: Hastings's Oregon Trail Rodeo, Fairbury's Rock Creek Trail Days, Lewellen's Ash Hollow Pageant, Gering's Oregon Trail Days, Bayard's Chimney Rock Pioneer Days. Fourth graders in the Lincoln Public Schools spend the academic year studying Nebraska history through Oregon Trail videos, maps, computer games, and dramatizations.

So celebrated is this slice of history that one might believe that this is the only thing that happened in some parts of Nebraska. Ash Hollow State Historical Park (mile 504, counting from Independence, Missouri, the principle jumping-off point) presents information about archaeological excavations in the area, chronicling six thousand years of human history, as well as the geological history of the site. Yet the primary reason that this place was set aside is because it was there that travelers crossed from the South Platte to the North Platte River and because there they finally found enough firewood and good water. But first, they had to make the treacherous descent of Windlass Hill, a three-hundred-foot hill at a twenty-five-degree slope, by wagon. A century and a half later, the ruts where wheel-locked wagons slid down the hill are still visible.

Likewise the museums at Chimney Rock National Historic Site (mile 576) and Scott's Bluff National Monument (mile 596) present information about the geological processes that formed these landmarks and their significance in American Indian history. Yet the primary reason these sites were preserved and memorialized is that they were easily recognizable signposts for those on the trail that the prairie was behind them and the mountains before them, that their journey was one-third of the way done.

Nebraska history texts and historical markers give an unmerited amount of attention to trail travelers like Susan O. Hale. This thirty-four-year-old woman from near Independence, Missouri, was traveling with her new husband when she sickened, probably from cholera, and died on June 2, 1852, near what is now the town of Kenesaw, located midway between Hastings and Fort Kearny (mile 319). Heartbroken, Mr. Hale refused to leave his bride in an unmarked grave, the fate of most who died on the trail. So he returned to St. Joseph, Missouri, bought a marble headstone, had her name chiseled on it and hauled it to her fresh gravesite in a wheelbarrow. A good story, but not the story of one of our own.

Nor is the often-repeated story of the Whitmans one of ours. Marcus Whitman and Samuel Parker, Presbyterian missionaries, immigrated to Oregon Country in 1835. The following year, Narcissa Whitman and Eliza Spalding, both the wives of missionaries, earned the distinction of being the first white women to follow the Overland Trail. In 1843, Reverend Whitman led about one thousand people, the first large migration from Independence to what we now call the Northwest. Apparently the reverend's motives weren't entirely spiritual. He believed that if he were to fill Oregon Country with white, Protestant Americans, U.S. claims to the place would outweigh Great Britain's. Though one frequently encounters the Whitmans in Nebraska histories and museums, their story more properly belongs to the place they left—New York State—and the place they believed to be their manifest destiny—Oregon, which they helped to settle, and Washington, where both were killed by the Cayuse Indians they were trying to convert.

Nor is the curious Ezra Meeker one of ours. In 1852 he, his wife, and newborn baby immigrated to what is now Washington in a covered wagon. In 1906 and 1910, he retraced the westering journey by wagon. In 1915 he reenacted it by car. In 1924 he followed the trail for 1,300 miles in an airplane. In 1929, just days short of his ninety-eighth birthday, while Meeker was preparing for his fifth trip along the trail in a car made to look like a prairie schooner, he died. I suspect that for Meeker, who said that he regarded the trail as "sacred," the adventures, the trials, and the community he experienced on his first journey west was his shimmering peak experience. Everything else in his life seemed lusterless and flat in comparison, including the less dramatic though much more usable story of what it's like to settle in a place and to succeed or fail at building a meaningful life there.

This is not to say that the stories about life on the road told by tourists, temporary residents, or those just passing through on their way someplace else aren't valuable. Those traveling the trail were responding in some great or small way to the expansionist dream of claiming and settling the western half of the central part of the continent: a United States that would include both coasts and everything in between. But even more they were relocating for the same reasons that we, at the beginning of the new millennium, do: they perceived the places where they had been living—in Meeker's case, Ohio, Indiana, and Iowa—as too crowded, too familiar, too lacking in the ability to meet their material, emotional, and spiritual needs. Such sentiments are still common. According to a recent *Lincoln Journal Star* article, Nebraska's "blue-chip" high school and college students are going out of state for education and employment not only because they want "to see some of the world," but because they perceive their home state as lacking in job opportunities, cultural enrichment, and tolerance of diversity. An old story.

Moving on might be a typically American response to this old story. In *Travels with Charley*, after visiting a trailer park near Cleveland, Ohio, John Steinbeck says that "every one of us, except the Negroes forced here as slaves, are descended from the restless ones, the wayward ones who were not content to stay at home." How could we not have inherited this tendency? he asks. But Steinbeck acknowledges that given our long history as hunters and gatherers, the urge to move on may be as old as humanity. "Only when agriculture came into practice . . . did a place achieve meaning and value and permanence." Thus, rootedness is a fairly recent development in human history, and because land ownership was a privilege reserved for the wealthy few, it was not a widely distributed tendency. Steinbeck concludes that "the deeper and more ancient . . . need" than rootedness is "the will, the hunger to be somewhere else."

The need to move on may be even older than humankind. In *The City in History*, Lewis Mumford writes that human life swings between the two poles of movement and settlement. "The contrast between these modes may be traced back to the original break between the mainly free-moving protozoa that formed the animal kingdom and the relatively sessile organisms that belong to the vegetable kingdom." Some organisms like the oyster, became "overadapted to a fixed position," losing its power of movement in the process, while many plants gained movement of a sort, through underground roots and seed dispersal. "At every level of life," writes Mumford, "one trades mobility for security or in reverse, immobility for adventure." Thus, billions of years after "the original break," we humans are still responding to Archeozoic promptings: staying in a place where we have a reliable food supply and good shelter; moving on in search of something better or different, or perhaps in search of movement itself.

The stories of those who followed the Overland Trail in search of the better or different tell what it's like to pitch a tent and stay awhile in a place that is not home. Through these stories, we can recognize the freedoms and burdens of our own being or not being in place. Through the stories of those who followed the trail we can learn how or how not to respond when our new residence doesn't resemble the conception of home that we brought with us. Through the observations of those who followed the trail we can recognize the merits or deficiencies of our own home place: once, the horrifying "treelessness" and almost infinite possibilities of the Great Plains; now, the vitality (or lack of it) at our city's core; the greedy or considerate or haphazard or calculated manner in which our edges expand; the strength and depth of class and racial divisions or unity; whether or not civic involvement and community-building involve something more inclusive and soul-satisfying than wearing monochrome clothing and cheering the same football team.

Sometimes the most instructive stories of the past are the ones least likely to have been told and retold. Some of the most instructive ones ask the hearer or reader to imagine the missing parts. On June 1, 1849, near Fort Kearny, mounted rifleman George Gibbs sketched in his diary the outlines of a story: "We found near the road two or three emigrants, who had concluded to abandon their journey and SETTLE. They had pitched their tent for a permanent location, plowed several acres of ground, and were about to put in a crop." I suspect that Gibbs capitalized every letter in the word "settle" because such a choice and action was so contrary, so unique. Unfortunately Gibbs recorded no other details about these people. Nor have I found references to them in any other diaries or histories.

Yet it is this partial story, rather than the more completely recorded stories of the Hales, Whitmans, or Ezra Meeker, that engages my imagination. I wonder about the motives of those "two or three emigrants" for quitting the grand, epic journey and staying on.

Perhaps they were overcome with road weariness. "I refuse to take another step. This place is as good as any," one of them might have said. Perhaps they had been offered a deal that they couldn't refuse: "I'll trade my blacksmithing tools for your wagon." Perhaps they couldn't part with the weighty possessions that were exhausting their oxen: the chest of drawers that Father had made for Mother or the three hundred to four hundred pounds of bacon and flour bought at St. Joe, or the cook stove, one of the most frequently abandoned possessions on the trail. Perhaps they were so poorly prepared for the journey that they could neither continue nor turn back. Perhaps they refused to leave the unmarked grave of a dearly beloved. Or perhaps they could see potential and sensed that one day Kearney would be one of Nebraska's loveliest cities, a railroad town, a university town, a cattle town, and because of its position on the central flyway, bird-filled each spring and fall.

I wonder what stories these unnamed settlers told their descendants or the streams of people passing through who were bold and curious enough to ask, "Why are you staying on?" Did the settlers offer justifications to those travelers who believed that the settlers had met a dead end, since there could be no great, good places east of Oregon or Utah? Or perhaps these settlers defended the place and their choice: "There's nothing I want that I haven't already got right here." Mostly I wonder how the decision to quit the physical journey and to commit to staying on shaped the thoughts and actions of these unnamed settlers.

Gary Snyder, who has written often about what it means to be at home, says, "There are tens of millions of people in North America who were physically born here but who are not actually living here intellectually, imaginatively, or morally." This comes as no surprise since we live out the stories that we hear or absorb. Many of the stories we tell teach that home is sought rather than created and that nothing can compare to the eight months that we spent on the trail. Snyder says that those who lack depth, fullness, and connection in their living need to be born again into this place. I believe that this conversion will occur more easily and with greater frequency if we change the stories we tell. The stories that will guide us on the journey toward intimacy with a place, a past, and a community, the stories that will take us home are stories of the trail's end. These are stories that we should tell and tell again, imagine, commemorate, and live.

Settle

To make coffee in my green-speckled, Sierra enamelware coffeepot, I add about one-third cup of grounds to a half-pot of filtered water. When the water is hot enough that it begins to roll, the aroma of freshly brewed coffee beckons me. But it is too soon to pour coffee, since the grounds are still in suspension. I remove the pot from the burner so that the water-saturated grounds will sink to the bottom of the vessel. Several minutes later, I pour dregs-free coffee. I regret that I don't have a glass pot so that I can watch the coffee water clarify and the grounds sink into a dark, dense layer.

The verb *settle* is derived from the Anglo-Saxon *setl*, "a seat, stool, or place of rest." At some point the Old English verb *setl* and the like-sounding Middle English verb *saughtel*, which means "to appease or reconcile," became synonymous. Thus, "to settle" means the moving downward of the heavy part or parts or the stilling of disturbing or agitating movements. Sedimentary rock, water-deposited pieces of plants, animals, rocks, and minerals that have settled and compacted, is the foundation of most of North America. One who has settled down, has ended her days as exile, refugee, sojourner, pilgrim, or vagabond. One who has settled her accounts has ended the dispute, paid her debts, and is ready to start anew. When rain settles the dust on the road, we open the windows, hang sheets on the line, and enjoy brighter faces, cars, leaves, feathers, sky. What is settled is set and still.

But not every stationary thing is settled.

14. Homestead National Monument Album

I.

"What manner of people are these?" asks the narrator of the 8–1/2-minute film shown in the Homestead National Monument theater.

Details of Daniel Freeman's early life are sketchy. He was born in Preble County, Ohio, in 1826; in 1835, his family moved to Illinois. In 1849, Freeman began practicing medicine there. He followed the progress of the homestead bill expectantly from the time Andrew Johnson first proposed it in the House of Representatives in 1845 until President Lincoln signed the bill into law on May 20, 1862. On many occasions, Freeman said he wanted to be the first man to take a homestead.

Freeman claimed that it was Secret Service work for the Union army that brought him to Nebraska in 1862 just before the homestead law went into effect. However, the National Park Service, which administers the monument, found no evidence of his military career, nor did Freeman deduct his time in the service from his homestead residency requirements, as veterans were permitted to do. After arriving in Nebraska Territory, Freeman marked off a quarter section in what is now Gage County, desirable because the soil was rich and Cub Creek ran through it. Moreover, it was just fifteen miles from the Oregon Trail and just a few miles from the Big Blue River, which meant more water, more trees, and the promise of a town. Legend says that a squatter was living near the creek when Freeman arrived. Freeman bought him off with a wagon and a team of oxen.

Immediately upon locating his land, Freeman broke ground, built a squatter's cabin, and made the sixty-mile trip on horseback to the Nemaha District Land Office in Brownville. The little Missouri River town teemed with settlers waiting to make their claims one minute after midnight on January 2 (the office was closed on New Year's Day), since a minute's delay could lead to an expensive, contested claim. Most of the prospective homesteaders attended a New Year's Eve party in the hotel, the Brownville House. There, Freeman made his appeal. He said that because he had to report to his military post in St. Louis on January 2, he would not be in Brownville to register his claim or to fulfill his dream of becoming the nation's first homesteader. The revelers took sympathy on him and unanimously agreed that under these circumstances, Freeman should be the first entrant. They persuaded clerk Richard F. Barret to open the land office just long enough after midnight on January 1, 1863, for Freeman to register his claim. No one knows whether Freeman's story of his military furlough deadline was true or not, but without it, he would have waited in line with the thirty others for a chance to be the first to file on January 2 at the Brownville land office.

In Freeman, I find the archetypal Western man: one who pulled up stakes, headed west, and there created for himself a new life, a new identity. A man who lived up to his name.

II.

Nebraska State Historical Society Photograph, March 19, 1935.

In the photograph, Senator George W. Norris and Representative Henry C. Luckey, both of Nebraska, hold the car door open. We see only the side of the face of the man in the backseat of the car, but that is enough to identify him as Franklin Roosevelt. Even though the president has more pressing matters to attend to—the Depression, the gathering forces of war, the Washington DC flood—he pauses long enough to sign a bill creating the Homestead National Monument near Beatrice, Nebraska. This 1936 piece of legislation specifies that the monument is to be "a proper memorial emblematical of the hardships and the pioneer life through which the early settlers passed in the settlement, cultivation, and civilization of the great West." Moreover, the secretary of the Interior was to "erect buildings to be used as a museum . . . [which] in his judgment may perpetuate the history of the country mainly developed by the Homestead Act" (Senate Bill 1307, 74th Cong., 1st sess.).

III.

"The history of the country mainly developed by the homestead act."

Zachariah L. Boughn, a historian who researched land acquisition in Cedar County, Nebraska, says it is a widely held myth that the Homestead Act and, to a lesser degree, the Timber Culture Act formed the cornerstone of Western settlement from the end of the Civil War until 1890, the year the frontier closed according to Frederick Jackson Turner. Boughn cites other historians who have exposed the vulnerability of the free-land myth. Fred Shannon, for instance, claimed that the role of homesteading in Western settlement was greatly overestimated and that the most active period of homesteading was much later than assumed. According to Shannon's figures, more land was homesteaded from 1910 to 1936 than in the preceding forty-eight years. By June 1, 1890, only 3.5 percent of the Trans-Missouri West had been homesteaded. This means that the government's offer of almost free land was not the "cornerstone of settlement" that many of our history books declare it to have been. Likewise, Paul R. Gates's statistics prove that the Homestead Act did not change the method of land acquisition for most settlers and speculators, since more land was purchased after the Homestead Act became law than before its passage.

Roy M. Robbins asserts that "homesteading on the high plains was pioneering at its worst." Droughts, fires, wind, grasshopper plagues, lack of trees, and overwhelming isolation caused failure and relinquishment of claims. During the first twenty years following passage of the act, 552,112 original homesteads were entered. But fewer than 30 percent (or only 194,888) were "proved up." Despite these facts, says Boughn, town and county histories, television and silver-screen Westerns, high-school history texts, novels both good and bad, and the articles of some historians continue to commemorate and perpetuate one of our favorite and most firmly ensconced myths.

IV.

"It is eminently proper that the events of this period should be preserved and while the place of commemoration might be selected anywhere in the country under the Homestead Act, yet it is fitting that the place selected for its preservation should be on the land which constitutes the first homestead entry made under the act" (Senate Bill 1307, 74th Cong., 1st sess.).

Although Freeman's farm was the first entered at the Brownville land office, other offices had their own first entrants. William Young testified that he filed a claim on his Palmyra, Nebraska, farm one minute after midnight, on January 1, 1863, at the Nebraska City office in order to save himself a thirty-mile return trip the next day. Young wrote in the January 10, 1885, *Nebraska City News*: "On the 26th of December, 1862, I was at the land office in Nebraska City and made out papers for a homestead. The homestead law took effect Jan 1 1893 [sic] so yo[u] see that just one minute after midnight Dec. 31, 1863, [sic] I had owned a homestead for sixty seconds. If Daniel Freeman took the same method to secure a homestead that I did and did his business at Brownville, then he is fifteen or twenty seconds ahead of me, Brownville being that much nearer sunrise than Nebraska City" (Mattison 4). Young's sloppiness with dates causes me to question his entire testimony.

So, too, Mahlon Gore filed his homestead claim at the Vermillion, South Dakota, land office, which was open on New Year's Day, one minute after midnight, January 1, 1863. Gore, a printer, had been working in his office at the *Dakota Republican* until 11:15 P.M. on New Year's Eve. On the way home, he noticed a light in the land office. Not knowing that he would be the only applicant in Vermillion on January 1, he stopped in to file, so he could avoid the rush later in the day. Unlike Freeman, he never received the title for his land. Gore had hired Henry Fisher to live in his house while he was on a trip in Michigan. After Gore's departure, Fisher notified the land office that Gore was not fulfilling his residency requirements. If upon returning from an unauthorized absence from his claim the homesteader found a contestant on his farm he had three choices: run him off, buy him out, sell the claim to him for the best possible price. Gore chose the latter.

But the most convincing claim to "number one" belongs to Orin Holbrook, who not only was the first to file at the Des Moines, Iowa, office on January 1, but was the first to file a final certificate (January 1, 1868) and to receive a patent (September 1, 1869).

V.

Metaphor: Carving.

Daniel Freeman was trained as a medical doctor, which in the nineteenth century required quite a bit of carving—especially if he provided medical services in the Civil War. If, indeed, he was in the Civil War.

Once settled on his homestead, which grew to include 840 acres, Freeman worked as a farmer, sheriff, and coroner, the latter an occupation also requiring knife work.

The intent of the Homestead Act was to slice and dole out the wilderness to almost anyone who was willing to work. Thus, any person who was the head of a family, or at least twenty-one years of age, and anyone who was a citizen (former slaves qualified) or who had filed his or her declaration of intention to become a citizen (European immigrants not only qualified but were aggressively courted by the railroads) was entitled to claim up to 160 acres of land valued at $1.25 an acre or 80 acres valued at $2.50 an acre, drawn from the vast public domain. Confederate soldiers were disqualified, since they had borne arms against the United States.

Carving a place in the wilderness was not enough for Freeman: he wanted to carve a place for himself in state and national history as well. As early as 1884 Freeman championed his quarter section as a suitable memorial to the Homestead Act. What he envisioned was a park, which happened to coincide with the interests of the people of Beatrice. In February 1909, Nebraska representative Edward Hinshaw introduced a bill in Congress to establish a national park on the Freeman homestead. A similar bill was reintroduced several times but was not passed until 1936.

Freeman also insured his place in history by opposing the use of the Bible in a local classroom. In 1899 he took his concern to the school board. When the board sided with the teacher, Freeman filed a suit against the school board in Gage County District Court. When the county court ruled in the board's favor, Freeman took his case to the Nebraska Supreme Court. On October 9, 1902, the state supreme court ruled in Freeman's favor. Because of Freeman's persistence, the state of Nebraska established a ruling against the teaching of religious doctrine in the public schools before the U.S. Supreme Court ever considered such a case.

VI.
Homestead National Monument Photographs.

Mr. and Mrs. Daniel Freeman pose with six of their eight children, circa 1887. The daughter and three sons towering above their seated parents are adults and all quite handsome. The daughter and son sitting between Daniel and Agnes are perhaps four and six years of age. Daniel is hoary headed, with a long, pointed beard. He could be his wife's father. The museum does not tell Agnes's story—where she came from, how she felt about tallgrass prairie, her husband's hunger for fame, a husband who was seventeen years her senior, or spending more than a quarter of her life as a widow.

The four Chrisman sisters stand before their soddy near Lieban Creek in Custer County in 1886. I suppose that these young, attractive, dark-headed women dressed up for photographer Solomon Butcher. Each wears a print dress; three hold large-brimmed hats. Each sister acquired three quarter sections—one under the Preemption Act of 1841, another under the Homestead Act of 1862, yet another under the Timber Culture Act of 1873—for a total of 480 acres each or 1,920 acres combined. Butcher notes that the sisters took turns living in the shacks or soddies on each other's land so they could comply with the residency requirement. I guess that an even greater motivation was the desire for companionship. The sisters are not the rare exceptions one might think. In her study of female homesteaders in North Dakota, Elaine Lindgren reports that 12 percent of all applicants for free federal land were women; 59 percent of them were under twenty-five years of age. In most counties, the percentage of women "proving up" was comparable to or higher than that of the men.

The display entitled "Women and Children," which includes the photo of the Chrisman sisters, attempts to challenge the prevailing stereotypes. But because the museum presents these women home-steaders separately from the other homesteaders, the display reinforces the myth that white men settled the plains. Moreover, it contrasts sharply with other messages in the museum about a woman's position. Directly across from the Chrisman sisters, for instance, is a wooden rotary washing machine. The placard describing the display states: "Not every settler could afford to buy his wife one of these!" Does Agnes Suiter Freeman belong more properly with the homesteading Chrisman sisters or with the wife who may or may not have received a coveted roller washer from her homesteading husband?

VII.

First placard in the display room: "Free land didn't begin with the Homestead Act."

European explorers and settlers described the lands of the Western

Hemisphere as *terra nulluis*—lands void of human habitation or, rather, void of humans with claims to the land and its resources. Either way, the result was the transfer of native titles to European crowns and immigrants. Those who did see the human inhabitants justified the dispossession by echoing the sentiments of John Quincy Adams, who asked, "What is the right of a huntsman to the forest of a thousand miles over which he has accidentally ranged in quest of prey? . . . Shall the fields and vallies [sic], which a beneficent God has formed to teem with the life of innumerable multitudes, be condemned to everlasting barrenness?" (Parsons 343). Since Adams saw farming as superior to hunting, he believed that the land should be reserved for or revert to farmers. But Adams and others who wanted to link land ownership with higher use ignored or were ignorant of the lifestyles and cultures of the Mandan, Pawnee, Omaha, Kansa, Arikara, Oto-Missouria, Hidatsa, and other long-established agriculturists.

Prior to the American Revolution, the Crown acquired Indian home-lands and gave them to the colonies. Settlers worked the land for a company, the Crown, or a proprietor and paid quitrent in lieu of the required feudal services. Sometimes land was given as a reward for military service or as an inducement to military enlistment or settlement—the latter, William Penn's method. But for the most part, settlers did not own the land. Under the Ordinance of 1785, one could purchase land directly from the government for a fee as soon as the Indian title was cleared and the land surveyed. But this system was neither as democratic nor as egalitarian as it appears, since the individual vied with speculators for desirable plots and the latter usually won. As in the Old World, a few individuals acquired most of the land.

Because Thomas Jefferson believed that those who work the earth were God's chosen people—depositories of "substantial and genuine virtue"—Jefferson's vision of the new republic required that as many as possible own and farm land. Jefferson argued that the best foundation for democracy was a nation populated with virtuous and independent yeomen. While Jefferson's dream does not translate into the present century, it did seem feasible at a time when the public domain included 1.8 billion acres. Indeed, Uncle Sam was real-estate-rich enough to provide a plot for every industrious home seeker. In 1841 Congress passed the Preemption Act, by which a squatter who lived and had made improvements on surveyed government land had the right to buy it at $1.25 per acre before anyone else, namely real-estate speculators.

Prior to the passage of this law, many virtuous, independent yeomen had lost their houses and farms to the claim-jumpers. The Preemption Act, which was repealed in 1891, put two hundred million acres of government land into private hands for a reasonable price and attempted to manifest Jefferson's dream.

The Homestead Act differed form the Preemption Act in that one paid with time, labor, red tape, and a little money, instead of a larger cash payment. A display midway through the loop in the visitor's center details the four-step process that home seekers had to complete before receiving a patent or title. First, one made an application, after which one had six months to move onto the land. Daniel Freeman's famous filing, written in a beautiful hand bordering on calligraphy, appears on the left. Second, one paid the fees (twelve dollars in Daniel's case). Third, following at least five but no more than seven-and-one-half years of continuous residence, the "proving up papers" had to be filed and the fee paid (six dollars in Freeman's case). Since Freeman did not file until January 20, 1868, he was the thirteenth to receive a title from the Nemaha District Land Office, which by then had moved west from Brownville to Beatrice in response to population shifts. Finally, the patent or title arrived (September 1, 1869, in Freeman's case). It was appropriate for framing.

The placard for the final display on the loop reminds us that the Homestead Act worked better on paper than it did in practice: "Many settlers failed to meet the requirement for ownership and the best lands were soon taken." While the land was free except for the processing fees, most settlers needed a substantial supply of cash to sustain them until the farm was well-established. Those who did not have capital often went bankrupt. William H. Beezley says that because homesteaders could not use their land against debts until they received the title, they were severely restricted in their access to mortgage funds and other types of credit. Likewise, residency requirements forbade homesteaders from leaving the land to take temporary employment. Nor were homesteaders permitted to sell parcels of land or timber for income. Beezley suggests that because the requirements for land ownership under the Homestead Act were so restrictive, many of those who failed to make the final entry on their claims obtained the title through some other land law or direct purchase. Moreover, those accustomed to the eastern United States or Europe were poorly prepared for the semi-arid, windy conditions of the Great Plains.

The goal of the Homesteading Act was to provide *small* family farms, a workable model in the East and Midwest. But a quarter section of sandy soil in the Nebraska Sandhills, where about twenty inches of precipitation fell annually, simply wasn't enough land to support a family. Thus in western Nebraska, the inappropriateness of the amount of land granted was a huge factor in the failure rate of so many homesteaders. The Kinkaid Act of 1904 stipulated that homesteaders in thirty-seven counties in the Nebraska Sandhills and Panhandle could enlarge their claims to 640 aces of nonirrigable land (initially, Kinkaid had requested 1,280-acre homesteads). Even so, one section might not be enough since each head of cattle requires fifteen to twenty acres of land in those regions. Those who succeeded in the more arid parts of the state were those who increased their holdings to include several sections to accommodate ranching, instead of farming, or found some other way to make money. For instance, Mari Sandoz's father, Jules, worked as a locator—one who helped new settlers find claims—as well as a farmer. Moses Kinkaid was a lawyer and a judge.

The last display in the visitor's center glosses over these failures and the difficulties of the Homestead Act: "Through homesteading the government transferred over 270 million acres to private ownership—over 10 percent of the total area of the United States." Between the years 1862 and 1883, only a little over half of those who filed in Nebraska, the state with the third most applicants, received the patent on their original entry.

In 1935, the supply of suitable land was almost exhausted, though veterans continued to receive free land in Alaska as late as the 1960s. According to an article in *The Old Farmers' Almanac* of 1990, state or local governments in Alaska, Maine, Minnesota, and British Columbia periodically parcel out relatively uninhabited parts of their states to "modern pioneers" willing to meet highly specific requirements. Because our collective images surrounding the Homesteading Act overlap with so many of the elements of the American Dream—land ownership, a house far from town and community, unbounded opportunity for gritty, hardworking, resourceful individuals—the law was not repealed until 1976.

VIII.
The Rest of the Story.

A May 26, 1936, *Omaha World Herald* editorial expressed the hope that the pioneer museum at the Freeman homestead would develop a realistic representation of land settlement policies and their consequences. "We are beginning to realize, in a vague kind of way, that our pioneering was not altogether good, that the perpetuation of some of the error in it now calls for rather drastic measures of correction. The museum should show in a graphic way both sides of the shield" (Mattison 22). Yet sixty-five years later, the museum has yet to achieve a balanced presentation of history.

One of the few display cases that mentions the presence of Native Americans on the land is entitled "Stage Set for Settlement." In one corner hangs a 1901 drawing by R. F. Zogbaums depicting soldiers and Indians fighting each other. Near a mounted wooden bow, a steel-tipped arrow, and a catlinite pipe, a placard says: "After 1865, more soldiers were sent to control 'hostile' Indians on the frontier. The tribes signed treaties making more land available for settlement." I feel as though I've just read the first and the last sentences from a thick book about the Indian Wars.

Not one of the placards or display cases lists the fifteen treaties that opened the future state of Nebraska to homesteaders one piece at a time between 1825 and 1882 and the effect of these agreements on land values. Not one of the placards or display cases tells that the Kansa Indians dwelt on the land near Cub Creek until the U.S. government purchased the land from them for one-half cent per acre.

Also missing is information about the 1864 Battle of the Little Blue. Most accounts that I've read of this battle state that in the early 1860s the Cheyenne, Lakota, Arapaho, and Brulé killed or captured several people on the Oregon Trail, burned their wagons, and drove off their livestock. Settlers near Beatrice feared the same for themselves. A militia of thirty-four men from Beatrice, one of whom was Daniel Freeman, responded to rumors of Indian uprisings. Most accounts that I've read of this battle fail to mention the provocations that led to these uprisings. Under the Kansas-Nebraska Act of 1854, the *"permanent Indian frontier"* was opened to settlement (italics are mine). Under the 1851 Treaty of Fort Laramie, Cheyenne, Lakota, and Arapaho leaders and representatives of the U.S. government agreed that the latter could establish roads and forts on Indian lands in exchange for fifty thousand dollars a year in provisions, merchandise, livestock, farming implements, and for protection of Indian lands from white plunder. For the most part, the U.S. government ignored the terms of the treaty. Warfare continued between whites and Indians and between different tribes. According to the commissioner of Indian Affairs, Indians continued "to suffer from the vast numbers of immigrants who pass[ed] through their country, destroying their means of support, and scattering disease and death among them" (Olson 132).

Travelers on the Great Platte River Road weren't the sole source of Indian aggravation and suffering. Roy Robbins says that, as with most other treaties, Congress delayed or misappropriated annuity money. Goods that were received were often inferior. Just as grievous, the Lakota did not learn until after the fact that an agreement under the 1851 treaty promising them annuities for the next fifty years had been reduced to just fifteen years. Minnesota Indian agent T. J. Galbraith said that the government's failure to live up to treaty promises was the reason for the hostilities along the Oregon Trail that began in 1862 (Robbins 230) and concluded with the surrender of the Lakota and the murder of Crazy Horse at Fort Robinson in 1877.

More suffering followed the passage of the Dawes Severalty or General Allotment Act of 1887, which encouraged Native American homesteading. The chief goal of this legislation was to encourage assimilation by destroying tribal communalism. An additional bonus was that carving tribal landholdings into 160-acre pieces freed up vast reserves of land for Euro-American home seekers. Never mind that such an act on the part of the U. S. government violated its own treaties. Never mind that the requirements for Native American land ownership under this act were so excessively stringent that they were almost impossible to meet. (Indians could not "prove up" until twenty-five years had passed, five times the length of time expected of black or white homesteaders.) Thus between the passage of the Dawes Act in 1887 and its reversal under the Indian Reorganization Act of 1934, 60 percent of Indian lands were lost through sales of lands declared surplus. Another 20 percent were lost through the disposal of homesteads. "A mighty pulverizing engine to break up the tribal mass," was how Theodore Roosevelt described the General Allotment Act (Berkhoffer 175).

IX.
Real Western History.

The real core of Western adventure, the driving passion for most Euro-Americans, was the pursuit of prosperity and independence. For most, this meant acquiring and defending a land title. New West historian

Patricia Nelson Limerick writes, "If Hollywood wanted to capture the emotional center of western history, its movies would be about real estate. John Wayne would have been neither a gunfighter nor a sheriff, but a surveyor, speculator, or claims lawyer. The showdowns would occur in the land office or the courtroom; weapons would be deeds and lawsuits, not six-guns. Movie makers would have to find some cinematic way in which proliferating lines on a map could keep the audience rapt" (55). Thus a restored land office or the first claim taken under the Homestead Act are the places that would best capture the essence of American history.

x.

Homestead National Monument.

When I visited Homestead National Monument on October 21, 2000, I found large colorful banners hanging near the entryway of the visitor's center. Each was entitled "Homestead Legacies"; each bore the name and likeness of a different person raised on a homestead: Virgil Earp (Arizona), Willa Cather (Nebraska), Jeanette Rankin (Montana), George Washington Carver (Kansas), Laura Ingalls Wilder and Lawrence Welk (South Dakota). East of the visitor's center, several miles of trails wind through the woods near the creek and through the prairie. Along the way signs mark the spot of Daniel's squatter's cabin, the original homestead cabin where the Freemans lived for nine years, and the family's two-story house, built with bricks made from Cub Creek clay. But none of the structures that Daniel built remain. The graves on the far western boundary that mark Daniel and Agnes Freeman's final resting spots are remarkable because of the difference in epitaphs. Daniel's: "Filed on first homestead in U.S.A. . . . Soldier, Doctor, Sheriff, and Farmer. A true pioneer." Agnes's: "A true pioneer mother."

The display in the visitor's center reveals the extent to which the driving passion for land has shaped the telling of history. One display case contains a coil of barbed wire and a placard explaining that in the conflict between cattlemen and homesteaders, "Barbed wire helped 'nesters' emerge victorious in the struggle for control." Two displays show advances in nineteenth-century farm equipment. On display is a sickle with which "a single farmer . . . could only harvest three-fourths to one acre of grain per day." The placard near the picture of a McCormick reaper says that with such a machine, one crew could harvest ten to twelve acres per day. Since dependence on one's neighbors is not part of the American Dream, the display does not note that a crew of ten to twelve men using sickles could also harvest ten to twelve acres per day. The school display, where one can browse through the formidable readings in a sixth-grade McGuffy Reader, says that a teacher might have had to make do with a couple of books and a slate brought from the East until "civilization" caught up with her and her students. Verna Armstrong's soft oil paintings dramatize progress, from claiming and conquering the Great American Desert to the domestic felicity that individual home and land ownership provides: a couple walks next to a wagon on the trail west; against a rising or setting sun, a locator shows them land and possibilities; the man breaks the prairie while his wife and children watch; the family participates in a circle dance outside the cabin; they gather round the fireplace for family time. But you will not find images and words that tell the complete story of what this monument commemorates—simultaneous acquisition and dispossession. It is as if the handwritten sign next to the roller washer— "Help Protect Your Past. Please Do NOT Touch"—refers to the version of history we are presented through the displays and placards.

Programs at Homestead National Monument broaden the scope of the museum. Among the yearly events at the monument are the annual storytelling festival in which regional and pioneer tales are told; the annual "Horsepower and More" program which presents the agricultural traditions and equipment of the homesteading era; living history demonstrations at Homestead Days; traditional schoolyard games at Freeman School Game Day; the harvest program, which shows how livestock was raised and meat prepared for the winter; the Winter Festival of Prairie Cultures, a month-long celebration of the ways in which different ethnic groups observed the winter holiday season; and the annual fiddling championships, featuring music of the homesteading era. (May 27, 2000, Meredith won first place in the junior division by playing "Boil the Cabbage Down," "Ash Grove," and "Irish Washerwoman.") Special topics further broaden one's understanding of the Homesteading Act. In February 2000, the monument presented a program about Nicodemus, Kansas, a town established in 1877 by African-Americans homesteaders, most of whom came from Kentucky. Unlike Nebraska's black homesteading communities in Harlan, Franklin, Hamilton, Cherry, and Custer Counties, which lasted a few years at the most, Nicodemus is still there. In fact, A. Gillan Alexander III is the third generation to own and work on his family's original homestead in Graham County, Kansas.

For me the most moving and telling part of the monument's presentation of history is neither in the visitor's center nor one of the special programs, where horses draw heavy equipment or women weave cloth or stories. West of the visitor's center and over a foot bridge spanning Cub Creek is a 100-acre tallgrass prairie, restored as closely as possible to its 1863 condition. Begun in 1939, it was the second prairie restoration project in the nation, the first undertaken by the National Park Service. It is a well-maintained prairie, burned on a five-year rotation and the sumac groves kept in check with the ax. For those of us who love grasslands, the Homestead prairie is worth the drive.

The first time I visited the monument was in late July in the early 1990s. The prairie was purple, orange, and green with hoary vervain, black-eyed Susan, wild bergamot, butterfly milkweed, and shoulder-high grasses. I positioned myself on a rise on the eastern edge of the prairie and faced southwest, where I could no longer see Highway 4, the houses and satellite dishes in the Pioneer Acres subdivision, the barbed wire fence reinforcing the Osage orange hedgerow that Daniel had planted, the smokestacks of Farmland Nitrogen or the Cominico Fertilizer plants. As I gazed upon the grassland bound by woodlands, I imagined that I was a former sharecropper, tenant farmer, slave, peasant, or a refugee from some crowded eastern place, who for the first time, was beholding this vast expanse of land, this "gate of escape to the free conditions of the frontier" as Frederick Jackson Turner called this modern Canaan. I imagined the lengths to which I would go to obtain and preserve the title to such beauty, wealth, status, and possibilities.

Hearth

The Anglo-Saxon word *hearth* and what it denotes has changed little in the past couple of millennia. Then and now, it refers to a brick, stone, or tiled floor of a fireplace, often extending out into the room. Metaphorically the hearth refers to the fireside as the center of home and family life.

What strikes me about the word *hearth* is that it contains within it two other Anglo-Saxon words, *heart* and *earth*. Though of different etymological roots, these words feel linked to me. In fact, if you circle each word within the word *hearth*, your circles will interlock. Earthen, heart-filled hearth, humankind's first altar.

Instead of building and tending a fire that transforms oxygen and wood into the heat and light that warms bodies, that converts hard, raw, cold food into something more palatable, that keeps away the terrors of the encroaching night, I perform work for other people that provides the money that buys the gas that fuels the motor in the furnace in a corner of my basement. This is the hearth that I keep. Though my house is too tiny and my income too small, I dream of buying a wood-burning stove or of hiring someone to build a fireplace.

Last winter, to take the edge off my heating bill, I bought a White-Westinghouse electric space heater at K-Mart. When the nine heating rods become radiant, glowing orange, and the fan blows the heat outward, my children and I gather around it.

15. Ideal Home

For most of my forty-four years, my ideal dwelling was a two-story, clapboard Queen Anne–style house nestled among trees at the end of a long driveway. On the wide, screened-in front porch of this imagined place hung a well-padded swing, where I spent many warm-weather hours reading, writing, napping, or conversing. The backyard, which sloped downhill to a creek, was deep and wide enough for chickens, a couple of goats, cats, dogs, clotheslines, bachelor buttons, zinnias, tulips, marigolds, irises, peonies, carnations, roses, and vegetables, all set out in tidy rows. Generous margins separated my nearest neighbors and me.

The front and back stairs in this ideal house led to the second floor; a flight of stairs led to the attic. On the second floor was a spacious bedroom for each member of my family as well as a guestroom. On both floors, was a commodious bathroom with a clothes chute. Sometimes we ate supper in the kitchen; sometimes we ate dinner in the dining room. The walk-in pantry provided shelf space for all of my pots, pans, and dishes, for several weeks' worth of groceries and rows of Kerr jars filled with fruits and vegetables from my garden. In the center of the library, a room with floor-to-ceiling bookshelves on each wall, stood an enormous oak table, but only one chair. Since no meals were served on that table, I never had to pack up my work. Noise, clutter, rambunctiousness, and the only television in the house were confined to the family room, where during the cold part of the year, a real fire snapped in the fireplace. The quiet, tidy parlor was ordered around an upright piano, the symbol of social harmony and domestic order.

This ideal was pieced together from the houses I encountered in Louisa May Alcott novels, movies depicting the homes of well-off

English people (Henry Higgins's house in *My Fair Lady*, Jane and Michael's in *Mary Poppins*, Rochester's in *Jane Eyre*) and the home of my childhood playmates, the Skrupas, who had a back porch, a downstairs front porch, an upstairs front porch, a walk-in pantry, a dining room, two living rooms and the "sick room," a bedroom used only if a family member was ill. Clearly this ideal was brought into being long before I could think abstractly or had any notion of the energy expenditures required to pay for and maintain a large house and yard. Until recently, this ideal determined for me what type of house could house a home.

Yet, I've never lived anyplace that even resembles my ideal home. Given my finances and earning potential, I probably never will. Given my disinterest in house maintenance, a huge house and yard in the country soon would be as disorderly and ramshackle as that of Mrs. Jellyby in Dickens's *Bleak House* or of Pippi Longstocking. Recently, I realized that if I remained faithful to this outgrown ideal, I would spend the rest of my days homeless.

When I decided to return to southeast Nebraska after three years of exile in the estranging-place, I did not need to go house hunting. My former husband offered to me, for less money than he was charging his present tenants, the little house that we had lived in the first two years of our marriage.

The thought of returning to the old neighborhood, a neighborhood in which I had a history, pleased me. I had become well acquainted with that part of the city long before I ever lived there. While Ian attended Sunday school at Antelope Park Church of the Brethren at the corner of Sumner Street and Normal Boulevard, I walked the surrounding neighborhoods. Then, I admired the various types of bungalows near Woods Park and St. Teresa's Catholic Church. I wondered how people could live in the tiny four-room houses near Bryan Hospital and Antelope Park. I envied the curved, glassed-in red brick porch on William Jennings Bryan's former home at 49th and Sumner. I appreciated the thoughtfulness of those who forty or fifty years ago had planted the pin oaks lining many streets and who had reserved space for the many parks in this part of the city—Neighbors, Roberts, Pansing, Woods, and sprawling Antelope Park. I'd return from my neighborhood rambles just in time to join Ian for the worship service.

I was also pleased to be returning to this neighborhood because many of my former neighbors were still there. Though "Mr. Vasek" had died, "Mrs. Vasek" still lived in her four-room house two doors south of me, where she had been joined by her daughter, son-in-law, granddaughter, and great-granddaughter. The two girls that Ian had played with years ago on swing sets and in inflatable swimming pools were now teenagers, who answered most of his questions about the junior high he'd be attending that fall. The neighbors one door south were unchanged, but their yard was substantially different. Canna lilies grew where there had once been an oak tree; a new deck, double garage, a high wooden fence, play set, and a trampoline consumed much of their backyard. Instead of one yappy dog that barks in the middle of the night, they now had two and would eventually acquire three more. The quiet neighbors one door north of me were just months away from paying off their thirty-year mortgage. "Marilyn," six doors north, was still the neighborhood greeter. "Helen" still lived across the street in the house she'd occupied for almost fifty years. "Jeannette," the only black woman in the neighborhood, still lived two blocks away. These old neighbors welcomed us home and we became acquainted with our new neighbors. I was also pleased that most of the services I needed or might need— a branch library, drugstores, grocery stores, a post office, my church, the community playhouse, an independent bookstore, a Dairy Queen, a hospital, a homeopath, parks, banks, and a hardware store—were still within an easy walking distance.

And, too, the Little House didn't require any "breaking in," since it was already memory-filled. On December 26, 1990, on an icy, bitterly cold day just seventeen days before Meredith's birth, Ian and I had moved into the Little House where my new husband had already lived for several years. Just a few days after Christmas 1992, the four of us left the Little House for a larger house in south Lincoln, where there were far fewer pedestrians, mature trees, and public parks. In the Little House, Meredith had spent her infancy and part of her toddlerhood; Ian had spent part of kindergarten, all of first, and part of second grade. In the Little House, Meredith had taken her first steps and spoken her first words; in the church parking lot across the street, Ian had learned to ride his bicycle. But also in the Little House, my former husband and I had fought, endured long silences, and threatened to end our marriage. I worried if these latter memories, set as they were in the kitchen, living room, bedroom, and basement, would make me sad.

I had other concerns about returning to the Little House. Though my former husband had made room for Ian and me when we moved in, in 1990, I never felt that the house was mine. My framed pictures of family members, of Walden Pond, of Brueghel landscapes, and Salvadore Dali's *Last Supper* had remained in boxes. I wrote, studied, and graded papers at the kitchen table, which meant that I had to pack up my books and papers in time for supper and unpack them again the next morning. How could I, as my former husband's tenant, feel that the house belonged to me? And, too, the Little House is but a four-room, 798-square-foot box. How could two children, an assortment of pets and an adult who works out of her home fit in the cramped, life-size equivalent of a green Monopoly house?

Yet when I discovered the types of houses that I could afford in the Lincoln rental market, houses neither as well-maintained nor in as safe or convenient a neighborhood as the one my former husband was offering, I saw the Little House with new eyes. I gratefully accepted his offer. My new landlord notified his present renters that he would not be renewing their lease. On July 22, 1998, my children and I moved into the Little House.

As soon as I unpacked my thirty-some boxes of books, set up my writing area, placed framed photos of my children as babies, my nephews, my grandfather as a young man, and myself as a high-school senior atop Great-Aunt Florence's sewing table, papered the refrigerator with coupons, schedules, and newspaper articles, served a meal (spaghetti) on my kitchen table, and positioned in a corner of the living room the antique rocking chair in which I had nursed and rocked to sleep both of my babies, the house was ours. Memories of the life that we had had in the Little House were dim and distant compared to the bright, near details of the life that we were and are living.

But the Little House was cramped. Ian's bedroom was in the carpeted, paneled basement where he received neither fresh air nor natural light. Meredith and I each had a bedroom upstairs. My copper tea set brought from Sweden by a great-great-aunt sat on top of the refrigerator with the foil, waxed paper, lunch bags, and bananas, since I hadn't a proper place to display it. The bathroom was fine as far as bathrooms go, except that there was only one. In violation of one of the principles of feng shui, the Chinese science of harmonious living—that sleeping and working should not occupy the same space—my bedroom was crowded with my computer, double bed, four file cabinets, and two dressers. The kitchen was so small that I had to pull the table away from the wall for family meals and then push it back afterwards so there would be room to walk from the living room to the back door and basement stairs. The young couple five doors down, who also rented a 798-square-foot box, said that they only entertained guests during the warm part of the year when they could cook and eat outside.

When I returned home, I vowed that I would remain in Lincoln at least until both of my children graduated from Lincoln high schools, Ian in 2003, Meredith in 2008. I vowed that I would take almost any job to make staying in place possible. Yet despite my pleasure at returning to my former address, I had no intention of staying in the Little House. Before my lease was up for renewal, I would find a house that more clearly matched my ideal.

When we discover that one of our most cherished ideals no longer or perhaps never did nourish us, we must revise or replace it if we are to live with vigor and integrity. Otherwise, we will be guided by and in the service of something false, outdated, sentimental, impotent. While this revision process can be liberating, it can also be perilous since once we have taken apart the ideal, we might not be able to bring forth a new one or repair the old one. What is perilous in this process is that in revisioning one of our ideals, we might feel compelled to examine and revise others, say, our image of family, nature, deity, or meaningful work. Before we know it we've torn down the whole house.

Nor is this a one-time process if we are alive and growing. Michael Dorris, who has written beautifully and insightfully about home, explains:

> The sad truth is that when home is deemed synonymous with permanence it is always illusionary. The pictures whose match we seek—the Norman Rockwell *Saturday Evening Post* cover of several generations gathered around a Thanksgiving table, the "family values" neighborhood of our second-grade reading book, the two-dimensional simplicity of the euphemistic good old days—have more to do with cherished fictions than with historical realities. Human life is, by its very nature, complex and dynamic. It requires frequent readjustment, compromise, and ingenuity. Moments, friezes, occur when empirical experience and fantasy align, but they are transitory, appreciated more often

in anticipation or retrospect than in process. Identifying home is then in essence an act of ongoing imagination.

Thus the process of liberating ourselves from culturally imposed values that are more likely to deny than fulfill our deepest needs and bringing forth an ideal that is worth seeking, worth possessing, worth defending, must be a recurring one.

Phoebe Goodell Judson's autobiography reveals the unsettled life that results when one is unable to make deep revisions in her image of the ideal home and then to commit to that new vision. In 1853 Judson followed the Oregon Trail into what is now Washington State. Her reminiscence, *A Pioneer's Search for the Ideal Home*, first published in 1925, offers an important corrective to the type of story we usually hear and tell about the immigrants: that following one grand and arduous relocation they found their ideal home and the good life awaiting their arrival.

Twenty-three-year-old Judson and her husband left their home in Ohio, where they'd lived since childhood, in order to obtain a grant of land that the U.S. government promised to the head of every household willing to settle in the "new country." The Judsons were willing "to encounter dangers, endure hardships and privations" to secure a home that they might call their own and that "would make [them] independent." An admirable motive. But home was not easily found, in part because Judson compared each place in which she was living with an image of home that she carried with her: "It should be built by a mountain stream that flowed to the Pacific, or by some lake, or bay, and nothing should obstruct our view of the beautiful snow-capped mountains," she wrote. "True, it would be built of logs, but they would be covered with vines and roses, while the path leading to it should be bordered with flowers and the air filled with their sweet perfume. 'Home, home, sweet home; Be it ever so humble, There's no place like home.'"

After arriving in the Northwest, Judson and her family moved several more times in search of this "ideal home." With each move, Judson believed that she had found it. But in each case, the realities of trying to make a comfortable life in that place convinced her otherwise. Judson recognized Grand Mound in Washington Territory, her and her husband's first attempt at settlement, as a place that "would have filled my conception of an ideal home, but for the unproductiveness of the gravelly soil." After only a year, the Judsons moved to the bottomlands of the Chehalis River where "the constant drudgery effectually took all the romance and poetry out of farm life." During the tumultuous 1860s, the Judsons moved to Olympia, Washington. With the discovery of gold in British Columbia and the prosperity that Judson and her husband hoped that discovery would bring to the Puget Sound area, they again moved, this time to Bellingham, which Judson found even more "lovely" than her former home near Lake Erie. In 1871, they moved to Whatcom Bay and became homesteaders. Several years later they moved yet again to the Upper Nooksack River. This, too, appeared to be the ideal site to Judson: "I never had seen a spot whose environments more perfectly fulfilled my dream of an 'ideal home.'"

When a "development boom hit Lynden" in 1889, Judson was both grieved and gladdened to see the firs and cedars felled to make way for a town. Yet she took pleasure in "see[ing] the silent wilderness grown pregnant with human life, and dotted with beautiful homes." She and her husband built a new and larger home for themselves, with two fireplaces. A "more enchanting spot upon which to rear it could hardly be surpassed on earth," she extolled. At this point Judson's image of the ideal home shifted from an isolated or idyllic house in the wilderness to a house in a community that was free of alcohol and gambling. As Jan C. Dawson observes, for Judson, "Scenery is now secondary to the economic and even social advantages of the new location." But the community changed, as did Judson's ideal. "In the final analysis," writes Dawson, "Phoebe Judson's search for an ideal home . . . remained a process rather than becoming a place, even when she was settled. It involved constant adjustments among several conflicting impulses." Though living in a new home in a thriving community, Judson confesses that her ideal home was a place "where sorrowing and sighing are unknown"—a place that could not be created on earth, a place that could only be known through death.

In contrast to Judson's inability to create a satisfying home are the stories of two of my neighbors. Helen has dwelt in the same house for over a half-century. Her map of her home territory includes personal and historical events superimposed upon geographical features. She tells me that once the land on which her house and mine are built was called Bryan's Acres, because it had been part of Fair View, William Jennings Bryan's farm, once a few miles east of Lincoln, now surrounded by the city. Now all that remains of Bryan's estate is his spacious brick farmhouse, crowded by a hospital on two sides and a hospital parking ramp on the other. I wonder if "The Great Commoner" saw his house now he would recognize it as home.

Following World War II, two Lincoln furniture dealers bought the land across the street from my house and filled a couple of city blocks with small, basementless, prefabricated houses. The investors offered a "100 percent loan" to GIs, which meant that Helen and her husband, a World War II veteran, put nothing down and only paid closing costs. "When we moved in here in 1950, this was the edge of Lincoln. I felt that we were out in the boondocks. In fact that part of the street was dirt road," Helen says, pointing south. "The block south of there was just a field, except for one house. The lawyer who lived there wouldn't sell his land, because he said that he didn't want to get up in the morning and see a bunch of garbage cans lining the street. Eventually he sold. He died a short while later." Now our neighborhood is crowded with houses, and on Monday mornings the street is lined with garbage cans. Now one has to drive far to find the boondocks.

Over a decade ago, the members of the church that is now the only other building on Helen's block, bought all of the houses on that block and razed them, so they could build the cavernous sanctuary where they presently offer four services on Sunday mornings. The remainder of the block is a parking lot. "Actually I wasn't the only one who held out. There was an old woman over there," Helen says, pointing to the southwest corner of the block, "who wouldn't sell at first." When she finally did, the church told her that her house wasn't worth as much as it had been when they first offered to buy it, since it was surrounded by asphalt. Imagine that!

"I wouldn't sell because my husband had Parkinson's disease. I was working full time at the VA Hospital as a dietician. Well, I was too busy to move and I had more important things to worry about than a parking lot. The church tried to get me to sell by telling me that after they cut down all the trees and knocked down all the houses that I wouldn't have any privacy. I told them that if that ever got to be a problem, I'd just put up a tall wooden fence." Helen also had less practical reasons for staying on. "I raised my three kids here. My husband died in this house. I've been here over a half-century myself. It's a safe neighborhood." In recent years, Helen has added a poor man's patio to the front of her house, a storage shed, a covered walkway between her house and garage, and a glassed-in, heated back porch. "My second son says that when I'm gone, he's going to buy out his brother and sister and move in here."

My neighbor Jeannette has remained in her ideal home for almost twenty years, even though she hasn't always felt welcome here. After she and her husband graduated from the University of Nebraska-Lincoln, they moved to Texas, where Jeannette worked as a counselor in a juvenile detention center and her husband as an accountant. When Jeannette became pregnant with their first child, they felt compelled to return home. In 1980, just a few months before their child was born, Jeannette and her husband bought a ranch-style house two blocks from mine. Shortly after she moved in, she learned of a plot by some of her neighbors—some who are still here and some who have moved away—to keep her and her family out of the neighborhood. "When they learned that a black family had made an offer on a house near theirs, they got together and made a counteroffer," she remembers. "But they were too late." While some neighbors came to tolerate or even accept Jeannette and her family, others did not. One morning she awakened to find someone else's garbage strewn across her lawn. On another morning, she awakened to find a FOR SALE sign stuck in her yard. And once a neighbor informed the police that the license plates on Jeannette's car had expired. "Why would you do that to your neighbor?" she asked me.

When Jeannette learned that her children were receiving little or no history that included African Americans at the nearby elementary school, she invited herself to be a guest speaker in their classes and volunteered to speak in other classrooms. "I got offers to speak during Black History Month, which shows that our history is still not thought of as *American* history. But it's a start." When her children were the victims of racial incidents, she went to the school and educated the educators. "I get tired of having to teach people what they already should know," she said. "Some days I dream of moving back to Houston where there are more black people and where the white people don't expect us to be invisible or just go away. But this is my home."

One spring, Jeannette's husband moved out and divorced her. Jeannette grieved; then she put together a résumé. No sooner had she begun applying for jobs than a fire destroyed part of her house. "In some ways, the fire was harder on the kids than their dad's leaving. People come and go in life, but home should be permanent. Even though I wanted to find a job that would get some money coming in and give me something else to think about, I put my job plans on hold. It was more important to make my home stable again for my kids." After Jeannette restored her house and helped her children became accustomed to spending every other weekend at their father's apartment, she took a job coordinating multicultural activities and workshops for a social services agency. "There's so much work to be done in our community," she says. "I'm needed here."

Unlike Phoebe Judson who kept moving in hopes of finding home, Helen and Jeannette tell stories about adapting or fighting in order to remain at home. I hope to be as strong and flexible, as courageous and imaginative. What is meaningful, obtainable, and transportable from my childhood image of an ideal home (pets, a garden, a kitchen table where family business, homework, socializing, as well as eating are carried on), I will keep. But those aspects of my childhood ideal that no longer serve me, I will cast off or rework. Despite my love of large houses with plenty of space and privacy for each member of the family, I need a small, or rather small, house, since I don't like to clean or mow and tend not to notice when things break. Despite my love of wild and open places, I feel safer surrounded by close neighbors and would perish in the absence of good, near libraries. Despite my love of bachelor buttons, peonies, tulips, and carnations, I now want an untidy profusion of native flowers—black-eyed Susans, purple coneflowers, Queen Anne's lace, tiger lilies. The only features of my childhood ideal that I can't relinquish are my desire for enough space for the spinet piano that Great-Aunt Pertsie bought me when I was thirteen, and which still sits in my parents' faraway living room, and enough space for a wood-burning stove or fireplace.

My revised image of my ideal home possesses features that I couldn't have imagined wanting when I was seven, twelve, or thirty. I want enough likelihood of long-term habitation that I can plant trees, knowing that I'll be in place long enough to enjoy their shade or to eat of their fruit. I want enough likelihood of long-term habitation that it is worth my while to learn the kinks in the plumbing, the most powerful place in the house for morning prayers, the choicest part of the yard for growing tomatoes, the histories, quirks, and passions of my neighbors, and how to make my city a more just and livable place for all of its inhabitants. I want enough likelihood of long-term habitation that I can not only tell but show my grandchildren the part of the backyard where Ian and his friends used to sleep in the tent, the living room window that Belle, our beagle, broke in excitement, the kitchen table that we had to move for family dinners, the muddy space behind the shed where Meredith tried to build a clubhouse, the jutting-out corner of the living room wall where Ian scratched his back so frequently that he wore off the wallpaper, the linen closet where our neurotically timid cat, Lilly, slept, the little hallway where Meredith's father realized that the crib he had just assembled for our newborn wouldn't fit through the door of the bedroom we then shared. I want enough likelihood of long-term habitation that I can imagine becoming what Barry Lopez calls one of the "local geniuses of the American landscape," one of those who has intimate knowledge of a tiny part of the earth's surface. Now I know where to go in the neighborhood to see buffalo grass, gargoyles, exposed Dakota sandstone, hundreds of hostas, each accompanied by a handwritten sign proclaiming that hybrid's name, a Czech shoe repair shop, ducks, geese, a hen and rooster, pieces of tree branches arranged to form freestanding or mobile sculptures, a vernal blue-purple pool of Sweet William phlox, flaming sumac, former farmhouses, and ample proof that this part of Nebraska is not flat. I can't even imagine what local knowledge I will acquire in decades to come. And I want enough likelihood of long-term habitation that I can imagine where I will spend a hopefully contented old age and the last moments of a hopefully well-lived life.

In truth the Little House is my ideal home. I only had to recognize it as such.

On January 31, 2000, I bought the Little House. What made the financial aspect of this momentous event possible was my work as the long-distance, acting director of the creative writing program at the Baltimore, Maryland, college where I am employed as an instructor. The four paychecks I earned as administrator and some of my life savings covered the down payment and closing costs on the Little House. Yet the loan officer judged my income from part-time teaching and the pieces of writing that I sold now and then to be too low and unstable for me to make monthly house payments—payments that were only ninety dollars more per month than the monthly rent I had been paying. My frugality, resourcefulness, and complete lack of debt made little difference to her. So, I did what I promised myself that I never would do again. I began working as a substitute teacher in the Lincoln Public Schools five or six days per month for eighty-five dollars per day. The potential for nine monthly paychecks per year for a type of work that the loan officer and underwriter understood, from an employer whose name they recognized, tipped the balance in my favor. My loan application was approved and the Little House was mine—or rather I began the thirty-year process to purchase the Little House.

House ownership is not a necessary condition for being at home. I've known many people who own houses but have little sense of place, history, and community. Conversely, I've known many people who don't own houses yet are living connected, inhabitory lives. But in my case, the permanent address, stability, and investment in the community that I associate with home ownership are necessary. Since I was seventeen, the longest I've lived in one place was a few weeks short of three years. This means that I have been even more mobile than the statistically average person in the United States who changes place of residence every four years. While such frequent moves offer a type of freedom, since they discourage attachment or commitment to a place, a community, or way of life, they also prevent the freedom that comes from embracing such commitments. When I bought the Little House I was ready to experience the type of freedom that comes from being in a place and a community in which I have a past, present, and a future. I was ready to commit that radical, counterculture act of staying home. With my needs for continuity and belonging met, I am free to become physically, intellectually, spiritually, and morally at home. I am free to delve more deeply into the ordinary. But if ever my Little House and this familiar neighborhood prevent me from living with vigor and integrity, I hope to have the vision and conviction to revise or replace my ideal with something more fitting.

To celebrate and commemorate finding my ideal home, my children and I planted two ash saplings in our front yard. Daphne, whose branches form an orb, casts loose shade on the ground before Meredith's bedroom windows. Apollo, whose branches form a long oval, barely casts a solid, narrow shadow before the living room windows. But my little trees will grow quickly. I water them weekly during the warm part of the year and speak to them often, telling them how much I love the ash tree's long straight trunk, its open crown, its leaflets that turn purple in the early autumn. I tell them that they are symbols of my intention to live here long enough that I'll see them replace the shade trees destroyed by the snow-and-ice storm of October 1996. I tell them that one day I'll sit in a lawn chair beneath their boughs and read and write or converse with friends, neighbors, children, or grandchildren.

I tell them that they are my gift of shade to my neighbors and to those who will live on this street after I am gone.

Now when I approach my home by car or on foot, my growing trees are the first things I see: constant reminders that I have found and am dwelling in my ideal home.

Neighbor

The Old English *neahgebur* is formed by compounding *neah*, meaning "nigh" or "near" and *gebur*, "a dweller." Quite simply, a neighbor is one who dwells near you. But what is near? In *Home from Nowhere*, James Howard Kunstler defines a neighborhood as "a five-minute walking distance (or quarter-mile) from the edge to the center, thus a ten-minute walk edge to edge, or one-half square mile." Kunstler's definition is too expansive for old "Mrs. Vasek," who lives two doors down from me. If she steps into her front yard, she has ventured far. Kunstler's definition is too narrow for me. I set out from my house each day for a three- to six-mile walk, heading in whichever direction exerts the strongest pull that day. This is my neighborhood. But is everyone I meet on my city rambles my neighbor?

When the testy lawyer asked Jesus a similar question, Jesus answered with the story of the Samaritan who stopped to help a man of unidentified race, rank, and religion, who had been robbed, beaten, and left for dead at the side of the road—a man ignored by a priest and a Levite, also traveling that road. Since the lawyer knew that he was required by Mosaic Law to love his neighbor as much as himself, he probably hoped that this teacher would offer a purely geographical definition. How much easier to love people whom we barely know (perhaps the lawyer and his near neighbors comfortably avoided the depths by only speaking of weather, garbage service, pets, grass, and gutters), but that seem so much like us than it is to love those others— the sojourners, the exiles, those left for dead on the side of the road, those on the other side of the ideological fence. While Jesus did not offer an easy, terse, bumper-sticker definition—"Support Your Neighbor.

Buy American"—he did offer a geographical definition of sorts. If a neighbor is anyone who extends mercy and lovingkindness to us; if a neighbor is anyone to whom we could extend mercy and lovingkindness, then every person in the parable—the half-dead victim, the oppressed Samaritan, the Samaritan's oppressors—is a neighbor. Therefore, if no one is too far from our home territory, too like or unlike ourselves to be considered our neighbor, then home, the point from which we determine all distances, is everywhere too.

16. Witness

The execution of Harold Lamont ("Wili") Otey was scheduled for 12:01 A.M., September 2, 1994. Otey, a forty-three-year-old African-American man, had been sentenced to death for the 1977 robbery, rape, and murder of Jane McManus, a twenty-six-year-old white woman from Omaha.

This was not Otey's first execution date. In 1991 a state court action regarding the fairness of Otey's clemency board hearing brought a stay just six hours before the execution scheduled for June 10, 1991. In 1994, I had hoped for another stay. But when I heard at 7:55 P.M. that the U.S. Supreme Court had refused to hear Otey's case and that no further legal action could be taken on his behalf, I knew his time to die was near. I did not know Otey; nor could I discern from the news reports if he was guilty or innocent. But I knew that taking a life was always wrong. On the evening of September 1, there was no other place I could be but at the deathwatch. Ian, who was ten at the time, my then sister-in-law, "Toni," and I gathered candles, matches, and flashlights and drove the one-and-a-half miles to the Nebraska State Penitentiary.

Though Nebraska had reinstated the death penalty in 1977, and though over a dozen men had received death sentences since that time, the last person to die in Nebraska's electric chair was Charles Starkweather in 1959. Officials anticipated that hundreds, perhaps thousands, of demonstrators would appear outside the prison to support or protest the resumption of executions in general and this one in particular.

By the time we arrived at the penitentiary, the parking lot had been cleared of vehicles and was divided by a snow fence into two sections: the west side for death penalty opponents; the east side for death penalty supporters. Each side had their own portable turquoise outhouses. The equipment vans from several television stations were set up near the prison. Uniformed men patrolled the area. All of this took me by surprise. I thought that we abolitionists would be the only ones there.

When I arrived at about 8:15, the groups of protestors on both sides of the fence were small and rather aimless. I chatted with people I knew from other death-penalty protests or from the university. We expressed our frail hope of a last minute reprieve from the Pardons Board, comprised of Governor Ben Nelson, Attorney General Don Stenberg, and Secretary of State Scott Moore.

During the next hour, I watched as a small crowd formed on each side of the fence. On a curb at the back of the parking lot on the west side of the fence sat a University of Nebraska philosophy professor, who had tutored Otey twice a month for nine years, and the professor's wife. Periodically they smiled and waved in the direction of the penitentiary. I scanned the driveway near the prison for the object of their attention. I scanned the prison windows. There in a second-floor window in the prison hospital stood a black man wearing a short-sleeved white shirt and a shaved head. After waving in the direction of the parking lot, Otey turned his back to the window and talked to a visitor; then he placed a black garland around each visitor's neck before he or she left. Again and again Otey repeated this motion. Finally I realized that he was hugging each visitor with his shackled hands. In the moments between the departure of one visitor and the arrival of the next, he raised his shackled hands and waved at those of us in the parking lot. I watched as people joining the vigil were swept by a wave of horror and compassion when they discovered Otey's presence at the window. Soon those of us on the west side of the fence also fell into a pattern: Otey turned to wave at us; we raised our candles and flashlights and waved back. Perhaps by the end of the evening when we were three hundred strong, he saw a rising, flickering galaxy of stars, a bright lifeboat, so to speak, every time he turned toward the window.

Over the course of the evening, the pro-execution crowd grew larger, more celebratory and raucous. By ten o'clock, I could no longer ignore them. They moved from one chant to the next: "Barbecue!" "USA!" "Fry the nigger!" "Go Big Red!" Some women banged on frying pans with big spoons or sticks. Four young men held a sign in the air that was longer than I am tall. It read, "Nebraska State Pen First Annual BBQ." On the left side was a drawing of a person with a light bulb for a head. Flames leapt beneath the abbreviation "BBQ." Other signs proclaimed, "The Death Penalty Equals Respect for Life"; "Nebraska—the Good Life for Whites" (a qualification of our state motto); "Buckwheat says Capital Punishment is OTEY" (Otey rhymes with okay); and "Hey Willie [sic], it's Fryday."

Those of us protesting the execution were a sober crowd that prayed, sang, and wept. Two nuns and another woman led the singing. "We Shall Overcome." "Amazing Grace." "This Little Light of Mine." Toni sang the Negro national anthem, solo. An old, white-headed white man, Hanno Klassen, a retired professor from Minnesota, bore a huge sign proclaiming, "Wili Otey, my friend of 16 years." He parted the crowd as if it were the Red Sea and sang a haunting chant about a new creation. Then all of us sang "Swing Low, Sweet Chariot," "I'm Going to Lay Down My Sword and Shield," "Were You There When They Crucified My Lord?" and some of the simple, meditative chants of the Taizé community. "Stay with me. Remain here with me. Watch and pray. Watch and pray." If I shut my eyes while I sang, I not only blocked out the clamor of the death party, but the songs became my prayers.

At about half past ten, Ian asked to use the outhouse. He and I moved to the back of the parking lot, near the snow-fence dividing line. While we waited in line for a toilet to open up, we watched the counter-demonstrators. College students waved signs proclaiming the fraternity or sorority to which they belonged or the dormitory floor on which they lived. One person wore a hood, whether that of an executioner or Klansman I cannot say. Later, I heard that some in the pro-execution crowd sported swastikas, others body-surfed. One man asked people if they wanted "fries with their Otey," as he passed out French-fried potatoes. I ordered Ian to pee in the grass so that we could return to the safety of our people.

At about eleven o'clock an Associated Press photographer positioned her tripod near the snow fence separating the west lot from the penitentiary and snapped pictures of the singing nuns, Hanno Klassen, my family (by then, my husband, his brother, and our daughter had arrived) and the pool of beautiful, candlelit faces behind us. The photographer's colleague, who had been photographing on the east side of the fence, wriggled to the front to ask her a technical question. Before leaving he remarked: "There's quite an IQ difference between these two crowds. It's like comparing Einstein to a carrot."

A few minutes before midnight, Otey waved at us and then he was gone. We sang, "He's got the whole world in His hands . . . He's got Wili Otey in His hands . . . He's got Jane McManus in His hands." Some sang, "He's got Ben Nelson in his hands," but others repeated the first refrain instead. At one minute after midnight, some of us spoke the Lord's Prayer. Then we stood in silence. A woman threw her head back and raised a cry of anguish that made my throat ache. While we wept and waited, we heard fireworks exploding and cheerleaders leading the crowd on the east side of the fence.

Even though the execution had not been officially announced, the crowd began dispersing shortly after midnight. I wanted to wait for the final word that Otey had passed over, but my husband feared the crowd dynamics. Indeed, as we were preparing to leave, at least a half-dozen police in riot gear ran into the demonstration area. I later heard that a fight had broken out near the outhouses when a white death-penalty supporter said to a black abolitionist, "See that hair? That's the same kind they shaved off of Otey's head before they put the electrodes on it." I believe that if a black man had ventured into the pro-death fold, he would have been torn limb from limb. I believe that if Otey had not gone to the electric chair, any other black man could have filled his seat and satisfied the crowd. In his poem, "Indiana March Song," Otey wrote: "i am doomed/ i must die to atone for your fears."

I did not learn until I arrived home that the prison employees had been so nervous that it took them longer than expected to attach the dozen straps that would hold Otey's body to the electric chair. The press did not report what had so unnerved them. The first of four surges of electricity entered Otey's body at 12:23. By 12:25 the deed was done. Otey was pronounced dead at 12:33. Witnesses say that he maintained his dignity and composure to the very end.

For several days after the execution, I was afraid. I was afraid of what I would dream when I fell asleep. I was afraid that three-and-half-year-old Meredith would retain a memory of the event, even though she had slept through most of the rabble and sadness in her father's or my arms. I was afraid that I would never again be able to drive the direct route downtown, since Ian refused to go near the penitentiary or to speak of what he had witnessed there. I was afraid that my husband and brother- and sister-in-law, black people from the Caribbean, people who did not call Nebraska home, would believe that the values they saw on display on the east side of the fence were not an aberration but widely held. Indeed, I feared that myself. And I was afraid that I could never again go to the grocery store, the public library, the bank, my classes at the university, or my children's schools without being afraid of encountering one of the fifteen hundred to two thousand people who had gathered on the east side of the fence on the evening of September 1, 1994. After all, most of those people were Nebraskans. Most were Lincolnites. Perhaps some were my neighbors, students, the parents of my children's classmates. What I'd learned of at least some of my neighbors on the night of September 1 left me feeling deceived and endangered. How could I reconcile my love for my home place with what I saw of some of its inhabitants? How could I keep my children safe among such people?

After the execution, I combed the newspapers for analysis of the exhibition outside the prison. No other news mattered. Those death penalty proponents interviewed by the press claimed they were at the penitentiary to see justice carried out. What I remembered was an orgy, a drunken, white lynch mob. For several weeks, letters appeared on the editorial page from those who were ashamed of their townspeople's actions. Some letters came from those who had gone to the penitentiary to support the execution. Karen Klein wrote that she changed sides when she saw the behavior of the pro-death-penalty crowd: "When I arrived at the pro-capital punishment side, I was so embarrassed by the behavior, I found myself on the anti-death side within five minutes. . . . It's scary to think that Lincoln is full of so many people with so much hate and nothing better to do than to purposely try to hurt other people's feelings." Michael Weisser, the cantor at the South Street Temple, articulated the most disturbing significance of the death celebration: "The crowd outside the prison opposed to the death penalty was peaceful. On the other side was a largely violent crowd. The contrast was so startling that you just know there's a link."

Seven years later, I am still frightened and puzzled by the spectacle that I witnessed just a few miles from my home. Sometimes I tell myself that the people on the other side of the fence are not representative of most of my neighbors. But, too, I suspect that many more people would have gone to that party at the prison if they could have gotten off work, found someone to stay with the kids, if they hadn't feared for their reputations or safety. Sometimes I tell myself that the mob mentality took over and that what happened was entirely spontaneous. But then I recall the amount of creativity, time, and money invested in the signs and costumes, the forethought involved in bringing alcohol, fireworks, frying pans, and French-fried potatoes to the demonstration. Not spontaneous. My friend on death row whom I visit one Wednesday morning each month says that perhaps evil spirits entered the crowd. On some days, this seems to me the most plausible explanation. But then, how do I explain the goodness, love, reverence, and community that I experienced on the west side of the fence and the tender compassion that we protesters showed each other during those difficult days following the execution?

I am grateful that as time passes the faces and chants and proclamations have become less vivid, less easily beckoned. I am grateful that most of the time I see my neighbors as common people, people like me who hold jobs, make house payments, try to raise decent children and be acceptable neighbors.

But sometimes I can't forget what I have seen.

Community

Community, from the Latin *communitas*, is derived from *communis*, meaning "common" or "general" and *unitas*, meaning "oneness." Thus, a community is a group of organisms with something in common. In the case of humans, that something could be vocation, familial origins, geographical residence, political or religious affiliations, shared privileges or oppressions.

A group of people only has to share a single feature to be referred to as a community. The Hispanic community. The gay community. The university community. But single-feature designations tend to ignore the chasm-creating differences that can exist within a group, such as that which gapes between the person who cleans dormitory rooms for $5.25 an hour and the university chancellor who receives about $100 dollars more per hour for his or her time and countless other dollars' worth of benefits, perks, prestige, and opportunities. The fact that both of these employees' paychecks are issued from the same payroll office does not, nor cannot, bridge this gap.

"Community" can also be more narrowly defined. Biologist Marston Bates said that "the essential element in the concept of the community is the interdependence of its various members to form a functioning unit. . . . The community, it seems to me, might be defined as the smallest group of such populations that can be studied and understood as a more or less self-sufficient unit." Yet even groups that meet Bates's criterion of interdependent members forming a self-sufficient unit vary substantially, especially when this definition is applied to human beings. The driving purpose of what I call a *basic* community is to tend to its members' physical needs as well as their needs for protection and socialization. Such basic communities (some pre-World War II neighborhoods, some extended families, some religious communities) tend to be tightly knit, homogeneous, and in agreement that the group will not question or discuss its values or dynamics. The members of what I call *nascent* communities have banded together in response to something extraordinary—a flood or tornado, a school shooting, a terrorist attack, a common illness, eight months on the Overland Trail, a law or amendment that threatens the group's well-being. Nascent communities offer temporary, communitylike experiences, which the members often remember fondly, perhaps as a peak experience in their lives. Once the crisis is over, the nascent community usually dissolves, though it has the potential to evolve into something deeper and more lasting.

Deliberate, intentional or conscious community is the rarest, deepest type. The members tend to each other's basic needs and support their needs for personal growth and expression. Such communities are not static but under constant revision, evolving as its members evolve. Members of conscious communities, those committed both to each other and to a common vision or purpose (the seven people from my church who meet each Sunday evening so that we can know, love, and uphold each other), bear witness to the grand illogic of a group: that the whole is always greater and more powerful than the sum of its individual parts.

17. Round

The earth lodge, the most typical human dwelling place on the Great Plains a couple of centuries ago, consisted of a circular exterior wall, a dome-shaped roof and an excavated earthen floor. The walls and roof were layered with willow branches, grass thatching, a shingling of sod and tamped-down earth. A six-to-ten-foot-long hall with a skin curtain at either end provided the only way in or out. From a distance, the individual lodge may have resembled a breast, a hummock, a half-walnut shell, a turtle carapace, a pustule, an overturned bird's nest, a hemisphere from which extended a stem, a cork, or a fuse. Sunken into the floor were four to ten poles—whole, barkless tree trunks, forked at the top and connected by crosspieces so that they supported the heavy slanting or domed roof. Anthropologist Gene Weltfish compared these long radial rafters to an umbrella frame, but I imagine them as the spokes of a cartwheel. Positioned in the ritually defined center of the lodge was the hearth; above it in the center of the roof like a navel, nipple, or hub was a hole that functioned as the chimney and only window.

The average Omaha, Oto-Missouria, Arikara, Mandan, Hidatsa, or Pawnee village was comprised of a few or many dozen of these closely set round houses, usually positioned on high ground above a river or stream. Some villages were quite large. In 1847 in present-day Nance County, Nebraska, William Clayton, found the ruins of approximately two hundred lodges of a Skiri Pawnee village. The inhabitants had abandoned their homes in 1846, after their old enemies, the Lakota, burned the village. When Moravian missionaries Gottlieb F. Oehler and David Z. Smith visited a Chaui Pawnee village in the Linwood,

Nebraska, area in 1851, they found between 140 and 150 lodges and a population of about 3,500. I have never encountered evidence in the reports of explorers, missionaries, or anthropologists of an earth lodge inhabited by just one person or of a family living in a lodge that was not part of a village. Evidently the cost of individuality at that time and in this place was too high.

Earth lodges varied in size from twenty to sixty feet in diameter, the size often depending on the status of the inhabitants. The original floor of one of the largest lodges of the Kitkehahki Pawnee village near Republican, Kansas, now the site of a museum, is fifty feet in diameter and includes an area of almost two thousand square feet. Whether small and intimate or spacious and cathedral-like, earth lodges offered a symbolic wedding of the womb and the celestial dome and a constructed reminder that all things that grow out of the earth are round. In 1904, anthropologist Alice C. Fletcher wrote that, during what she called the Hako ceremony, the Pawnee priest drew a circle with his toe (Fletcher does not say in what, but I guess the dirt) to represent the eagle's use of its claws to build its round nest. But even more, the priest's actions represent those of Tirawa or "vault of the heavens," the supreme deity and first cause, creating the world for people to live in. "If you go on a high hill and look around," the priest told Fletcher, "you will see the sky touching the earth on every side, and within this circular enclosure the people live. So the circle Tirawa-atius has made for the dwelling place of all the people. The circle also stands for the kinship group, the clan, and the tribe."

The lodge was structured so that the inhabitants could not forget the near presence of the sacred. Between the hearth and the altar, was *wiharu*, the place where "the wise sayings of those who have gone before us are residing." The inhabitants could not walk over this sacred spot; rather, they took the long and indirect way, walking around the hearth until they arrived at their destination. The rectangular, raised-earth altar was positioned on the west side of the lodge so that it received the day's first light. A bison skull rested upon the altar; a sacred medicine bundle hung above it from the rafters.

The interior of the lodge was a female space. Indeed, women owned and maintained the earth lodge and everything in it. The duties of the average woman living on the Great Plains a couple of centuries ago included, according to geographer David J. Wishart, "a repetition of arduous daily tasks. The women erected and dismantled the tipis, built and repaired the lodges, produced the staple crops, collected wild plants, hauled fuel and water, dug and transported salt, processed skins and furs, bore and raised children, and in general looked after the household." This meant cooking, cleaning, periodic fumigation, maintaining the cache pit, making pottery, clothing, and stone implements. The female lodge dwellers were a community that slept, worshipped, and worked together, day after day.

In the absence of walls, earth lodge dwellers erected imaginary ones, which partitioned the space yet preserved the open, hollow roundness. Weltfish says that the earth lodge was divided into two duplicate halves, the north and south sector, the walls of which were lined with the beds or sleeping compartments. The female residents of each sector alternated in carrying out essential household functions. The north and south sectors were each divided into three "stations." Immature girls and recently married woman slept and worked in the two western stations, old women and children in the two eastern ones, mature women in the two central stations.

One did not spend the entire round of the seasons in or near the earth lodge. The traditional yearly schedule for Plains Indians was to live in their lodges in the late winter and spring, when they planted their crops. For the summer bison hunt, they moved onto the grasslands and lived in tipis or "side dwellings," half-bowl-shaped, skin-covered frameworks of bent saplings that were open in the front. When living on the prairie, the Pawnee were divided into small groups centered around one bison hunter. At summer's end, they returned to their river houses for the harvest. In the winter, they returned to the grasslands for the hunt. And so on. The earth lodge was a domicile, the dweller's fixed and permanent residence, the home to which one planned to return even when living elsewhere. Yet when people came home from the hunt, they might not inhabit the same lodge they had left a few months earlier. I do not know why and how they regrouped. Certainly they perceived themselves as a homogeneous group, a community defined by blood ties, common mythological and geographical origins, common external threats, obligations, values, and traditions. The village was a large extended family; any lodge in the village could become home.

When I stand before the replica earth lodge at the Museum of Nebraska History or the preserved earth lodge near Republican, Kansas, when I study earth lodge floor plans in James R. Murie's *Ceremonies of the Pawnee* and Weltfish's *The Lost Universe: Pawnee Life and*

Culture, when I pour over copies of photographs of earth lodges from the Smithsonian Institution's anthropological archives, I imagine myself into one of these little earths. But I—who has always dwelt in angular spaces with firm, visible partitions, doors that lock, and only a few other people sharing the enclosed space, the chores, the larder, the collective past, and the sacred—find the interior of the earth lodge appealing and disturbing. I imagine feeling warm contentment in a houseful of people obligated to respond if someone gets sick in the night, has a broken-down car, a story to tell, an enemy to face, and who guarantee that there will never be too many empty chairs at the holiday table. I imagine feeling hot frustration in a houseful of people whose cohesion depends upon never speaking of, perhaps never even imagining, schedule changes, other theories of creation, architectural innovations, the deep, forbidden allure of an outsider or the necessity of a hidden corner niche where one can daydream, cry, sulk, sing old songs with new words, and for once, dance alone. I imagine at night, before I surrender to sleep, feeling both safely held and too tightly bound as I gaze toward the hub of the cosmic wheel and watch a mote of the heavens pass by.

Relic

On a high shelf above the stove, I keep a small wooden box that once belonged to my maternal grandmother, Mae Parris, the last relative of her generation. This box came to me not after she died on July 11, 2000, but after she broke up housekeeping and entered a nursing home—the only time I ever saw her cry. The wood is the color of cedar, though it doesn't smell like cedar. On the top front of the box, "Recipes" is written in green cursive, with a cluster of green leaves at both ends of the word. On the bottom front of the box lid are red and yellow apples and a red and yellow pear. Inside the lid is a Bisquick recipe cut from a magazine for Easy Drop Danish Cookies. In the front interior of the box are recipes cut from newspapers and magazines for Hominy Casserole, Lightning Fudge, Cottage Cheese Dressing, Create-A-Crust Apple Custard Pie, Easy Cheesy Turkey Loaf.

Behind the clippings are perhaps 150 index cards, about half of which contain recipes written in Granny's own hand. She wrote legibly and rarely misspelled a word, commendable for a woman who did not go to high school. As I read the cards, I discover a charming quirk: my granny's words start on the line but slant upward, as if moved by the slightest impulse to be airborne. When a *t* appears as the final letter in a word, the tail swings up and back as if to cross the *t* but stops short of this goal and arcs outward instead. Another suggestion of flight.

I do not remember eating many of the foods for which these cards provide instructions: Ham Jambalaya, Carp Burgers, Egg Noodles, Ozark Venison Stew, Carmel Dumplings, Grape Wine with a Balloon, Sauerbraten Rabbit, Bran and Cheddar Cheese Batter Bread. But the cards remind me that Granny loved anything that included cornmeal (three recipes for corn bread; two for cornbread dressing; one each for cornmeal dumplings, corn dogs, and hush puppies), anything escalloped (cabbage, corn, apples, oysters), moist, fruity cakes (numerous, batter-spattered, edge-worn recipes for apple or peach cakes) and rhubarb pie (two recipes, both for a cream filling).

This keepsake, this surviving fragment, this movable shrine, this relic is a fitting reminder of what I knew about my granny (in her letters to me, I saw her handwriting become looser, more prone to spelling errors and flight as she aged) and that about which I knew little (the hearty noon meals that she cooked for herself and my grandfather after they both retired). This recipe box reminds me why the ancient Greeks trekked to those temples claiming to possess Orpheus's lyre, Helen's sandal, or the stone that Kronos swallowed, why medieval Christians sought those shrines claiming to possess John the Baptist's jawbone, Jesus' foreskin, threads from Mary's tunic or a piece of the true cross, why Bob Marley devotees trek to 56 Hope Road in Kingston, Jamaica, where they can see Marley's herb garden, his blender, his rusted bicycle. Pilgrims know that the part is equivalent to the whole, that through a *relic* (*reliquiæ* is Latin for "remains") the saint, prophet, martyr, hero, or loved one lives. A single recipe card, say, for Ironworker Bean Soup, evokes a kitchen where my grandfather is sitting at the table reorganizing his tackle box, a lost reliquary, and my grandmother is at the counter, chopping onions, garlic, parsley, and celery ("tops and all," the card says) to add to the white beans, ham bone, mashed potatoes, catsup, and water simmering on the stove.

18. Mammoth Bones

Henry S. Kariger noticed his chickens pecking at something white that had eroded out of the hillside on his farm near Wellfleet, in southwestern Nebraska, a place where wind and water had worn small canyons into the plain. On a couple of occasions, Kariger crushed the exposed bone to provide lime for his large flocks. But when he unearthed molars, a jawbone, and vertebrae while digging a foundation, he had a hunch that what he found was more than just chicken feed.

On November 14, 1921, Kariger sent a letter scrawled on lined paper to Erwin Hinckley Barbour, the director of the Nebraska State Museum at the university in Lincoln:

> Dear Sir: Having dug up the skull and lower jaw of some large animal It has one Large tooth in each jaw. Meas: 4–1/4 in wide and 10–3/4 in length. and weighing I should say about 20 lbs. They look like a big rasp. The rest of the body seems to be in the ground. there yet. Could you give me any information of what it could be. or what to do with it.
>
> > Will be Greatly Obliged
> > Yours Truly
> > H. S. Kariger,
> > Curtis, Nebr.
> > Box 195
> > P.S. The upper jaw weighs close to 100. lbs. and the Lower half 75 lbs.

Fifteen days later, Professor Barbour wrote to Kariger: "You have described the animal in a way that makes it certain that you have one of the mammoths. I am entirely sure of this without seeing it." Barbour warned Kariger against further attempts at removing the bones: "You ought by all means to see that the portions which you have are put away where they cannot be handled, otherwise they will go to pieces. I wish this could have been found in the spring. In that event I would leave at once and visit you and see if it could be saved." Barbour offered to pay Kariger for the specimen, explaining that "a good skull, with the lower jaw and the tusks and teeth in position, is sometimes worth two or three hundred dollars or more." The content of Barbour's letter to Kariger differs little from that which he sent to the hundreds of other Nebraskans who reported having found the bones of now-extinct creatures on their property. The only curiosity about Barbour's letter is that he waited fifteen days to respond to Kariger about what Barbour would eventually call "the catch of the season."

Perhaps Barbour was so matter-of-fact about Kariger's discovery because finding mammoth bones in Nebraska was, and is, fairly common. Indeed, Nebraska is an elephant graveyard. At the turn of the millennium, a sign in Elephant Hall at the University of Nebraska State Museum says that approximately ten thousand extinct elephants have been found in Nebraska, the state with the most complete fossil record of elephant evolution. The odds that one has fossils of an extinct proboscidean beneath her house are one in ten. In 1914 alone, Barbour found three new species of stegomastodons at Devil's Gulch in Brown County. Though many of the people who uncovered elephant bones on their property weren't aware of the relative abundance of such remains and so tended to believe that what they had found was rare, the paleontologist had to take such claims seriously. Loren Eiseley, who hunted bones for Barbour from 1930 to 1933, offered a caution in *The Night Country*: "Ninety-nine out of every hundred of these stories is spun out of thin air. It is the hundredth chance that the bone hunter plays for. That means, really, that he cannot afford to neglect anybody's story; the worst of them may contain a germ of truth or, at the very least, a bone."

Perhaps Barbour's response was slow because he really was excited about this most recent find. He had been hoping to obtain what he did not have—a *complete* mammoth skeleton. Indeed, he might have found Kariger's claim that "the rest of the body seems to be buried in the ground" so tantalizing that he was sleepless with excitement and worry. A speedy response on Barbour's part would have indicated value. Since mammoth bones are often poorly fossilized, they break down rapidly when exposed to air. Barbour had seen too many specimens destroyed when the landowner tried to extract the fragile bones himself "with crowbars and poles and in one instance, at least, a team was hitched to a valuable skull, and it was pulled from its bank with disastrous results." Another obstacle was that Eastern collectors could pay higher prices than the University of Nebraska for Nebraska fossils or rights to hunt in bone beds on private property in Nebraska. In a September 11, 1922, letter to Chancellor Samuel Avery, Barbour reported that "ten institutions" were collecting in Nebraska that year alone. Perhaps he feared that if Kariger thought that the skeleton he had found was valuable, he would sell it to one of the Eastern institutions that already had acquired so many Nebraska fossils: the Carnegie Museum, the American Museum of Natural History in New York, the Field Museum of Chicago, the natural history museums at Yale, Columbia, Princeton, Harvard, or Amherst.

Perhaps Barbour's excitement was tempered by the knowledge that there was so little room in the 1908 Museum Building for items either donated or collected on paleontological expeditions. If, say, he acquired a complete skeleton of an exceptionally large Columbian Mammoth, he would not be able to display the fully assembled skeleton in the cramped facilities. Why hope to obtain what might have to remain packed away in attics, cellars, downtown storerooms, and the underground steam tunnels between university buildings?

Barbour was also busy. He chaired both the Geology and the Geography Departments, taught classes, directed the state museum, conducted field work, headed the Nebraska Geological Survey, which he had founded, fulfilled his various civic commitments (among others, the Lincoln School Board, the Lincoln City Park Board, the Executive Board of the Boy Scouts), sought to obtain funds and approval for a new museum building, and helped raise his four granddaughters whose parents sent them from their isolated ranch in northwestern Nebraska to Lincoln, where they attended public schools and the university while living with Barbour and his wife. Barbour frequently cited some of these duties as the reason for a lack of promptness in his correspondence, arrival at the sites of fossil finds, or gaps in his prolific publication record. Perhaps there simply wasn't time to respond to Mr. Kariger before November 29.

When the Columbian Mammoth lived in what is now Nebraska 130,000 to 11,000 years ago, the vegetation and insects in the region differed little from what one finds here now. But the large birds and mammals were strikingly different. Like the grasslands and savannas of Africa in recent millennia, the grasslands and savannas of the Great Plains were home to herds of big herbivores. In Nebraska during the Ice Age, this included bison, pronghorns, horses, llamas, musk oxen, grand sloths, caribou, camels, and elephants. Sabertooth cats, giant dire wolves, lions, panthers, giant short-faced bears, and wolverines kept the herbivores from complacency. Condors, teratorns, carrion storks, eagles, hawks, and vultures feasted on the leftovers of the kill.

The Columbian Mammoth was particularly well-adapted to both the grasslands and to deep winters. The hard, enamel-covered ridges and soft, tooth-cement-filled valleys of the mammoth's grinding teeth wore down at different rates. This rough, uneven surface enabled the mammoth to eat poor, tough food, which in turn allowed it to tolerate a wide variety of environmental conditions. Mammoth dung found in Bechan Cave in Utah reveals that grass made up the bulk of the three hundred to five hundred pounds of forage that the mammoth needed to consume each day; sedges and rushes about one-third; the remainder included "birch, rose, saltbush, sagebrush, blue spruce, wolfberry, and red osier dogwood," according to author Gary Haynes. In his natural history of the Black Hills, Edward Raventon notes that the mammoth had a "simple, non-ruminant, fermentation digestive system" that allowed it "to quickly process a high proportion of [this] low-quality food."

Like living elephants, mammoths were probably social with a clear hierarchy of dominance, living in herds of about thirty individuals comprised of well-organized matriarchal family groupings. And they were smart. No animal the size of an elephant, facing such aggressive, intelligent, agile predators as saber-toothed cats and giant dire wolves, could have survived unless it possessed a brain of "superior quality." The only predators whose intelligence the mammoth couldn't match or surpass were the spear-hurling, bipedal mammals, who also crossed from Asia into North America.

Initially the exchange of letters between Kariger and Barbour appears to have been fueled by each man's personal interests. Barbour wanted a complete mammoth skeleton for the museum; Kariger wanted money.

"You ask what I want to do with it," Kariger wrote on November 30, 1921. "I have decided that I shall sell to who ever will give the most for it." Kariger said that he had been told that "the specemin is very likely a Giant Sloth and that there was not a specemin of that kind in North America." Apparently, this led him to expect a bonanza.

On December 9, Barbour wrote to Kariger that a mammoth usually brought $150 to $300, "according to excellence of preservation." On December 28, J. D. Figgins, the director of the Colorado Museum of Natural History in Denver, wrote to Barbour that Kariger had written to him "some weeks ago" saying that Barbour had offered him $250 to $375 for "parts of the skull, lower jaw, and vertebrae." Kariger had enclosed photographs of these bones. Though Figgins also was eager to obtain a complete mammoth skeleton and had sent one of his employees to Wellfleet to investigate Kariger's claims, he was unwilling to enter a bidding contest. In his December 29 response to Figgins, Barbour appears disturbed by Kariger's efforts to find the best price for his bones. "I dislike the false attitude of Mr. Kariger. He left out of my letter what I really told him it apparently was worth. His letter to me was not of the right stamp." When I look at photographs of the tiny house where Mr. and Mrs. Kariger and their three children lived; when I see the rugged loess hills behind their house, land that is difficult to cultivate despite the good soil; when I consider the widespread inflation and spiraling prices of the post–World War I years, I cannot fault Henry for trying to obtain the best price for his treasure. Two to three hundred dollars in 1921 was the equivalent of two to three thousand dollars in 2000. Perhaps someone in Henry's family was chronically ill. Perhaps he wanted a piano for his wife and children. Perhaps he wanted to make a down payment on a business in town so that the anxieties brought about by high taxes, decreasing farm values, fluctuating crop prices, hail, drought, and the exhaustion of sun-up to sun-down work days would no longer burden him. Barbour never confronted Kariger about his offer to Figgins for fear that ill feelings might disrupt the negotiations.

When Kariger came to the 1922 Nebraska State Fair in Lincoln, he brought most of the mammoth remains with him in his truck. Given the care that Barbour usually took before transporting bones and fossils (strengthening the bones with shellac; casting and crating them), I cannot believe that he had approved of this plan. On September 9, Barbour bought two tickets to the fair where he secured the bones. (I imagine the exchange between the two men occurring outside the swine competition barn, after pie and coffee and before the horse races, though perhaps Barbour was too eager to inspect his new acquisition or perhaps Kariger was too eager to receive his payment to endure such ceremony.) Barbour seems to have been terribly excited at what he found, because on the same day as the exchange he wrote to his friend Henry Fairfield Osborn, vertebrate paleontologist and curator at the American Museum of Natural History: "This week we got a splendid columbi (jeffersoni). The skull with its fragments will be fairly complete with mandible almost complete. The teeth are perfect. We have both scapulae, both humeri, atlas and axis vertebrae, other cervicals and vertebrae of the back and tail, sacrum complete, tibia and fibula, parts of pelvis, and the right to continue digging until we find the balance." Barbour was getting ahead of himself. Since Henry Kariger's father owned the land, Henry could not grant Barbour the right to dig. Three months would pass before Barbour would receive the official right to dig. Nonetheless, two days after receiving the bones Barbour wrote to Chancellor Avery of "the catch of the season."

On December 2, Barbour received news from Kariger that must have delighted and horrified him: "The other day the hill in which I found mammoth, caved off exposing one of the tusks which is not in very good condition and about four feet is broken off and the hogs got at before I discovered it, but I have taken care of it." Barbour would eventually discover that "taken care of it" meant that Kariger had removed the bones from the ground. On December 11, Barbour wrote to Kariger that if Kariger left the other tusk in the ground until spring, he would pay him a bonus.

In a February 8, 1923, letter, Barbour reproached Kariger: "If the material had been left in the ground as I directed in the first place it would have been worth twice as much to you as it was after you went to all the expense and labor you did to secure this specimen, so whatever happens don't let anything destroy what remains." Perhaps Kariger had caused damage when he excavated and transported the bulk of the skeleton to Lincoln, and Barbour wanted to avoid a similar situation. Then, Barbour asked Kariger to return, at his earliest convenience, the book that he had loaned him, since "There are several men waiting for [it]." The book was the 1913 issue of the *Nebraska Geological Survey* in which Barbour's article about the tooth of a Howard County Columbian Mammoth appeared.

Kariger was mindful of the almost two months that had passed since their last communication. On February 17 he wrote: "Received your letter of the 8th. Was surprised to hear from you. Thought you had forgot all about the mammoth."

Several theories have been offered to explain the disappearance of ancient elephants, including chemical changes in the makeup of the ocean, viral epidemics, a lethal burst of energy from an exploding star, and extrabiblical evidence that there wasn't room on Noah's ark for the behemoths. Yet only two theories have marshaled a convincing amount of evidence. The climate change hypothesis holds that the transition from a glacial to a warmer, drier interglacial climate broke so many links in the food chain that the big, native herbivores and those who preyed or scavenged upon them starved to death. Biodiversity expert Edward O. Wilson says that within the mere space of a millennium or two at the end of the Ice Age, 73 percent of the large mammal and avian genera that had lived in North America and 80 percent in South America were gone. Yet in Africa where the effects of climate change were less severe, elephants and other big mammals and birds survived.

The overkill or blitzkrieg hypothesis, according to its chief proponent, Paul S. Martin, holds that the big herbivores disappeared not because they lost their food supply, but because they became one. Within a thousand years after the arrival of skilled, big-game human hunters from Asia, the big, relatively innocent, North and South American mammals had been hunted to extinction. In support of this theory, Wilson points out that when humans arrived and settled in New Zealand, Madagascar, Australia, and the Americas, regardless of what was happening with the climate, a large part of the megafauna soon disappeared.

Other scientists combine the climate change and overkill hypotheses into one grand explanation. Some say that because of the effects of climate change, the big mammals were headed toward extinction before humans arrived and that the activities of human hunters merely hastened the inevitable. Some say that when the Pleistocene ended, so too did a 2.5-million-year period of intense global weather change. In the relative calm that followed and that persists to this day, humans built villages and then towns, domesticated plants and animals, and smelted metal. In response to a more stable and abundant lifestyle, the human population soared. Thus, the mammoth's shrinking habitat was due both to climate change and human encroachment.

Barbour left Lincoln for the Kariger farm in a museum truck on June 17, 1923, with student William T. Hall. The approximately 250-mile trip took two days and required a night over at the Clarke Hotel in Hastings. On June 18, Barbour and Hall arrived in Curtis where they spent the night at the Graham Hotel, ate an early lunch, used the garage, and bought supplies. The expense account for this trip offers the only clues as to how Barbour and Hall would search for and handle the mammoth bones that they hoped to find. In Curtis, Barbour purchased a quart of denatured alcohol to thin the shellac that he would use as a bone-strengthener. He bought seventy-five cents' worth of flour for the flour-water batter into which he would dip strips of the cloth and newspapers that he had bought in Curtis. Then he would wrap the strips around the bones to separate them from the plaster casts that kept them safe during transport. On June 20, Barbour bought five feet of gas pipe fitted to an auger, which he used to obtain soil samples. On June 23, he paid fifteen dollars for Kempton dynamite, detonating caps, and a fuse, so that he could blast away the hill in which the mammoth's bones, and probably the remains of many other organisms, were embedded. Barbour paid Kariger twenty-five dollars for five days of services with a team of horses, a plow, and a scraper, which removed the overburden at the site.

From June 19 to 23, Hall and Barbour roomed and boarded with the Karigers, for which Barbour paid Mrs. Kariger twelve dollars. I imagine the university men eating with the farm family at the kitchen table. I imagine that in the evenings, while the Kariger children played with the toys that Barbour had brought them, the adults discussed the news: the Teapot Dome Scandal, the construction of the new stadium down in Lincoln where the university football team would play, Howard Carter's discovery of Tutankhamen's tomb, the Nebraska Supreme Court's ruling against a Hamilton County man who had been convicted of teaching German to a child.

Or perhaps Barbour taught the Karigers about mammoths: where they came from, when they lived, why they vanished. Perhaps he told them that, judging by the wear on and the placement of their mammoth's teeth, he was about forty-five years old at his death, ten to twenty years short of a mammoth's average life span, and that his front leg bones were still growing when he died. Perhaps Barbour explained why the Kariger mammoth's cranium was gone. A mammoth skull had to be big enough to support ligaments, muscles, heavy tusks, and a trunk, yet light enough so that the elephant could hold up its head. Thus the tissues surrounding the brain and extending into the upper jaw, the bones beneath the eyes, and other parts of the skull were latticed with air-filled cavities. While finding mammoth jawbones, palates, and tusks is fairly common, since these bones are hard and thick, finding an intact mammoth skull is not, since the thin bone and honeycombing is highly erodable.

In what might have been a whimsical, hopeful, or instructive moment, Barbour blew life into the dry bones by carving the outline of a mammoth into the wall of the excavation pit, much like those etched or painted by Paleolithic artists on cave walls in what is now France. I wonder if together, Barbour and the Karigers imagined a fleshed-out, ten-ton creature grinding, snuffling, rutting, snoring, running, trumpeting, charging, and dropping to the earth for the last time. I wonder if the Karigers regretted having removed and sold the bones of the marvelous creature that had been buried in the loess for the past thirty thousand years. I wonder if they wondered what would become of the remains of their mammoth now that they were no longer theirs.

Kariger's excavation had been so complete that there was nothing left for the university men to remove. On June 23, Hall and Barbour returned to Lincoln empty-handed. Money for the trip was drawn from a fund established by Hector Maiben of Palmyra, Nebraska, who had given Barbour about six thousand dollars for collecting and exhibiting mammal bones. Barbour's list of withdrawals from the Maiben account included: $123.11 for the trip and supplies; $250 for the purchase of the Columbian Mammoth; $1 for two tickets to the Nebraska State Fair. Total reported costs for obtaining the Kariger mammoth: $374.11.

Barbour had named the Kariger mammoth *Elephas maibeni*, *Elephas* being the genus that included mammoths and modern elephants, *maibeni* being the Latinized last name of the patron who funded the purchase and excavation of this specimen. But in the mid-1920s, Osborn, the chronic divider and subdivider of proboscidean genera and species, bestowed upon Kariger's mammoth the scientific name *Archidiskodon imperator maibeni*, Maiben's Imperial Mammoth. Eventually this name would be replaced with *Mammuthus columbi*, though the nickname, "Archie," derived from Osborn's Latin name, *Archidiskodon*, meaning "primitive tooth plate," would stick.

In 1925, Barbour arranged Archie's forelimbs, vertebrae, and ribs so that they formed "a palaeo-zoologic arch" over the head of the stairs in the old Museum Building, under which students and visitors had to pass if they were to enter the main floor of the museum. The rest of Archie's bones remained packed away. Barbour had not displayed the 2.5-foot-long tip of Archie's left tusk because a complete set of tusks from a Columbian Mammoth from Campbell was already on display. It is for the best that he did not attempt a restoration of Archie's tusks at this point. Kariger had told Barbour that he had seen the imprint in the ground where one of the tusks, so curled that the tip almost touched the base, had lain. How had Kariger known that a tusk had made this mark? Had he seen it before he crushed it for chicken feed, before his hogs ate it, or before he unearthed it? Or had he dreamed it but forgot that the image was self-made? Though Barbour had not seen this unlikely imprint himself, he accepted Kariger's description as fact. The charcoal sketches of a herd of Lincoln County Columbian Mammoths that Barbour drew and published in the August 1925 Nebraska State Museum *Bulletin* show tusks so tightly coiled that they are almost circular. Such a tusk would be a cumbersome nuisance. Yet in the same issue, Barbour's line drawing of the head of the Franklin County Columbian Mammoth depicts a skull and part of the gently curving tusks. These practical appendages could plow snow off dry, flattened grasses, chip ice off drinking water, dig, strip bark, uproot trees, and gore or intimidate attackers or competitors.

After the move from the crowded Museum Building into spacious Morrill Hall in 1927, Henry Reider and his assistant, Frank Bell, under Barbour's supervision, began articulating and installing Archie's remains and filling in the absences with plaster reconstructions and actual bones from mammoths found in Trenton, Reynolds, and Cumro, Nebraska. On November 1, 1932, the *Daily Nebraskan* reported that some of the bones were so heavy that "chains have been used to hoist them into place, with iron bars in the center of them to support the great weight." On December 2, the *Daily Nebraskan* reported that most of the bones had been moved to the main floor of Morrill Hall "where the base is being made preparatory to mounting the skeleton." On December 9, Barbour wrote to Childs Frick of the American Museum: "Yesterday, our big Archidiskodon went up into its case. The pelvis and vertebral column are in place, and before Christmas, the whole thing will be done. It is simply so big that every once in a while we take fright for fear there is some mistake." A February 19, 1933, photograph in the museum shows the nearly completed skeleton within scaffolding. On the upper level, student Eugene Vanderpool, in a mid-calf-length apron, which protected the white shirt, tie, and dress pants that Barbour required his male preparators to wear, stands near the tip of Archie's tusks, holding what looks like a large wrench. Chief preparator Henry Reider, in a billed cap and apron, crouches inside Archie's rib cage. An unidentified man with a hammer and chisel works on Archie's left scapula. On the bottom level, Barbour, in an elegant suit with a white handkerchief in the left breast pocket, trim beard, pince-nez glasses, and feet in third position, points at a bone on Archie's left hind leg, as if explaining some osteological detail to Frank Bell, who looks on attentively. By 1933, the preparation and mounting of the skeleton was complete.

Despite my thirteen-year acquaintance with Archie, when I enter Elephant Hall, I am still overwhelmed by his presence. But after my initial astonishment at his height (13.7 feet to the top of his domed skull, according to Bell's measurements), the sweeping thrust and inward twist of his tusks (they are twice as long as I am tall), and the breadth of his pelvic canal (wide enough for me to crawl through), I begin noticing finer details. The eleven-foot four-inch tusks that extend from the comparatively tiny skull are supported by guy wires attached to the ceiling. The tip of the left tusk, the only part of either tusk that was once part of Archie, is wrapped in brown bands; the remainder of this tusk and the entire right tusk are plaster-of-Paris reconstructions. The lustrous, buff-gold bones are cracked in places, smooth or rough in others. Into the eye sockets, I imagine the tiny eyes and thick eyelashes of Indian elephants. Extending from the empty nose socket, I imagine a creased mass of ponderous flesh and muscle. Though no one knows what the ears of Columbian Mammoths looked like, since no soft tissue evidence remains, I imagine small, cupped humanlike ears like those of the woolly mammoth's, extending from the tiny ear holes.

I look up into the rib cage. It is an overturned cradle, the hull of a boat, a cathedral ceiling, the arc of the heavens. A long strip of wood on each side of the inner rib cage is affixed to each rib with crisscrossed black threads; a pole bolted to these strips at the widest point of the hull appears to keep the rib cage from collapsing. Round, white pads separate each rib from the spine at the point of attachment. Inscribed into some ribs is a tidy string of black numbers and letters. Two gold-brown bolts on the left scapula (and probably on the right one, too,) secure an upside-down u-shaped strip of metal and a crossbeam that supports the spine and scapulae. Between Archie's hind legs rises a pole that supports his pelvic bones. Between his front legs rises a pole that supports the sternum, which appears to be "free-floating," since none of the cartilaginous ribs to which it once was attached exist, and a cervical vertebrae. Yet another pole links the forehead and the ceiling; metal strips attach the mandible to the cranium. Pads of fat and gristle once supported the sole of Archie's enormous feet so that he always stood on tiptoe. Now, steel poles mounted to the floor support each raised sole and rise into each leg, suggesting the unseen interior scaffolding that supports this mammoth's frame.

Archie is at once a natural wonder and a human-crafted, a human-engineered, piece of work.

Henry Kariger's letters express deep affection for Barbour, following his stay at the farm. On July 6, 1923, Kariger wrote to "My Dear Dr. Barbour" of his relief upon learning that the professor had returned home from Wellfleet without much trouble. "The children sure enjoy their toys and send their many thanks. We sure enjoy reading the magazines. . . . Will keep on the out look for any bones that might appear out of the bank."

On May 21, 1924, Kariger wrote to "Dear Friend. Mr. Barbour" of his recent discovery of what he believed to be a neck bone. "I haven't tried to find any others as I told you if I found a nother I wood give you a chance Now I am going to live the farm soon So If you want a chance at this take action on this at wanc." In this letter, Kariger's script is tighter, devoid of punctuation, and more riddled with spelling errors than in past letters, as if something had unsettled or distracted him. Barbour may have believed that the continued correspondence and the invitation to hunt for more bones was an attempt on Kariger's part to maintain a connection that for Kariger had been lucrative and intellectually stimulating. But Barbour did not return to Wellfleet. Instead, he sent undergraduate William M. Strong. After dynamiting and hand-leveling the hill on June 11, 1924, Strong found only "a few foot bones of very small mammal"—nothing warranting further investigation. Later that day, he went to Curtis and caught the eastbound train to Lincoln.

The next letter from Kariger is typed on letterhead stationary: H. S. Kariger/ Pool and Billiard Hall/ Confectionery in Connection in Bertrand, Nebraska, and is dated February 9, 1925. Kariger writes that he had read an article in the *Omaha Daily News* and wanted to know if there was "any truth in it." He closes: "Hoping Dr. you and Mrs. Barbour are enjoying the best of health." Over six weeks later, Barbour's secretary, Marjorie Shanafelt, wrote to Kariger on Barbour's behalf about the article in question, which concerned people in Siberia eating the flesh of recently found, recently thawed mammoths. After assuring Kariger that while dogs and wolves might eat the well-preserved meat, it is unlikely that humans would, Miss Shanafelt closes with: "We are pleased to note your interest in these matters, please write in anytime and do not be discouraged if we do not reply immediately." This is the last letter that Kariger would receive from Barbour.

In his last letter to Barbour on December 15, 1925, Kariger sent holiday greetings to Barbour and his wife and thanked him for a book about the Columbian Mammoth. This was the August 1925 *Bulletin* that contains photographs of Archie's various bones and Barbour's conjectural restoration of the coiled tusks, as well as mention of Mr. and Mrs. "Karriger," as Barbour incorrectly spelled their name, who had "discovered, dug out, and preserved" the bones. Stored with the Kariger letters of 1925 is a photograph of the Kariger children, two girls of about nine and seven and a boy of about three or four, standing at the bottom of the porch steps. On the back is written, "Just to show you how fast children grow up." Signed, "Mrs. Kariger."

On their annual trips to the state fair, the Karigers may have stopped by Morrill Hall to see Archie—the largest mounted elephant in the country, if not the world. Or they may have traveled the 175 miles from Bertrand to Lincoln for the sole purpose of visiting their mammoth. I wonder if they felt embarrassed, amused, or nostalgic when they read the story on the placard of how they had made mammoth-bone chicken feed or when they saw the photograph of their little Wellfleet house accompanying the display. I wonder if, despite their anger, puzzlement, irritation, or relief about the misspelling of their surname on museum placards and in newspaper and journal articles, they were still drawn to the display of the hard remains of this thirty-thousand-year-old mammoth, who had lived where they once lived and whose presence had so enriched their lives. I wonder if, when they saw Archie, they remembered that his bones had bought them respite from the bill collectors, some bright indulgence, or a new life away from the farm, as well as the acquaintance of a man who could open the earth and there read stories about the unimaginably distant past. I wonder if, when Henry Kariger wrote his first letter to Professor Barbour on November 14, 1921, he had a hunch that these bones would bring him and his family something far more lasting and gratifying than anything money could buy.

Metaphor

Metaphor is derived from the Greek *metapherin*—*meta*, "over," and *pherein*, "to bear"; hence *metaphora*, "a transferring or bearing over to one word the sense of another." The heart is a lonely hunter. Life is a pilgrimage.

But a metaphor is more than just a way to decorate a literal statement. Aristotle spoke of metaphor's ability to induce insight. That insight comes through a recognition of the similarities and the differences between the two things being compared. For instance, the metaphor "Mother Nature" says that nature (the nonhuman, nonhuman-made universe and its phenomena) is a female parent. Perhaps this comparison first evokes images of a mother pouring out milk and unconditional love. Or of Mary at the foot of the cross, abiding by the son she only partly understood. Or of the spider that allows her just-hatched offspring to devour her body. Or of Eliza in *Uncle Tom's Cabin* who, upon hearing that her owner was going to sell her little son Harry, gives up the only home she has ever known to secrete him to safety. By the time Eliza, with her child in her arms, reaches the Ohio River, her feet are bare and bloody. Nonetheless, she leaps from ice floe to ice floe until she and her son are on northern soil, safe from the slave hunters. Ah, the self-sacrificing, give 'til it's gone, motherly nature.

But, then, we remember other types of mothers. Susan Smith, who is spending the rest of her life in a Georgia prison, drowned her two young sons because she says that she was distraught over an unrequited love. Joan Crawford meted out beatings and bizarre punishments to her children, according to her daughter Christina. Some dogs eat their tender, newborn pups. The mother opossum gives birth to as many as twenty fetuses, some of which will die shortly after birth since the mother only has thirteen teats. Some female fish lay their eggs and swim away forever, leaving the father fish to guard the eggs until they hatch. Just what kind of mothers are these?

We speak of Mother Nature as a fruitful, bountiful woman. Yet there is something about her that seems alien and inscrutable. For her good as well as our own, we have conquered, mastered, subdued, and cultivated this munificent but erratic woman. Her grasslands ("virgin" and otherwise) are broken and forced to bear alien fruits. When her land does not bear marketable products, we deem it barren and worthless— a nuclear waste dump. Her land is considered "undeveloped" until it hosts an auto dealership, an industrial park, or housing subdivision. In societies where women have been and continue to be considered Other, in societies where nature is considered inferior to art, culture, science, and other human creations, the Mother Nature–Mother Earth metaphor justifies and reinforces the dual domination of nature and females. But what we must never forget is this: Mother Nature is a metaphor of our own making. She has not borne us; rather, we have borne her.

If you doubt the power of a single metaphor, spend the rest of this day considering how different our treatment of each other, our philosophies, the health of our planet would be, if for the past several millennia we had personified nature as a father instead of a mother.

19. Common Miracles

Meredith and I lie belly down on one of the narrow cement spits that extend into the lake, a spot frequented by fishers who fill wire baskets with carp, yellow perch, bluegill, and an occasional turtle. But we are casting our nets for a different catch.

On this June morning, in this calm and shallow inlet, dozens of one-half-inch, dark brown water striders dart over the water surface. Two sets of long, graceful spider legs appear to extend from the same spot on their slender thoraxes. Since the hind pair is longer than the other pair, together the four legs form an unbalanced cross-stitch. If you look closer you will see that a third pair of short, thick legs are folded beneath the bug's head. If you look very closely at a winged strider (some adults are not winged), perhaps while it is sitting on a spatterdock leaf, you will see that two pairs of wings fold flat over the back. One pair is comprised of a thin membrane; the other is leathery at the base and membranous at the tip, justifying the scientific name for the order, Hemiptera, or the "half wings."

These bugs, which entomologists know as *Gerris remigis*, are called by several common names in addition to "water striders." Those people who have only seen the eight long legs of two mating bugs call them "water spiders." Some call them "skaters" because they glide on the lake surface as ice skaters do, "water darters," because of their sudden, fast movements, or "wherrymen," because their movements resemble those of a person rowing a light, narrow racing boat. Others call them "good luck bugs" for reasons I can only guess. Former NEBRASKA*land* editor Don Cunningham says that as a child, he called them "penny skippers." In the western Nebraska town where he grew up, he and his friends gathered hundreds of water striders from the irrigation canal and kept them in fruit jars where, somehow, the bugs were supposed to turn into pennies. But my favorite name for the water strider is "Jesus bug," so named because of its ability to "walk" on water.

In the biblical story, Jesus, who was sad and weary after hearing about John the Baptist's execution, sent his disciples by boat to the other side of the lake, while he withdrew to the hills alone. Sometime before daybreak, Jesus saw his disciples in the middle of the lake, struggling to row against the wind and waves. Jesus walked across the lake to help them, scaring them witless in the process. "Lord, if it is you," demanded doubtful Peter, "bid me come to you on the water." Peter walked on the waves (I imagine slow, cautious steps that became increasingly bold) until he noticed the strong wind and became afraid. As he started to sink, he called out for help. "O man of little faith," Jesus chastised as he grabbed his sinking friend, "why did you doubt?" I wonder how much faith is involved in the water strider's ability to stay on the surface? If, say, someone broke the news to her that walking on water is miraculous and that she can't possibly be doing what she's doing, would she sink too?

The "miracle" that permits the water strider to move about on that fine line where water and sky meet is surface tension and several unique adaptations. Surface tension results from the greater attraction of water molecules to each other than to the air above. Thus water molecules cling tightly to each other, trying to pull the whole mass of the lake into as small a space as possible, creating what appears to be a tough elastic film on the water surface. In *The Naturalist's Year*, Scott Camazine explains that surface-dwelling insects have water-repellent bodies or body parts and other adaptations that permit them to glide effortlessly on the surface layer, while those insects who lack such adaptations are fatally imprisoned. The water strider's oarlike legs, for instance, are lined with unwettable hairs. Even if she accidentally breaks through the surface and is submerged, she pops back to the surface like a cork, buoyed by the air trapped between her leg hairs. Thus the Jesus bug can dart upon the water's surface, while merely dimpling the elastic film. What appear to be large pads or Mickey Mouse–size shoes on the end of her thin legs are really just indentations in the water surface caused by the weight of the insect and the resistance of her feet to breaking the surface tension. The claw, which appears at the tip of each foreleg in most insects, is positioned far enough back on the water strider's forelegs that it does not break the surface tension. If the strider does get wet feet, she crawls onto a pondweed leaf and dries out before returning to the water. The only other time the strider leaves the surface is following courtship (males and females communicate their intentions to each other by ripples in the surface film). The striders leave the surface to mate on a submerged branch or rock near the shoreline; then the female lays her eggs in parallel rows on the same spot. Two weeks later, the eggs hatch and the nymphs swim toward the light, break through the surface tension, and assume their place on top of it.

Surface tension is not as kind to those insects lacking the necessary adaptations. If a mosquito, midge, or spider falls or gets washed into the lake, it is fatally trapped by the tension. The water strider is poised to profit from such tragedies. Sensory organs on her velvet-covered legs detect the vibrations of the struggling prey. She rows her middle legs, creating a gliding motion, then, using both back legs, makes rapid jumping movements toward her dinner. The strider pounces, grabs her victim in her two front legs, and jabs her jointed sucking beak into it, injecting a poison that first stuns her prey and then dissolves its innards. Finally, the strider sucks out the juices, converting the energy they contain into her own gliding and darting movements. All that remains of the prey is a cast-aside husk floating on the surface. And who preys on Jesus bugs? Ducks, fish, dragonfly naiads, diving beetles, the swallows who skim the lake surface at dusk, and any other surface feeders.

In short, the water strider spends most of her life creating and responding to ripples.

It is ninety degrees on this late August morning. Bees are feeding on the sweet, white spheres of buttonbushes that border the lake, and dragonfly wings shimmer in the sunlight. The Jesus bug community stippling the water surface has grown so large that it looks like a heat rash. My daughter and I lie belly down on the cement tongue and gaze into the water. The blending of spheres so lulls me that I lose my perspective. Minnows glide through clouds. Scarflike stems of elodea wave over the reflection of our faces. I hear the splash of something entering the water. It is a primal sound that I want to respond to, though I cannot say why or how. One diminishing ripple after another rolls across our reflections. Black water striders, all lines and dots, are our cast net, moving to capture this moment.

Quintessence

In the fifth century B.C., the philosopher Empedocles said that all matter is composed of four elements: earth, air, fire, water. This four-part division seems logical to me, since I can reduce everything in my house—refrigerator, soap, carpet, file cabinets and their contents, plastic bottles of vitamins and minerals, a bouquet of hawk feathers, vegetables packed in tin cans—into a combination of these elements (from the Latin *elementum*, a "first principle").

Aristotle is credited with adding the fifth element, the quintessence, (*quinta*, "fifth," and *essentia* or "essence," from the Latin *esse*, "to be"), also known as *ether*, to the other four. Aristotle explained that while the four elements of the earthly region move in a straight line—either up or down or up and down—and eventually stop moving, the motion of the celestial bodies is circular and eternal. For Aristotle, who insisted on a firm division between the order and harmony of the heavens and the chaos and baseness of the earth, it was appropriate and logical that the quintessence, this purest and highest essence, exists only in the heavens.

Centuries later the Scholastics, those medieval Christians who revised Greek thought until it was consistent with and supportive of Christian thought, expanded the possible location of the fifth element. For the Schoolmen, *quintessence* referred to the eternal, immutable celestial objects in Aristotle's heaven as well as "the highest and most nearly perfect essence or power possessed by a natural body." For the alchemists, the quintessence—the universal remedy, the elixir of life, the great miracle worker—was latent in all bodies and could be extracted either by distillation or some more arcane process. In the nineteenth century, the fifth element, or ether, had lost its spiritual significance, but was no easier to locate and had even more fantastic properties. Then physicists believed that ether—which differed from ordinary matter in that it could not be seen, tasted, felt, or weighed—filled all of space and was the medium through which light and other forms of electromagnetic energy traveled in waves. Now we use the term quintessence in our everyday speech to refer to the purest, most concentrated essence, the most nearly perfect manifestation of a quality or thing.

The quintessence is the drop of oil within the kernel, the heart of one's heart, the landscape within the landscape. And we humans are, in Hamlet's words, the "quintessence of dust."

20. Spiral-Bound

A thick woody vine twines about a utility pole. Barely noticeable among the oval leaves are tiny, greenish white blossoms, clustered at the branch tips. By late summer the flowers will have developed into pea-sized fruits, nearly round, finely wrinkled, and brilliantly orange. Some frosty fall day, the husks will split into thirds and bend back to reveal the reddish berry within.

When it first emerges from the ground, bittersweet is nothing special. It grows straight up like asters, corn, cottonwood trees, and most other plants. But by the end of the summer, the bittersweet vine is a good ten to twenty feet long and girded so tightly around its supports that it can kill a sapling. The vine clambers over the ground or twines around fences, trees, shrubs, rain spouts. When it twines around other bittersweet vines, it forms thick, woody cables.

A spiral traces a continuous curve around a fixed point or center, while simultaneously receding from that point along a cone, helix, or screwline. While this is not the shortest route between two points, it is stronger and more flexible than a straight line. I suppose that is why the spiral is such a common form in nature: pig tails, mammoth tusks, the horns of some goats and antelopes, the hairs of some humans, the spiraling, emerald-colored disks at the end of the tail of the king bird of paradise, some spider webs, various whorled mollusk shells, the descent of a leaf or airplane, the Great Spiral in Andromeda, two million light-years away, and *Daimonelices*, lovely, stone corkscrews, the fossilized burrows of gopherlike beavers who lived in northwestern Nebraska during the Miocene.

Through the microscope, one can see other spirals: the coiling double helix of human genetic material, right-winding bands of chlorophyll in spirogyra, the green algae that scums lakes and ponds, and spirochetes, the slender, spiral bacteria that causes syphilis, relapsing fever, and some chicken diseases. Through a hand lens one can see that some moths and butterflies sip nectar and other liquids through a prolonged set of mouthparts. When she's not using it, the butterfly rolls this drinking straw into a spiral beneath her face. But the loveliest spiral of all is the cochlea, a snail-like structure in the hollow cavern of the inner ear. This "masterpiece of miniaturization," as Thomas D. Rossing calls it in *The Science of Sound*, "contains all the mechanisms for transforming pressure variations into properly coded neural impulses."

The spiraling movement of the bittersweet vine begins as soon as the vine tip clasps a support and coils about it. In *Ingenious Kingdom: The Remarkable World of Plants*, Henry and Rebecca Northen explain that some vines and tendrils actively search for supports through "circumnavigation," a searching rotary movement. A stem grows longer and the tip continues to "feel around" by making bigger and bigger sweeps, until at last it finds something within its grasp that it can twine about. Vines and tendrils that find a support to coil around grow thicker and stronger. Those that do not wither or die.

One side of a twining shoot grows faster than the other due to the force of gravity and a chemical change that occurs in the growing cells when one side of a tendril is rubbed through contact. As the vine grows, it revolves in two directions at once. Just as the earth rotates on its axis as it orbits the sun, the side of the vine that grows faster pushes the stem around, which then makes a little turn in upon itself. Because of this spiraling action, the vine remains taut instead of slackening and sagging as it grows. Also, the spiraling brings the branchlets closer to the support so that they, too, can twine or cling. In the event of high, damaging winds, the vine is stronger and more resilient than the tree that supports it.

Nebraska botanists John E. Weaver and Frederick E. Clements observed that since climbing plants are most abundant in forests, and uncommon in open grasslands or deserts, the climbing habit must have resulted from the struggle for light. Over time, plants devised ways of bringing their photosynthetic organs or leaves into maximum exposure to light with the least expenditure of materials for stems or trunks. A grapevine, for instance, with a stem diameter of only a few centimeters, is given over largely to conduction. Yet it may have a foliage area equal to that of the tree that supports it. True opportunists.

Carolus Linnaeus said that plants differ from humans and other animals only in their lack of movement. But anyone can see that every tendril tip has the power of independent movement. Moreover Charles Darwin noted in *The Movements and Habits of Climbing Plants* that plants "acquire and display this power only when it is of some advantage to them," further suggesting the plant's autonomy and will.

I am sitting on a fallen tree trunk near Salt Creek. The sky appears in shards between the mesh of hackberry and bittersweet leaves overhead. I trace the vine with my eyes from the point where it leaves the earth to its first turn. It disappears behind the trunk, then wraps about the visible portion, appears and reappears, again and again, the movements appearing to augment each other. "Life begins less by reaching upward, than by turning upon itself," writes philosopher Gaston de Bachelard. "What a marvelously insidious, subtle image of life a coiling vital principle would be!"

Vladimir Nabokov also found the spiral to be an excellent symbol. Nabokov conceptualized his life as a colored spiral in a small glass ball. The twenty years he spent in his native Russia (1899–1919) formed the thetic arc, "the small curve or arc that initiates the convolution centrally." His twenty-one years of voluntary exile in England, Germany, and France (1919–40) formed the antithesis, "the larger arc that faces the first in the process of continuing it." The period he spent in his adopted country, the United States (1940–60), created a synthesis or new thesis, "the still ampler arc that continues the second while following the first along the outer side." For Nabokov, this three-part structure expressed the essential spirality of all things in their relation to time. "Twirl follows twirl, and every synthesis is the thesis of the next series."

Whirling dervishes move in loose, transcendent spirals during their worship as they dance to the music of a reed pipe. The twenty-first key in the major arcana of the Tarot pack, "The World," bears a likeness of an androgynous person carrying a spiral wand in either hand. Each wand turns in opposite directions, representing the principles of integration and disintegration. I shut my eyes and watch the wands twirl, hurling sparks as their velocity increases. William Butler Yeats conceived of history, which he said repeats in two-thousand-year periods, as a spiral or gyre. A widening gyre is Yeats's image of chaos (when the falcon, "turning and turning in the widening gyre," can no longer hear the falconer, "Things fall apart; the centre cannot hold"). But a tight gyre is his image of the perfect ascending form.

Blindly, mutely, the green mind moves outward, then turns in upon itself, advancing two steps, retreating one, spiral-binding the wood and everything in it, as it makes pure spiraling leaps from the earth to the sun it seeks. If heaven is something that must be ascended into, I suspect that it can only be achieved through the even coils of a tight, perfect spiral, well-rooted in the earth.

Heaven

The earliest meaning of the word *heaven* was probably spatial: heaven is (or the heavens are) the canopylike expanse over the earth in which the sun, moon, and stars appear to float. Early people believed that their deities resided up and away in some celestial abode, far from earthly cares and burdens. Siva's heaven was in the highest, most glorious summits of the Himalayas. In Babylonian astronomy the heavens were divided into seven stacked layers, with the seventh heaven being the highest. Both the Hebrews and the Muslims adopted this idea. Thus, Yahweh and the most exalted angels resided in the seventh layer— heaven's heaven. In both the Hebrew and Christian Scriptures, heaven is God's throne; the earth is God's footstool.

But, too, heaven is a state of being. It is the goodness, light, and bliss that come from being in God's presence. In contrast, hell (*helan*, in Old English, "to hide, cover, or conceal") is the place of darkness, evil, suffering, and sorrow: the place where God is not. Many of the biblical passages that mention heaven could either be referring to a literal place not of the earth or to an inner, God-present state. "Blessed are the poor in spirit, for theirs is the kingdom of heaven" (Matthew 5:3). "Provide yourselves with purses that do not grow old, with a treasure in the heavens that does not fail, where no thief approaches and no moth destroys" (Luke 12:33).

The line between literal and figurative language is neither clear nor fixed. "Dead" metaphors, for instance, have lost their tangy metaphoric sense and have become bland literal usages. Time is not money, but because we perceive both as valuable commodities and limited resources, we say that we spend, budget, borrow, invest, waste, lose, or run out of time. Though the Christian god has some of the attributes of a father, it is not one. Though nature has some of the attributes of a mother, it is not one.

We forfeit some of our freedom and flexibility when we forget the figurative or nonliteral nature of our metaphors. For instance, a belief in heaven as a literal place beyond the blue encourages the attitude that the earth is not one's home. When Woody Guthrie visited the migrant worker camps in California in the 1930s, he found the Carter Family's version of the old Baptist hymn "The World is Not My Home" to be extremely popular:

This world is not my home
I'm just a-passing through
My treasures and my hopes are all beyond the blue
Where many Christian children
Have gone on before
And I can't feel at home in this world anymore.

According to Guthrie's biographer, Joe Klein, Guthrie believed that the effect of this song "was to tell the migrants to wait, and be meek, and be rewarded in the next life. It was telling them to accept the hovels and the hunger and the disease. It was telling them not to strike and not to fight back." Guthrie was "outraged by the idea that such an innocent-sounding song could be so insidious."

Not fighting for justice is only part of it. If we live as if the world is not our home and that heaven is over yonder, we will always be sojourners, never settling into a place, never putting down roots; nor will we feel compelled to complete the circle by returning a portion of what we've been given. If we live as if the world is not our home, we will never embrace the entirety of our being—earth, water, fire, air, as well as quintessence. If we live as if the world is not our home, we will spend our lives waiting for our invitation to the feast to arrive instead of taking our seat at the laden table. If we live as if heaven is over yonder, we will miss the pieces of heaven scattered before us. Why not fall on our hands and knees and gather as much heaven as we can bear?

Or, Guthrie may have missed the point. Instead of deceiving themselves, those who take the metaphor of the God-filled, heavenly state as a literal, out-of-this-world place, indeed those who take any of their metaphors literally, might be engaging in the ultimate creative act: bringing into existence that in which they have placed their faith.

21. My Place of Many Times

Time dragged on Sunday afternoons. The six Skrupa children, my playmates who lived across the alley, either were visiting or being visited by relatives; our three television stations only broadcast sports, or so it seemed; and after instructing my brother and me to be absolutely quiet, my parents put our little brother to bed for his nap and then retired for theirs. So, I sat on the couch with my book or tablet and crayons across my lap and watched the filigree minute hand on our Ansonia mantle clock creep across the Roman numerals. Eventually, the clock took a deep, mechanical breath and struck the half-hour. A slice of eternity had passed; the long ascent to the hour had begun. I kept vigil because I knew that if I did not, the clock would grind to a halt, and Sunday afternoon would last forever.

Sunday evenings, my father and one of my brothers, opened the round, glass door that covered the clock dial, inserted the key, and wound the gears. If the clock had to be reset, my father moved the hands, pausing to let the clock strike each hour and half-hour. It was a ceremonious end of the old week, a ceremonious beginning of the new week.

The black onyx and marble Ansonia was an eight-day clock, which left me wondering if the weeks had been a day longer in 1881 when our clock was crafted. If so, it fit what I already knew. With the aid of her *Old Farmer's Almanac*, my Grandma Knopp had taught me that a natural year consisted of thirteen moons, though our calendar divided the year into twelve units. At school I had learned that one day is actually twenty-four hours and one minute long, a subtlety our calendars could not acknowledge on a daily basis. Consequently, every fourth year we added an extra day to our calendars to compensate for the time lost annually when the 365-¼-day cycle of a true year was rounded down to 365 days. Apparently our methods of translating movement through time into movement through space are imperfect.

The first few times our Ansonia broke, my father took it to elderly "Mr. Holmquist," whose house fibrillated with the unsynchronized ticking of dozens and dozens of clocks. Since Mr. Holmquist was the only person in Burlington, Iowa, perhaps in all of Des Moines County, who could fix old clocks and because he was meticulous, he was backlogged with work. When we dropped off our ailing clock, he taped a tag with our last name and telephone number to the case and set our Ansonia on a shelf crowded with other tag-bearing clocks. "I'll call you in a few weeks," the old horologist said, as he twitched his thick glasses up on his nose. To shorten the time that we were without the ticking, chiming, and the ceremonial winding of the Ansonia or one of the other old clocks my parents had collected at auctions and antique shops, my father began tinkering with their works himself. As Mr. Holmquist's heart problems worsened, his repairs took even longer. An acquaintance of my parents brought her broken clock to my father. Then someone she knew brought his clock for repairs, and so on. Eventually, Mr. Holmquist referred all of his customers to my father.

In time, my father acquired more clock repair jobs than the dining room table could accommodate, so he converted a small room in the basement into his workshop. There he sat on a high stool, hunched over his workbench, a magnifying lens strapped to his head, clock guts strewn before him, the radio alternating between the country-western station, to which it was almost tuned, and static. The shelves above my father's workbench sagged with radio alarms, electric kitchen clocks, watches, boxes of main springs, hair springs, driving mechanisms, escape wheels, weights, screws, pins, uncategorized junk, and S. LaRose parts catalogs. On his shop door hung a calendar, always turned to September and the picture of the two hounds forever running through the autumn woods, as if time had stopped. The calendar proclaimed two years, 1938 and 1973, one on either side of the word *September*. The days of the week and the numbered dates of those two years corresponded exactly, reminding us that repetitions occur in the seemingly linear march of time.

The clocks my father "fixed" couldn't agree on anything. If I stopped in his workshop, his Place of Many Times, to tell him that supper was ready, I might hear the eagle-topped banjo strum nine times, a "black" clock with corner columns, brass feet, and no hour hand strike quarter past something, a discordant Hartford kitchen clock gong twice, and an octagonal Seth Thomas Regulator gear up but stop short of making a pronouncement. This place was as disorienting as I imagine a clockless, windowless prison cell with unrelenting artificial light to be, or a Salvador Dali painting where a limp watch slides over the edge, another hangs from a tree branch, and an orange pocket watch is being devoured by black ants.

Then, I could not understand why my father wanted to surround himself with the clicking and clicking of wheels upon wheels—reminders of time's demands and passage. For years, my father awakened at 5:08 so he could hear the first local news and weather of the day on KBUR at 5:15. He craved a home where supper was served daily at five o'clock sharp instead of whenever the food, the children or guests, and the cook (my mother) were ready. Through his example he taught me to arrive too early for most events, a deep habit that took many years and two children of my own to unlearn. And he was always in a hurry to get things done, as if life is but a series of deadlines. In fact, the "got-to-do" list that my father carried in his head consumed so many of his quickening hours that he eventually abandoned clock repairs and his Place of Many Times.

When my father retired after thirty-seven years welding locomotive boilers, Burlington Northern Railroad presented him with the perfect gift: a costly wooden shelf clock with a hinged glass door, a gold pendulum, and a key for winding. My father is pleased to have a working clock to wind on Sunday evenings. He's pleased to hear the hour and half-hour met with chimes, since his banjo, the Regulator, and the Ansonia have been mute and motionless for years. And perhaps he, too, is struck by the symbolism of this gift. My father is deeply marked by the Protestant work ethic, which holds that by scrupulously saving time, by using it with piety and care, and by turning it to profit, one shows his or her respect for God's gift of time. Thus, my father worked all day at the railroad; in the evening he cleaned the house, tidied the yard, or fixed what was broken. Daily, he redeemed time.

At first, retirement changed little in his life. My father chopped up dead trees, cleaned the garage, burned down the chicken coop, planted fruit trees, and relined the chimney. But now little remains on his "got-to-do" list. Prior to his retirement, a surgeon opened my father's heart and repaired a broken valve. But clocks recover more completely than humans do from such repairs. Weekly blood tests, drugs, and tiny strokes caused by surgical "debris" restrict my father's activities. Now daily time is marked not by units of work but by doses of medicine. Yearly time is punctuated not with holidays and vacations, but by hospital stays for his heart problems or by disruptive hormone injections for the prostate cancer that just won't go away. "There's not much left of me anymore," my father confessed at his retirement party, after taking his 10 P.M. handful of bright pills. Now he has time for clock repairs, but no inclination. And so, his time passes slowly.

During a recent telephone conversation, I unwittingly complained to my father that I haven't enough time for my writing because of the various lessons, meetings, and appointments that I drive my children to and from, because of the demands of my writing students, because of my commitments to church, social welfare, and the people I love. "Helps to pass the time, don't it?" asks my father, who falls asleep each afternoon to the tick of his retirement clock.

But my time passes too quickly. Even when my work is caught up, my children are occupied, and I have time set aside in which I can read, write, or play, my sense that my remaining days are not only fewer in number but are moving faster and faster, nips at my heels and stirs my guts. Instead of being devoured by time, I want to feast at a banquet table, forever unfurling abundantly before me, time never-ending. I want to believe that clocks stop when I am not looking. I want a Sunday afternoon so slow and uncommitted that it seems to be centuries long.

I seek ways to slow time's passage. I prioritize the items on my got-to-do list and work through them efficiently. I scrub the bathroom while I talk on the telephone. I exercise while I help with homework. I stay up late and rise early to write. I carry student manuscripts with me, so I can work while I wait in the grocery line or in doctor and dentist waiting rooms, "on hold" with a telephone receiver in my hand, in my car waiting for Meredith to finish school, dancing class, violin lessons, and play practice, for Ian to finish school, Civil Air Patrol, work, church youth group. But when I am most intent on saving time, of filling each moment swiftly and completely, I am more breathlessly out of time, more obsessively watching the clock, more time's slave.

I imagine ridding my home of watches, clocks, televisions, radios, and other time-telling machines. In this unmetered atmosphere I would eat when hungry, sleep when tired, begin work when fresh and ready, end work when tired or the job finished. My schedule would become increasingly eccentric—short night's sleep, but frequent daytime naps, no meals, but frequent nibbles, fourteen hours of work one day, none the next. Gradually I would become wilder and more honest, governed by my felt sense of rightness, harvesting nothing but ripe moments. Yet because the clock not only reports the time, but synchronizes activities as well, my children and I would find ourselves excluded from those events outside our home with more precise starting points than "when the pot of beans that I put on the stove this morning is done cooking" or "when the starlings go to roost." To synchronize ourselves, we would develop other ways of measuring duration. Like the amount of time it takes to wash one load of clothes on the permanent press cycle (twenty-seven minutes). Or for a woman of my height and physical condition to walk three level miles at a comfortable pace (sixty minutes). Or for Meredith to play her entire violin repertoire (two hours). Or for Ian to tire of talking on the telephone (three hours). Not precise measurements, but measurements nonetheless. But in time, I might walk slower or faster, Meredith might play longer and once Ian buys a car, he might spend less time on the telephone.

I attempt "voluntary simplicity," the process of scaling down my desire for material things and services. Since, as Henry David Thoreau says, "the price of anything is the amount of life you pay for it," I figure that I can gain time by taking back that time I once sold. So I eliminate cable TV, machine-dried clothes, short, short trips in the car, garbage service, newspaper and magazine subscriptions, restaurant and convenience foods, first-hand clothes, and so on. In the time that I've "saved," I hang laundry on the clothesline, walk my errands, recycle almost everything, walk to the library to read the magazines and newspapers I'd rather not do without, prepare food and wash dishes for meal after meal, plant, weed, harvest, and put up vegetables, comb the clothes racks at garage sales and Goodwill stores. In other words, I break even.

Philosopher Jacob Needleman says that the key to finding more time is not to make more lists of when and what we must do or do without but to pay more attention to the life we have. Likewise Swami Vivekananda assures that when the mind is concentrated the idea of time vanishes and we "come and stand in the one present." So, I hang sticky notes over the kitchen sink, on the car dashboard, on the wall across from the toilet, on the face of my alarm clock to remind myself to "Be here now." Occasionally, I enter a bright glade of timelessness. Yet despite my efforts, I'm still more likely to experience the Eternal Now unexpectedly: while completely absorbed in deep communion with another person, while writing (that time-stopping act of committing past and present moments to paper), during single-minded prayer (when the divine light strikes the soul, says St. John of the Cross, many hours pass yet it seems but a moment), immersed in the sights and sounds and smells of Nebraska's tallgrass and mixed-grass prairies.

Until I've turned once and for all from the time of ticking machines to the truer time of the soul, the best I can do is to create a place where I can slip free of time's grip. In this place, I will set an "accurate" Seth Thomas tambour to remind me of Isaac Newton's "Absolute, True, and Mathematical Time," which he conceived of as a uniform linear process, one moment succeeding another, each moment the same for the entire universe. The glass door covering the dial will reflect my own face; through the wooden door in the back, I will observe the working of the parts. This clock will permit me to hear and watch the reciprocal movements of the balance wheel and escapement, the swaying of the pendulum, reminding me in ways that the silent hidden gears of electrical clocks cannot that seconds, minutes, and hours are mechanical creations. This clock will permit me to touch and tinker with the inner workings, so that literally and figuratively, time—or at least the measure of time—will be within my grasp.

To remind me of the fluidity and indefiniteness of relative time I will hang a copy of Salvador Dali's *The Persistence of Memory*. When this painting was first exhibited at the Museum of Modern Art in New York, viewers were disturbed because Dali's "wet watches," appeared to be destroying the very idea of time. It's not the erosion of time, but the bending or warping of time that I see—an image of which twentieth-century physicists might approve. According to the special theory of relativity, time measurements made by observers in different states of motion not only do not agree with one another, but the measurement of any one observer is no more correct than that of any other. A distant event may take place in the "past" of one observer and in the "future" of another. Thus, "now" does not extend beyond "here." This means that it is impossible to define the exact time at which a distant event takes place. Dali's melting watches will remind me, and those who come to visit me, that, like music, time speeds, slows, stops, starts again, and sometimes repeats itself. Like a rubber band, time stretches and stretches and then snaps back. In truth, time is dependent upon my experience of it.

And in my Place of Many Times, I will set the silent, unmoving mantle clock that I found in my parents' garage to represent the frozen time of fear, anxiety, waiting. I will set a clock that runs too fast to remind me how time contracts in the presence of a deadline. Next to it I will set a clock with a handless dial to represent the suspended time of complete and joyful absorption. To represent the unbounded time I encounter in dreams and literature and memory, I will fill the walls with old and future calendars—other years that can be entered and exited at will. To represent nature's cyclical time, I'll hang charts from *The Old Farmer's Almanac* regarding the approximate times of sunrise, sunset, moonrise, and moonset for my Nebraska home, and the phases and dates of the year's thirteen moons. To remind me of the enormity of the span of time in the life of this planet, I will sit an hourglass, half filled with fine crumbled grains of ancient rocks.

On Sunday afternoons I will go to My Place of Many Times and shut the door against the falling shadows. In this created place I will refute absolute time, moment after varying moment. In this place I will have time on my hands to meter and to mete.

Homewell

When I returned to my growing-up place for a visit from whatever faraway place I was living at the time, my granny and my Great-Aunt Pertsie would each say, "I've sure been homesick for you." This struck me as a moving, though odd use of the word *homesick*. To be homesick is to yearn for certain people, but always within the context of a place and often a time. I guess that these two sisters believed that no matter where they were, if one piece of their image of their belonging-place was missing, then they weren't completely at home. Homesick wasn't the right word for that feeling, though I know of no word in our lexicon that is. Perhaps *home-scattered* or *home-torn* could have named what these two women felt so sharply.

Nor is there a word in the lexicon that names that state when all the essential pieces of home are together. But today, January 23, 2001, I have brought forth the word that my great-aunt and granny needed and am introducing it into general currency. *Homewell* is not only pronounceable and spellable but is a compound word whose meaning is decipherable at first glance, at first hearing. (Is there a word for the aural equivalent of "glance"?) Yet, the longer you abide with the word *homewell*, the more the meaning unfolds. The Anglo-Saxon word *home* is "that place where we lay our bodies down" and "our individual abode within a community." The Anglo-Saxon *wel* or *well* means "agreeable or suitable to one's wish or will." Now, it not only means suitable or proper, but "good health" (I feel well today) or "favored" (She is quite well-off). The Anglo-Saxon verb *wellan* or *wyllan*, means "to bubble up, to flow, spring or gush from or forth." The Anglo-Saxon noun *wella* or *well* is a deep hole or shaft sunk into the earth in order to tap an underground supply of water. Metaphorically it refers to the source of an abundant supply. When you are *homewell*, you feel rooted, nurtured, aligned, synchronized, whole, plugged in, and flowing. When you have *homewell*, what is essential—hearth, home, love, community, belonging, memory, creativity—is with you.

"Now that we are all here," my granny and my great-aunt meant to say, "we are homewell."

22. Everyplacetime

Yesterday it happened when I saw a profusion of dayflowers growing along an alley in an older neighborhood in Lincoln. As I focused on the two round blue petals, the tiny, lower white petal, the yellow pistils and stamens and the lance-shaped leaves of a single plant, something from the edge of my visual field, something I could neither see nor name, beckoned to me. I yielded my focus and allowed my attention to shift to the softer periphery where the eye cannot see objects with definition or detail but is alert to movement and light. As soon as I shifted from figure to ground, I realized that the colony of dayflowers before me was more than just that colony of dayflowers. Suddenly and simultaneously, I was in every place and time that I've observed dayflowers: the moist shady area along the north side of the garage behind the house in southeastern Iowa where I grew up; an old untended part of a cemetery in Union County, Illinois; by a farmhouse cellar door near Nebraska Highway 77; along the sides of a damp culvert in Baltimore, Maryland. This "Everyplacetime" experience persuades me to believe that other places and times never stopped existing, despite what I've been taught from the crib: that a particular place is an immovable location that can be reached only by moving toward it through physical space, that once a moment in time is past, it can be reentered only through memory.

I first experienced Everyplacetime when I was thirty and living in Des Moines, Iowa. It was a late autumn afternoon and I was absorbed with the beauty of dark, bare tree branches against the pink sky. Without warning the scene before me became every other branched-veined sky at sunset. This might have been disturbing if it had not been accompanied by a sense of warm homecoming and contentment. For the next several days, whenever I had a free moment—when my young son was sleeping, when my high school students were working quietly—I drafted one poem after another in which I tried to capture what followed the shift from Oneplacetime into Everyplacetime. But the experience was ineffable. In fact no piece of writing, including this one, has ever satisfactorily captured it. How can I explain that, while the experience of simultaneity begins with the crossover from tight focus to peripheral vision, the shift is more than just a physical process? How can I describe that tightrope-walking moment when I teeter between believing that my life is a succession of discrete placetimes that never can be reentered once they are past and that the long ago and faraway are present in the now and the here? How can I recreate in words the shape of Everyplacetime when I don't even know what prompts me to move in and out of ordinary perception? Am I called back by the audience in my head that always needs persuading that I am smart, compassionate, witty, and above all right? Am I called back, in Richard Wilbur's words, because of my soul's tendency to "shrink/From all that it is about to remember"? Or is it something else?

Explaining how Everyplacetime differs from mere remembering is a far easier task. When I return physically to the site of childhood scenes, I'm weighted with a sense of how much time has passed since I attended end-of-the-school-year picnics or church ice-cream socials at Perkins Park, or had an everyday life in houses now inhabited by people I do not know. When I chance upon relics like those from my childhood in a junk shop or yard sale—a ballerina lunch box, a cow-shaped creamer, an onyx mantel clock, a Scholastic Books copy of *Black Beauty*—I am consoled by the object's ability to evoke a combination of time, place, and people; yet, too, such nostalgic journeys make me sad because of what is beyond my reach. Everyplacetime, however, brings with it the solacing conviction that a particular intersection of time and place has been there all along and is always available. The only obstacle is my own tendency to forget this truth.

Often the shift is triggered by plants that I have known most of my life, especially those associated with a specific time and place: generous, fragrant peonies that Grandma Knopp took to Aspen Grove Cemetery each Decoration Day; the wrist-thick bouquet of violets that I picked on the hill behind Lou Peck's house because I was too shy to play tag with the big kids; the yellow spatterdock (lily pads, Granny Parris called them) that covered the Mississippi River sloughs near

Montrose, Iowa; spongy, buff mushrooms that Nancy Skrupa and I picked from "Aunt" Sadie's front yard, smashed on her sidewalk, and then told our frightened mothers that we had eaten; the more or less elliptical leaves on the dying elms that lined Marietta Street; tough-stemmed Hupinger's flowers (chicory) that grew along the road leading to stinky Hupinger's cereal factory, where Grandpa Parris worked; "sweet and sour," my childhood name for oxalis whose shamrocklike leaves I nibbled for their tartness; and penny plants (broadleaf plantains) whose fruiting body I believed to be the tapered spikes that formed the borders on wheat pennies. Other cues come clean of any associations except that they were part of the backyard world of my childhood. When I gaze intently upon goldenrod, cottonwood leaves, ferns, tulips, lichens, sweat peas, radishes, dandelions, irises, rhubarb, pumpkin vines, hollyhocks, wrinkled mint leaves, wild roses, the blossoms of any fruit trees, and blond, jointed corn stalks, the transformation occurs.

More recently acquired associations are also imbued with that magical, mythical quality that characterizes my most pungent childhood memories. I had never been so acutely aware of the scent and hue of lilacs as at twenty-six, when I brought home a huge bouquet from Sioux Falls, South Dakota, a few weeks after the lilacs near my southeastern Nebraska home had turned brown. When I fell in love with grasslands at age thirty-two, one of the first forbs I became acquainted with was the leadplant. Now, the small, gray oval leaflets and the wands of tiny, dark purple blossoms among the tall grasses evoke in me the same surprise and recognition as when I unexpectedly find my own face reflected back to me in a store window or a pool of water. Likewise I never encountered a beech tree that I can remember, until I was thirty-nine and a frequent hiker in the Shawnee National Forest. Though I no longer live near that forest, I sometimes shut my eyes and remember the smooth and warty gray beech trunks, old, benevolent beings, whose heavy-lidded "eyes" watched me as I moved through the forest.

It wasn't until the arrival of Everyplacetime that I realized how willful plants can be. Unlike passive, human-made creations that pay little attention to me, plants have chosen me to be the recipient of their blessings. Unlike human-made creations that wear out, get lost, or break, my power plants are common, persistent, and renewable. Unlike human-made creations that lack the vitality to engage my attention throughout the different phases of my life, plants' ability to convert light into root and seed, scent and color, food, medicine, poison, and their ability to appear in such an astonishing diversity of forms, continues to fascinate me. Plants are agents, instigators or conduits that offer reunion with some great unnameable, that reveal to me that space and time are not hard, rigid containers but soft, porous membranes. How right that what provokes my shift into Everyplacetime is not strains of music, lines of poetry, aromas from childhood, or an image of the deity, but the earth's own green-growing garments. If one defines the transcendental as a realm that exists apart from the material universe, my shift into Everyplacetime is anti-transcendental, since the experience comes from the earth and binds me more tightly to the earth.

Once Everyplacetime rose unbidden; now I cultivate it. When I garden, I don't pull more weeds than are absolutely necessary, because they are too powerful to waste. When I walk, I choose less tended-to neighborhoods where red cedars, yarrow, fleabane, pokeweed, Sweet William phlox, and Queen Anne's lace are more likely to grow in abundance. During the warm months of the year, I read and write at a folding table and chair in the weedy, unmown part of my backyard. When I grow weary of words, I gaze upon dandelions, Virginia creeper, henbit, geraniums, tomatoes, and the mulberry tree, until I lose my focus and shift my awareness into the edges of vision where different placetimes blend and swirl around me.

My partnership with plants offers respite when I'm in a placetime that I'd rather not be. It sustained me during the three sad years that I spent in the estranging-place, too far from my prairie home. It sustains me during the two, edgy out-of-place weeks that I spend each August teaching writing in Baltimore (edgy, because I can't find cottonwood trees or open spaces; out of place, because I'm too far from my children and the center of the continent). Still, I have only to find thistles, marigolds, wild grapes, crab apples or portulaca if I want to leave the confines of Oneplacetime. Even when I'm far from home, for a few blissful minutes, I can evoke home.

Everyplacetime may be an end unto itself, the reward for years of amateur botanical studies, two decades of sitting meditation, and frequent musings about the meanings of "home." Or it may be just the beginning. Perhaps the experience will grow in frequency and intensity until all boundaries have dissolved. Then when I behold a feathery fern frond, I'll find myself slithering through Devonian swamps where giant ferns with stems as thick as tree trunks tower above me, and know that I am home. Then when I behold a dayflower, a delicate beauty whose flowers bloom and expire within the space of a single morning, I'll find myself traveling a quiet road in the Chinese countryside, and know that I am home. Then when I behold a rare, lovely orchid, I'll find myself centuries in the future, strolling through a crowded tropical city where this adaptable blossom, once found only in the extinct rain forest, now grows in lavish, pink ruffled colonies on trees, wooden fences, and utility poles, and know that I am home.

Perhaps someday there will be no placetime on this dear planet that does not belong to me and I to it.

References

1. HOMECOMING

Bigwood, Carol. *Earth Muse: Feminism, Nature, and Art*. Philadelphia: Temple University Press, 1993.

Brown, Dee. *Bury My Heart at Wounded Knee*. New York: Rinehart, 1971.

Erdrich, Louise. "Indian Boarding School: The Runaways." *Jacklight: Poems by Louise Erdrich*. New York: Henry Holt, 1984.

LeClaire, Peter, and James H. Howard. *The Ponca Tribe*. Washington DC: U.S. Government Printing Office, 1965.

Tuan, Yi-Fu. *Topophilia: A Study of Environmental Perception, Attitudes, and Values*. New York: Columbia University Press, 1974.

2. FAR BROUGHT

Adams, Dennis. "Woodland Resources." *A Walk in the Woods*. Lincoln: Nebraska Game and Parks Commission, 1993: 58–63.

Andreas, Paul. "Arbor Day." *Omaha World Herald Magazine of the Midlands* 21 April 1968.

Aughey, Samuel. *Sketches of the Physical Geography and Geology of Nebraska*. Omaha: Daily Republican Book and Job Office, 1880.

Carey, John. "Little Habitat on the Prairie." *National Wildlife* 38 (2000): 52–58.

Harden, Randolph. "Letters from Pioneer Nebraska by Edward Randolph Harden." *Nebraska History* 27 (1946): 18–46.

Lowitt, Richard, ed. "Shelterbelts in Nebraska." *Nebraska History* 57 (1976): 405–22.

Madson, John. *Where the Sky Began: Land of the Tallgrass Prairie*. Boston: Houghton Mifflin, 1982.

Malin, James C. *The Grassland of North America: Prolegomena to its History, with Addenda and Postscript*. Glouster MA: P. Smith, 1967.

Mooter, Dave. "Urban Forest." *A Walk in the Woods*. Lincoln: Nebraska Game and Parks Commission, 1993: 66–69.

Myres, Sandra L. "Women and the 'Mental Geography' of the Plains." *The NEBRASKA Humanist* 9 (1986): 39–45.

Olson, James C. *J. Sterling Morton*. Lincoln: University of Nebraska Press, 1942.

Rice, Ginger. "Tree Planters Gave Land a New Shape." *Journal and Star* 16 April 1972: B2, B3.

Stegner, Wallace, and Page Stegner. *American Places*. New York: Dutton, 1981.

Travnicek, Ivan. "Government Encourages Planting of Trees through Many Programs." *Sunday Journal and Star* 16 April 1972: B10.

3. THE MEMORY OF TREES

Backster, Cleve. "Evidence of a Primary Perception in Plant Life." *International Journal of Parapsychology* 10 (Winter 1968): 329–48.

Erdrich, Louise. "Skunk Dreams." *Best American Essays 1994*. Eds. Tracy Kidder and Robert Atwan. Boston: Houghton Mifflin, 1994. 110–20.

Frazer, Sir James George. *The Golden Bough: A Study in Magic and Religion*. Abridged edition. New York: Macmillan, 1922.

Haller, John M. *Tree Care: A Comprehensive Guide to Planting, Nurturing, and Protecting Trees*. New York: Collier, 1986.

Meltzer, Milton. *The Landscape of Memory*. New York: Viking-Kestrel, 1987.

Merkulov, A. "Sensory Organs in the Plant Kingdom." *Nauka i Religiya (Science and Religion)* 7 (1972): 36–37.

Peattie, Donald Culross. *Flowering Earth*. Bloomington: Indiana University Press, 1991.

Williams, William Carlos. *Selected Poems*. Ed. Charles Tomlinson. New York: New Directions Books, 1985.

4. AFFINITY

Curry, William. Telephone interview with author. 27 August 1999.

Dick, Everett. *Conquering the Great American Desert*. Nebraska State Historical Society Publication 27 (1975).

Dutton, William S. "These Farm Inventors Made a City Boom." *Popular Science* March 1955: 120–25, 294.

Edel, Leon. *Writing Lives: Principia Biographia*. New York: W. W. Norton, 1984.

Frame, Donald. *The Complete Essays of Montaigne*. Stanford University Press, 1981.

"Frank Zybach (1894–1980): Inventor of the First Center-Pivot Irrigation System." Biography for induction ceremony into the Nebraska Hall of Agricultural Achievement. 22 April 1982. Nebraska State Historical Society MS 259, series 1, box 2.

Hicks, Nancy. "As Drought Lingers, State Slows Irrigation." *Lincoln Journal Star* 10 June 2000: A1, A8.

Laukitis, Al J. "Inventor Created Instant Rain for Farmers." In "Twentieth-Century Legacy: 100 People Who Helped Build Nebraska." *Lincoln Journal Star* 15 July 1999: X9.

Manning, Richard. *Grasslands: The History, Biology, Politics, and Promise of the American Prairie*. New York: Viking, 1995.

Olsen, Tille. *Silences*. New York: Delta, 1978.

Sageser, A. Bower. "Windmill and Pump Irrigation." *Nebraska History* 48 (1967): 107–18.

Sheffield, Leslie F. "Economic Analysis of the Costs and Returns for the Production of Corn Using Center-Pivot Irrigation Systems, Southwest Nebraska." Diss. University of Nebraska, 1971.

———. "Technology." *Flat Water: A History of Nebraska and Its Water*. Eds. Robert D. Kuzelka, Charles A. Flowerday, Robert N. Manly, and Bradley C. Rundquist. Lincoln: Conservation and Survey Division, Institute of Agriculture and Natural Resources, University of Nebraska, 1993. 87–196.

Sheffield, Leslie F., and Brad Rundquist. "Circles of Green on the Plains: Frank Zybach, Valmont, and the Center-Pivot Revolution." *Flat Water: A History of Nebraska and Its Water*. Eds. Robert D. Kuzelka, Charles A. Flowerday, Robert N. Manly, and Bradley C. Rundquist. Lincoln: Conservation and Survey Division, Institute of Agriculture and Natural Resources, University of Nebraska, 1993. 132–33.

Strange, Marty. *Family Farming: A New Economic Vision*. Lincoln: University of Nebraska Press, 1988.

Swinton, Val. "Zybach Contraption Doing Well, Thank You." *Lincoln Sunday Journal and the Star* 24 April 1983: B2 and B5.

Thorson, Samuel. "Nebraska Cradle of Wizard of Irrigation." *Lincoln Sunday Journal and Star* 22 April 1973: B12.

U.S. Bureau of the Census. Washington DC: Government Printing Office, 1952, 1982.

Webb, Walter Prescott. *The Great Plains*. Boston: Ginn, 1931.

Worster, Donald. *Rivers of Empire: Water, Aridity and the Growth of America*. New York: Pantheon, 1985.

———. *The Wealth of Nature: Environmental History and the Ecological Imagination*. New York: Oxford University Press, 1993.

5. A Salt Marsh Reclamation

Barbour, Erwin Hinckley. "Wells and Windmills in Nebraska." Department of the Interior Water-Supply and Irrigation Papers of the U. S. Geological Survey 29. Washington DC: Government Printing Office, 1899. 11–85.

Cox, William. *History of Seward County, Nebraska, Together with a Chapter of Reminiscences of the Early Settlement of Lancaster County*. Lincoln, Seward, Nebraska State Journal, Graphic Printing, 1888.

Duggan, Joe. "Endangered." *Lincoln Journal Star* 19 March 2000: E1–2.

Farrar, Jon, and Richard Gersib. "Nebraska Salt Marshes: Last of the Least." *Lincoln Journal Star* 12 January 1992: J1, J6.

———. "Cross Section of a Salt Marsh." *Lincoln Journal Star* 12 January 1992: J6

Harvey, Augustus. *Nebraska as It Is*. Chicago: C. S. Burch, 1878.

Horton, Agnes. "The History of Nebraska's Saline Land Grant." *Nebraska History* 40 (June 1959): 89–103.

Leopold, Aldo. "Marshland Elegy." In *A Sand County Almanac with Essays on Conservation from Round River*. New York: Balantine Books, 1991.

McKee, James. *Lincoln: The Prairie Capital*. Woodland Hills CA: Windsor, 1984.

McKibben, Bill. "Not So Fast." *Literature and the Environment*. Eds. Lorraine Anderson, Scott Slovic, and John Grady. New York: Longman, 1999. 464–67.

Snyder, Gary. *The Practice of the Wild*. San Francisco: North Point Press, 1990.

Steinauer, Gerry. "Alkaline Wetlands of the North Platte River Valley." *NEBRASKAland Magazine* 72 (June 1994): 18–43.

Thoreau, Henry David. "Walking." *The Heath Anthology of American Literature*. Ed. Paul Lauter. 2nd ed. 2 vols. Lexington MA: D. C. Heath, 1990. 2079–2100.

Body

Asma, Stephen T. "A Portrait of the Artist as a Work in Progress." *The Chronicle of Higher Education* 19 January 2001: B17–18.

Berthoff, Anne E. *Reclaiming the Imagination*. Upper Montclair NJ: Boynton/Cook, 1984.

Moyers, Bill, ed. "The Chemical Communicators: Candace Pert, Ph.D." *Healing and the Mind*. New York: Doubleday, 1993.

Consumer

Mason, W. H., and G. W. Folkerts. "Some Basic Ecological Principles." *En-*

vironmental Problems. Eds. W. H. Mason and G. W. Folkerts. Dubuque IA: William C. Brown, 1979.

BEAUTY

Adler, Mortimer J. *Adler's Philosophical Dictionary*. New York: Scribner, 1995.

Burke, Edmund. *On Taste; On the Sublime and Beautiful; Reflections on the French Revolution; A Letter to a Noble Lord*. New York: P. F. Collier and Sons, 1909.

Hutcheson, Francis. *An Inquiry into the Origin of our Ideas of Beauty and Virtue*. N.p.: 1725.

8. INHERENT VALUE

Bealsey, Conger. "The Return of the Beaver to the Missouri River." *Nature's New Voices*. Ed. John A. Murray. Golden CO: Fulcrum, 1992.

"Endangered Fish Coming Back in Missouri River." *Lincoln Journal Star* 8 January 2000.

Hovey, Art. "Platte Flow Solution as Elusive as Fish is Ugly." *Lincoln Journal Star* 8 March 2000: A1 and A11.

Nash, Roderick Frazier, ed. *American Environmentalism: Readings in Conservation History*. New York: McGraw-Hill, 1990.

"Nebraska's Threatened and Endangered Species: Pallid and Lake Sturgeons." Brochure in *NEBRASKAland Magazine* 71 (October 1993).

9. IN THE AIR

Keen, Richard A. *Skywatch: The Western Weather Guide*. Golden CO: Fulcrum, 1987.

Nelson, Hallie Myers. *South of the Cottonwood Tree*. Broken Bow NE: Purcells, 1977.

Palecki, Michael. "Could the Sandhills Start Moving Again?" *NEBRASKAland Magazine's Weather and Climate of Nebraska*. Lincoln: Nebraska Game and Parks Commission, 1996. 112.

Ross, Bob. *The Kingdom of Grass*. Lincoln: University of Nebraska Press, 1992.

Wilson, Edward O. *The Diversity of Life*. Cambridge: Harvard University Press, 1992.

ADAPTATION

Ehrlich, Gretel. *The Solace of Open Spaces*. New York: Penguin, 1985.

10. NECESSARY, HONORABLE WORK

Camazine, Scott. *The Naturalist's Year*. New York: John Wiley, 1987.

NICHE

Elton, Charles. *Animal Ecology*. New York: Macmillan, 1936.

11. BACKDROP

Barbour, E. H. Letter to C. H. Morrill. 26 June 1928. Morrill Hall Archives. Nebraska Hall, Lincoln NE.

Coe, Lulu Mae. "Frescoes in Morrill Hall Are Being Painted by Former Lincoln Artist, Probably the Only Woman in the Country Practicing the Once Lost Art." *Lincoln Sunday Star* 3 May 1927: D1, D6.

Corner, George. Interview with the author. 29 August 2000.

"Daemonelix, Corkscrew Fossils, Given a Striking New Setting at Morrill Hall." *Omaha World Herald* 28 July 1938.

Davis, Harriet. "Elizabeth Dolan Tells of Processes Involved in Painting Morrill Hall Murals." *Daily Nebraskan* 18 April 1928: 1.

Didion, Joan. *The White Album*. New York: Simon and Schuster, 1979.

Dolan, Elizabeth. Untitled, unpublished manuscript. Bennett Martin Public Library, Lincoln NE.

Eiseley, Loren. *The Immense Journey*. New York: Random House, 1957.

Hull, Mary Pollard. "Elizabeth Dolan Has One-Woman Show." *Omaha Weekly Bee* 1 August 1939. N. pag.

———. "Miss Dolan Shows Art at Joslyn." *Omaha World Herald* 1 August 1937. N. p.

Mahoney, Eva. "Murals in Morrill Hall Bring Fame to Nebraska Woman." *Omaha World-Herald* 24 June 1928: 3.

Mayer, Ralph. *The Artist's Handbook of Materials and Techniques*. 5th ed. New York: Viking, 1985.

Mechlin, Lelia. "Regional Conference at Lincoln." *The American Magazine of Art* 19 (January 1928): 16–20.

"Morrill Hall Backgrounds Form Rare Beauty for Fossil Remains of Nebraska and Africa." *Sunday World-Herald Magazine* 24 June 1928: 3:1.

"New Mural in Lincoln Y.W.C.A. Building Adds to Laurels of Miss Elizabeth Dolan." *Sunday Journal and Star* 19 February 1933. N. pag.

Olsen, Tillie. *Silences*. New York: Delta, 1989.

Osborn, Henry Fairfield. Letter to E. H. Barbour. 11 March 1933. Morrill Hall Archives. Nebraska Hall, Lincoln NE.

Schultz, C. Bertrand. Letter to E. H. Barbour. Undated. Morrill Hall Archives. Nebraska Hall, Lincoln NE.

Smith Holmes. "Elizabeth Dolan's Habitat Backgrounds for the University of Nebraska." *The American Magazine of Art* 20 (1929): 460–62.

Stevens, Connie. "Elizabeth Dolan." *Perspectives: Women in Nebraska History*. Nebraska Department of Education and Nebraska State Council for the Social Studies (June 1984): 174–82.

Voorhies, Michael R. "Our Oldest Mammals." *The Cellars of Time: Paleontology and Archeology in Nebraska*. Lincoln: NEBRASKAland *Magazine* 72 (January/February 1994): 34.

12. TRUE TRAVEL

Bird, Isabella L. *A Lady's Life in the Rocky Mountains*. 1873. Norman: University of Oklahoma Press, 1960.

Camus, Albert. *Notebooks, 1935–1942*. New York: Marlowe, 1994.

Grant, Michael. *American Southwest: People and Their Landscape*. San Diego: Thunder Bay Press, 1992.

Lawrence, D. H. *Phoenix: The Posthumous Papers*. New York: Viking Penguin, 1936.

Lisle, Laurie. *Portrait of an Artist: A Biography of Georgia O'Keeffe*. New York: Seaview Books, 1980.

Muir, John. "Twenty Hollow Hill." *Wilderness Essays*. Ed. Frank Buske. Salt Lake City: Peregrine Smith, 1980.

Theroux, Paul. "Stranger on a Train: The Pleasures of Railways." *Sunrise with Seamonsters: Travels and Discoveries, 1964–1984*. Boston: Houghton Mifflin, 1985.

HISTORY

Goldbarth, Albert. "After Yitzl." *The Best American Essays 1988*. Ed. Annie Dillard and Robert Atwan. New York: Ticknor and Fields, 1988.

Watzman, Haim. "Archaeology vs. the Bible: A Reluctant Israeli Public Grapples with What Scholarship Reveals about the Old Testament's Version of History." *The Chronicle of Higher Education* 21 January 2000: A19–20.

13. TRAIL'S END

Carlson, Brian. "Students Continue to Leave State in Search of Opportunity." *Lincoln Journal Star* 24 December 2000: A1, A9.

Mattes, Merrill. *The Great Platte River Road: The Covered Wagon Mainline Via Fort Kearny to Fort Laramie*. Lincoln: Nebraska State Historical Society, 1969.

Mumford, Lewis. *The City in History: Its Origins, Its Transformations, and Its Prospects*. New York: Harcourt, Brace and World, Inc., 1961.

Settle, Raymond W., ed. *March of the Mounted Rifleman: Ft. Leavenworth to Ft. Vancouver, 1849*. Lincoln: University of Nebraska Press, 1989.

Snyder, Gary. *The Practice of the Wild*. San Francisco: North Point Press, 1990.

Steinbeck, John. *Travels with Charley in Search of America*. New York: Viking, 1962.

14. HOMESTEAD NATIONAL MONUMENT ALBUM

Beezley, William H. "Homestead National Monument: Its Establishment and Administration." *Nebraska History* 43 (1962): 59–75.

Berkhoffer Jr., Robert F. *The White Man's Indian*. New York: Vantage Books, 1979.

Boughn, Zachariah. "The Free Land Myth in the Disposal of the Public Domain in South Cedar County, Nebraska." *Nebraska History* 58 (1977): 359–69.

Collins, Jim. "Free Land: Where It Is and How to Get It." *The Old Farmers' Alamanac*. Dublin NH: Yankee, 1990.

Dick, Everett. "Free Homes for the Millions." *Nebraska History* 43 (1962): 211–27.

"Freeman School." Washington DC: National Park Service. U.S. Department of the Interior.

Gates, Paul R. "The Homestead Law in an Incongruous Land System." *American Historical Review* 41 (1936): 66.

Limerick, Patricia Nelson. *The Legacy of Conquest: The Unbroken Past of the American West*. New York: W. W. Norton, 1987.

Lindgren, H. Elaine. *Land in Her Own Name: Women as Homesteaders in North Dakota*. Fargo: North Dakota Institute for Regional Studies, 1991.

Mattison, Ray H. "Homestead National Monument: Its Establishment and Administration." *Nebraska History* 43 (1962): 1–27.

Olson, James C. *History of Nebraska*. 2nd ed. Lincoln: University of Nebraska Press, 1974.

Olson, James C., and Ronald C. Naugle. *History of Nebraska*. 3rd ed. Lincoln: University of Nebraska Press, 1997.

Parsons, Lynn H. "'A Perpetual Harrow upon My Feelings': John Quincy Adams and the American Indian." *The New England Quarterly* XLVI (Sept. 1973): 343.

Robbins, Roy M. *Our Landed Heritage: The Public Domain, 1776–1970*. Lincoln: University of Nebraska Press, 1976.

Shannon, Fred A. "The Homestead Act and the Labor Surplus." *American Historical Review* 41 (1936): 637–38.

Sheldon, Addison E. *History and Stories of Nebraska*. Lincoln: University Publishing, 1919.

Turner, Frederick Jackson. "Contributions of the West to American Democracy." *Frontier in American History*. Melbourne FL: Krieger, 1985.

Welsch, Roger L. *Sod Walls: The Story of the Nebraska Sod House*. Lincoln: J & L Lee, 1991. (Original photograph of the Chrisman sisters)

15. IDEAL HOME

Dawson, Jan C. "Landmarks of Home in the Pacific Northwest." *ISLE* (*Interdisciplinary Studies in Literature and the Environment*) 2 (Winter 1996): 1–23.

Dorris, Michael. "Maintaining a Home." *Paper Trail: Essays*. New York: HarperCollins, 1994.

Judson, Phoebe Goodell. *A Pioneer's Search for the Ideal Home*. Lincoln: University of Nebraska Press, 1984.

Lopez, Barry. "The American Geographies." *Orion Nature Quarterly* 8 (Autumn 1989): 52–61.

NEIGHBOR

Kunstler, James Howard. *Home from Nowhere: Remaking Our Everyday World for the Twenty-First Century*. New York: Simon & Schuster, 1996.

COMMUNITY

Bates, Marston. *The Nature of Natural History*. Princeton NJ: Princeton University Press, 1950.

Friedman, Stephen. *City Mover*. New York: McGraw-Hill, 1989.

17. ROUND

Murie, James R. *Ceremonies of the Pawnee*. Ed. Douglas Parks. Lincoln: University of Nebraska Press, 1989.

Weltfish, Gene. *The Lost Universe: Pawnee Life and Culture*. Lincoln: University of Nebraska Press, 1977.

Wishart, David. *An Unspeakable Sadness: The Dispossession of the Nebraska Indians*. Lincoln: University of Nebraska Press, 1994.

18. MAMMOTH BONES

All correspondence is from the Morrill Hall Archives, Nebraska Hall, University of Nebraska, Lincoln, Nebraska.

Barbour, Erwin Hinckley. "A Tooth of the Columbian Mammoth." *Nebraska Geological Survey* 4 (1913): 58–65.

———. "Curtis Trip, Maiben Account, Hall and Barbour, Curtis Mammoth." Morrill Hall Archives. Nebraska Hall, University of Nebraska, Lincoln NE.

———. "Mammalian Fossils From Devil's Gulch." *The University Studies of the University of Nebraska* 14 (1914): 185–202.

———. "Museums and the People." *Publications of the Nebraska Academy of Sciences* 8 (1913): 3–12.

———. "Skeletal Parts of the Columbian Mammoth *Elephas Maibeni*." *Bulletin* (The Nebraska State Museum) 10 (August 1925): 95–118.

Bell, Frank. Measurements of Completed Mounted Skeleton. Accession Catalogue. Morrill Hall Archives. Nebraska Hall, University of Nebraska, Lincoln NE.

Corner, George. Interview with the author in Lincoln, Nebraska. 29 August 2000 and 2 April 2001.

Eiseley, Loren. *The Night Country: Reflections of a Bone-Hunting Man*. New York: Charles Scribner's Sons, 1971.

Daily Nebraskan 1 November 1932. (Title and page number not available.)

Haynes, Gary. *Mammoths, Mastodants, and Elephants: Biology , Behavior, and the Fossil Record*. Cambridge: Cambridge University Press, 1991.

"The Inflation Calculator." www.westegg.com/inflation/.

Martin, Paul. *The Last 10,000 Years: A Fossil Pollen Record of the American Southwest*. Tuscon: University of Arizona Press, 1983.

"Museum Renovations Improve Life for Long-Dead Mammoth." *Omaha World Herald* 7 July 1993.

"Near Reconstruction of Large Fossil Elephant." *Daily Nebraskan* 2 December 1932.

Raventon, Edward. *Islands in the Plains: A Black Hills Natural History*. Boulder CO: Johnson Books, 1994.

Strong, William. Field Notes for 10, 11 June 1924. Morrill Hall Archives. Nebraska Hall, University of Nebraska, Lincoln NE.

Ward, Peter. D. *The Call of Distant Mammoths: Why the Ice Age Mammals Disappeared*. New York: Copernicus, 1997.

Wilson, Edward O. *The Diversity of Life*. Cambridge: Harvard University Press, 1992.

19. COMMON MIRACLES

Camazine, Scott. *The Naturalist's Year*. New York: John Wiley, 1987.

20. SPIRAL-BOUND

Bachelard, Gaston de. *The Poetics of Space* New York: Orion, 1964.

Darwin, Charles. *The Movements and Habits of Climbing Plants*. New York: D. Appleton, 1988.

Nabokov, Vladimir. *Speak, Memory: An Autobiography Revisited*. New York: Putnam, 1966.

Northen, Henry, and Rebecca Northen. *Ingenious Kingdom: The Remarkable World of Plants*. Englewood Hill NJ: Prentice-Hall, 1970.

Rossing, Thomas D. *The Science of Sound*. Reading MA: Addison-Wesley, 1990.

Weaver, John E., and Frederick E. Clements. *Plant Ecology*. New York: McGraw-Hill, 1938.

HEAVEN

Klein, Joe. *Woody Guthrie: A Life*. New York: Alfred A. Knopf, 1980.

21. MY PLACE OF MANY TIMES

Needleman, Jacob. *Time and the Soul*. New York: Currency/Doubleday, 1998.

Thoreau, Henry David. *The Variorium Walden and the Variorium Civil Disobedience*. New York: Washington Square Books, 1972.

Vivekananda, Swami. *Living at the Source: Yoga Teaching of Vivekananda*. Eds. Ann Myren and Dorothy Madison. Boston: Shambhala, 1993.

Wilbur, Richard. "Love Calls Us to the Things of this World." *Things of this World*. New York: Harcourt, Brace and World, 1956.